AN, arrived at Daufuskie [Bloody Point,

la] Habersham and myself and my gardener,

the rest remaining at Bloody . . . At 2

key, sandwiches, rolls, crab . . . en salad

, snowball pound cake, 6 bottles of champagne,

(bamboo) for the ladies from my house, and nap

spoons, saucers, etc. Returned to Savannah, rea

othing untoward happened. March 20, 1880—

y rail relieved by carriages. (Gave the steward of

eon, Josiah Murray and brother waited. Ann

. Oyster on the shell, boned turkey truffled, sandw

ges, apples, prunes, dried [crystallized] ginger,

ld, but coffee. Wines, even sherry and champa

bee, lunching Enroute on boned turkey, sandwic

wberries and strawberry ice cream, snowball po

D1030636

The Savannah COOKBOOK

DAMON LEE FOWLER

John Robert Carrington III, Photographer

Gibbs Smith, Publisher
TO ENRICH AND INSPIRE HUMANKIND
Salt Lake City | *Charleston* | *Santa Fe* | *Santa Barbara*

First Edition
12 11 10 09 08   5 4 3 2 1

Text © 2008 Damon Lee Fowler
Photographs © 2008 John Robert Carrington III

All rights reserved. No part of this book may be reproduced by any means
whatsoever without written permission from the publisher, except brief
portions quoted for purpose of review.

Published by
Gibbs Smith, Publisher
P.O. Box 667
Layton, Utah 84041

Orders: 1.800.835.4993
www.gibbs-smith.com

Designed by Linda Herman/Glyph Publishing Arts
Printed and bound in China

Library of Congress Cataloging-in-Publication Data
Fowler, Damon Lee.
 The Savannah cookbook / Damon Lee Fowler ; photographs by John Robert Carrington III.
— 1st ed.
     p. cm.
 Includes bibliographical references.
 ISBN-13: 978-1-4236-0224-8
 ISBN-10: 1-4236-0224-2
 1. Cookery, American—Southern style. 2. Cookery—Georgia—Savannah. I. Title.

TX715.2.S68F6885 2008
641.5975—dc22
                          2007042889

For All Savannah Cooks

At Home and Away

Past, Present, and Future

Especially the Staff at Kitchenware Outfitters:

David and Barbara, Caroline, Colleen, Deanna, Eliza, Josh, Judy, Kathy, KC, and Susan

And For TLH, who saw it through

Contents

Preface

A BLAZING SUN GLINTED blindingly off the hood of my little white car and glittered on the wide, muddy river that rolled underneath the causeway connecting Highway 17 to the old Tallmadge Bridge. Though still late morning on the first day of June, the air, heavy with the briny, black-mud aroma of the marshes, was already thick with humidity and hot as July. My hands clutched the wheel as the rusting gray-green cage truss of the old bridge towered ahead. It was the biggest bridge I'd ever driven over, and try though I might to keep my eyes fixed on the road directly in front of the car, not looking to the side was impossible. Just to the left was my first glimpse of Savannah—a tall bluff hugging the river's south flank. Fronted by a dark wall of weather-beaten brick and stucco warehouses, the river bluff was divided in half by an imposing neo-classical building crowned with a blue-green dome. Beyond lay a checkered blanket of living green and tin roofing, softened by a heat haze punctured here and there by the odd cupola or old church spire.

Just as the car crested the bridge and started the long descent into town, something happened that changed my life forever. No, the car didn't go hurtling off the side of the bridge. But, in a way, what did happen had nearly the same impact: looking out over those acres of weathered roofing, live oaks, and graceful spires, a sudden and distinct sense of homecoming washed over me. "I'm home" went through my head and even passed my lips in a stunned whisper.

Somehow, I negotiated the last of the bridge and merged onto a wide, divided avenue shaded by spreading oaks and bordered by tall, elegant houses of time-worn brick and stucco, raised on high basements and capped by deep, bracketed eaves. It all seemed strangely familiar, so familiar that I drove to the address scrawled in the notebook on my lap as if I had been doing it all my life. The moment soon passed, of course, and the streets and park-like squares again became what they really were—a wonder of places I'd never seen before. But that sense of homecoming has never left.

That was nearly thirty years ago. I'd come to Savannah to serve out a preservation internship with the Savannah Landmark project and would spend the rest of a blazing, record-breaking summer documenting dozens of dilapidated, barely habitable houses in the beleaguered old Victorian District. But that, it turned out, was to be only a small part of the experience. Every moment of free time was spent exploring this ancient city, seeing all the usual sites of a tourist, and discovering hidden corners that visitors rarely see—falling in love with a place and its people that have changed my life.

There were nervy transplants who had gotten the old house bug and upended their entire lives for a temperamental if beautiful mass of old wood, brick, and crumbly plaster; placid natives who wore their gentility as casually as a faded seersucker jacket and looked on this newcomer fervor with a kind of wry, if grateful, amusement; brash pretenders who made a splash with newly acquired "family" portraits and silver and then disappeared in the night like marsh vapor and skittering palmetto bugs; unpretentious old salts and marsh rats who had more money and real pedigree than the lot of them; everyday folk who were as generous with their meager tables as if they were millionaires. I knit friendships that have lasted a lifetime and made acquaintances that have taken thirty years to forget.

There was a kind, old-Savannah matron whose family came with Oglethorpe, still my standard for elegant graciousness and civility: an earthy, self-taught African American chef who put her children through school serving fragrant hot lunches to dock workers from a converted bread truck; an imposing belle from South Georgia who, like me, had arrived in Savannah with the same sense of homecoming and never left; a housewife who collected kitchen antiques, made wonderful peach and tomato preserves, and handed out pithy advice to the lovelorn, whether they wanted it or not; and a wild artist who taught me how to drink Irish whiskey and think with imagination.

Lacing its way through it all was the distinctive fragrance of a cuisine like nothing I've encountered before or since. Rich with the produce of its many waterways, heady with elements of the South African Gold Coast, Mediterranean Southern France and Greece, the Sephardic Jewish cooking of Iberia, and even the cuisines of China and Southeast Asia, it gradually took hold of my imagination and has not let go.

Here were the celebrated local blue crabs, spiced and stuffed into their back-shells or baked in creamy, cheddar-topped gratins, briny-sweet oysters roasted in their shells or simmered in rich cream, delicate inlet shrimp simply cooked in butter or folded into sweet corn pudding, whole flounder filled with deviled crab dressing, Madeira-laced bouillon chilled into a rich yet cooling amber jelly, whole

Vidalia sweet onions baked to perfection in little more than their own juices, okra and tomatoes redolent of garlic and hot peppers, red rice studded with bits of bacon or spicy smoked sausage. Running through it all was a steady, insistent quartet of garlic, onion, sweet bell pepper and spicy cayenne.

It was a cuisine that casual visitors rarely ever tasted—and they still don't. Savannah has not traditionally been a restaurant town, at least not like its sister cities Charleston and New Orleans. There have always been restaurants, to be sure—even some quite good ones—however, they didn't and don't serve the kinds of dishes that Savannahians make at home. Why would they? Those catering to locals serve the kinds of things they wouldn't make at home, and those catering to visitors tend toward the generic food that can be found at any seaside resort. Besides, excepting business lunches and the rare dinner for out of town guests, Savannahians do not consider a restaurant a proper place for real entertaining. That, in their estimation, can only be done at home. Even in the wilting, record-breaking heat of that long-ago summer, when live-in help was a thing of the past and air-conditioners could not always keep up with the heat generated by a three-to-four course dinner, they nonetheless made those dinners and served them elegantly, yet without pretension, on tables laid with crisp linen, old silver, and family china. Even modest families would not have received company with any but the best of their larder and china cupboard.

It is a cuisine and form of entertaining that has but rarely been written of in regional cookbooks and novels. Yet it is the very soul of the place that I fell in love with so long ago, the place that has filled my heart and imagination for a lifetime.

Here, on these pages, in these recipes, is its story.

Damon Lee Fowler
Savannah
September 2007

Acknowledgments

AFTER NEARLY THIRTY YEARS, so many Savannahians have touched my life and kitchen that attempting to name them all is foolhardy. I will most likely forget to mention someone important, but here goes nothing.

First of all, no one can write about Savannah cooking without being influenced by Martha Giddens Nesbit. Food editor of the *Savannah Morning News* and *Evening Press* for a decade, author of two important cookbooks, and later food columnist both for the paper and for *Savannah Magazine*, she has had a profound influence on our food culture and has transformed the way Savannahians cook, eat, and think about food.

This book is about Savannah's home cooking, so I have reluctantly left the work of our many brilliant chefs for another time. That said, many of them, especially those who cater and teach cooking, have had a profound influence on my food writing and on Savannah's home cooking. John Baker III, Rose Campbell, Jack Coburn, Cynthia Creighton-Jones, Walter Dasher, Nita Dixon, Paula Deen, Nick Mueller, Isser and Ava Gottlieb and sons, Laurence, Michael, and Richard, Myrtice Lewis, Susan Mason, Trish McLeod, Jo Ann Morrison and Camille Searcy, Joe Randall, Joyce and Jim Shanks, Elizabeth Terry, Geneva Wade, Sema Wilkes, and Robbie Woods have shared their professional and home kitchens with me. Some are native born, some came here by choice, some were dragged here and fell in love with the place after the fact; all have had a distinctive influence on our cooking.

Several years ago I was consulted on a cookbook project at The Olde Pink House Restaurant, and thanks to Donna Bayless and Beth Double, received an insider's view of one of Savannah's oldest continuously operating restaurants. I was also able to study recipes from some six decades of its history, from its days as a tearoom in the 1920s to its present incarnation as a fine dining establishment.

We wanted to capture the flavor of Savannah's historic downtown in the photography and were offered more homes than we could use. Bonnie and A.J. Carter, Joan and Gary Levy, Bonnie Gaster and Bob Edleman, Connie and Walter Hartridge, and Esther Shaver-Harnett and David Harnett opened their homes, kitchens, and china cabinets to us, and the Episcopal Churchwomen of St. John's Church made the historic Green-Meldrim home available. Barbara Wilson, Kathie Anderson, and Tim Hall loaned tableware.

These generous hearts didn't just let us in the door. Bonnie Carter made the pound cake and worked with us through the longest session of the project. Joan rolled up her sleeves and peeled and chopped fruit and vegetables, sliced brisket, and scrubbed pots. Bonnie Gaster was there from start to finish, making gumbo and sharing shellfish wisdom while her husband Bob ran errands and kept us supplied with coffee (and other beverages). Connie ironed linens, polished silver, and helped arrange settings. Esther left her busy bookstore to dig out tableware and opened her pantry for things forgotten. Shirley Cannon, housekeeper at the Green-Meldrim, was an invaluable sous chef and insisted on making her tomato sandwiches herself.

Specific recipe contributions are credited where they occur, but I must particularly thank Emma Adler, Anita Clay, Teeny Fulenwider, Nancy Gerard, Connie Hartridge, Joan Levy, and Anna Habersham Wright Smith for sharing important, fragile manuscripts rarely seen outside family circles. Anna shared the original manuscript memoir of Savannah's famed nineteenth-century cooking teacher, Leila Habersham, and the most extensive manuscript record of Mrs. Habersham's school known to us.

Without Ashby Angell there wouldn't have been recipes for Burra Peg or Pepper Sherry, and thanks to her, and to the Jefferson Foundation at Monticello, bird's eye peppers are again growing in local soil. Historians Jennifer Lindner and Dale Reed helped track down the source for Burra Peg. *Gourmet* senior editor Jane Daniels Lear grew up in Savannah and has been a wonderful resource.

I first came to Savannah thanks to my graduate professors at Clemson University, Dr's. Harold Coolidge and Cecelia Veolker, who encouraged me to apply for preservation internship with Savannah Landmark. And without the tireless work of Lee and Emma Adler, who conceived Landmark's mission, that internship would not have existed. Later, Jim King and Brenda Bowers persuaded me to come back here to live. I'm grateful to them all for bringing me home.

While working on this book, David and Barbara Freeman let me join the staff at Kitchenware Outfitters and provided a regular teaching venue in the cooking school. They and their staff have become good friends and helped critique many a test run. It was my best friend Tim Hall, however, who has been subjected to the tedium of almost every test, including the mistakes that didn't make the cut. He kept me objective and encouraged me to keep going.

For nearly a decade, I've been the feature food writer for the *Savannah Morning News*. My readers have been a never-ending joy.

Thank you all.

Cooking in Savannah: A History in Food

THE SOCIAL, ECONOMIC, AND POLITICAL HISTORY OF SAVANNAH, from its founding in February 1733, through its role in the Revolution, Early Republic, rise of King Cotton, War Between the States, and seesaw years of Reconstruction, Depression, and two world wars, to the decline and rebirth of its historic downtown, are well rehearsed. That's always in the background when we step into the kitchen or sit down at the table—whether the kitchen is humble or grand, or the table is polished mahogany, well-worn pine, melamine-topped chrome, or a rough picnic spread with old newspaper.

There is little point in repeating them here except where they've affected what people eat. You do not need to know what year the first steamship was launched from its port, or when the last rogue slave ship made a run for it. You don't need to know when we became an unwilling host to Union General William T. Sherman, or how many international dignitaries and presidents have been welcomed with open arms, or even how many waffles they ate (though, if you must know, President Taft appears to have set the record). And you certainly don't need to know how many ghosts are supposed to inhabit the old Habersham house on Reynolds Square. As interesting as those things may be, they don't always tell you much about the actual cooking, where it came from, and why it was served to those dignitaries in the first place.

This is what you do need to know: the political fact that Georgia became an English colony in 1733 ensured a predominantly English table; the economic facts of rice plantations and West African slaves added the infusion of heady rice dishes like Hoppin' John, red rice, and okra pilau, as well as sesame and okra; the socio-political fact of Austrian, French, and Spanish religious persecution brought Salzburger Lutheran, French Huguenot protestant, and Jewish émigrés, and with them sauerbraten, nudeln, fricassees, and the subtleties of Spanish Sephardic cookery; early twentieth-century social upheavals in the Mediterranean and Asia meant new communities of Greeks, Sicilians, and Chinese—adding barbecued lamb, tomato gravy, and stir-fried collards to the table; war and economic upheavals know no class or race—they empty tables across every social strata, forcing ugly changes that are often permanent but drawing uneasy bedfellows together in ways that prosperity will not, knitting a common thread through kitchens of all races and classes. Those are what the historical facts mean to Savannah's kitchens and tables.

Oh, and the Habersham house on Reynolds Square, better known as The Olde Pink House? What you need to know is not that it hosts at least three ghosts, but that it is one of the oldest public dining rooms in the city, that for more than half a century set the standard with simple but delicious tearoom fare that is still a legend more than thirty years after the tea cloth was traded in for white linens.

But let's back up and take a broader view. The first element in the culinary mix is also the most illusive—the foodways of the Native Americans who first inhabited this bluff. We know very little of the Yamacraw in pre-Colombian times. A tribe that by all accounts was already dying out when the first English ship landed, their history was an oral tradition that was broken before it could be taken down. Their culture was already deeply affected by Europeans before Oglethorpe and his settlers took the first step onto the bluff. A few already spoke English, and there would surely have been a little contact with the Spanish, since some of Georgia was still claimed by Spain as part of Florida. Their foodways are largely lost to us, and what they were like is the subject of only sketchy speculation. The "native" influence, then, was predominantly what lay beneath their feet—the fertile soil where rice and produce grew like weeds, the marshlands teeming with crab, oysters, and shrimp, and barrier islands thickly populated with deer, squirrel, rabbits, quail, ducks, pheasant, wild turkeys, and terrapin. All these things became defining elements of Savannah's table, but excepting possibly the oyster roast, the Yamacraw had little effect on how they were cooked.

The first major culinary influence, then, was English. To be fair, not everyone on that first boat was English (there was at least one Italian), but overall, the cooking was solidly British, and for the first few decades probably differed from that of the mother country only in being more rudimentary and basic—poverty was rampant in the early days of the colony, and kitchens were rather crude. Surviving diaries and correspondence complain bitterly of unreliable provision deliveries and of basics that were in constant short supply. It would not remain so; within little more than thirty years, import records show an astonishing food culture emerging, but that is getting a little ahead of things.

Less than six months after the English arrived came the first Jews—mostly of Portuguese and Spanish Sephardic extraction. Their cooking adapted quickly, its Iberian character possibly subdued by the fact that the colony was intermittently at war with Spain, but little attention has been given to the fact that they had many rice dishes in common with the Africans. Next came the Salzburger Lutherans, establishing Ebenezer community a few miles upriver and one of Savannah's early protestant congregations in 1735. With them came their traditional Austro-Germanic cookery that survives in a bare handful of adapted dishes. Perhaps it is because these groups were here longest that their cooking assimilated more completely than that of later émigrés.

The next major culinary influence came when the ban on slavery was rescinded in 1750. By then, rice was emerging as a major money crop in the Lowcountry, and, not surprisingly, a goodly share of the slaves brought into Savannah came from the rice-growing countries of Africa's Gold Coast. For the next century, the food culture of these slaves had a major impact on all of Savannah's tables, transforming the solid foundation that the English had laid. With the slave trade came trade in other goods—sesame seeds (known locally by the African name "benne"), okra, cowpeas, and probably eggplant. With the slaves came the knowledge of how to cook these things, as well as rice and such South American imports as tomatoes, hot and sweet pod peppers, and peanuts, which had long since been introduced to Africa, and which many historians believe to have come into the South by way of African trade.

As the colony began to flourish in the 1750s and '60s, prosperity created a demand for other imports (discussed in the pantry section, page 3). By the early nineteenth century, when the rise of cotton culture made Savannah one of the busiest and richest ports in the country, the essential character of the cooking was established. The prosperity of the antebellum period enriched it, creating a cuisine and way of entertaining that has not just been the stuff of legend, but the frame upon which much of modern Savannah's food culture has been built.

Since the beginning, the winds of war and economic upheaval have blown other immigrants to our shores. Each group has brought elements of their native food cultures—French Protestants and Catholics in the late 1700s and early 1800s; Irish Catholic political and economic refugees in the 1820s and '30s; the Chinese beginning in 1889. In the first decades of the twentieth century, sizable communities of Greeks and Italians arrived, fleeing poverty at home, and the Chinese community continued to grow as more immigrants migrated from the West Coast.

These communities were small, but they didn't have to be big in numbers to have a large impact. For example, a single family of Russian Jews opened a bakery that had a major influence on Savannah's food culture for more than a century. The

Two Old-Fashioned Picnics,
From the Journal of George Wymberley Jones De Renne.*

April 12, 1878—Went down the river on Daufuskie and Tybee, in a steamer (The Centennial) chartered by me at $50.00 for the day.

We left the wharf, foot of Drayton Street, at 9:15 AM, arrived at Daufuskie (Bloody Point) at 11:15. Visited that place. Mr. Stoddard, Mrs. [Leila] Habersham and myself and my gardener going in a carriage with me to Melrose for the two hours, the rest remaining at Bloody Point . . . At 2 PM we crossed to Tybee, lunching Enroute on boned turkey, sandwiches, rolls, crab salad, chicken salad, orange sherbet, strawberries and strawberry ice cream, snowball pound cake, 6 bottles of champagne, 2 of sherry, 2 of whiskey, lots of ice. Five rocking chairs (bamboo) for the ladies from my house, and napkins, plates, dishes, tumblers, wine glasses, knives, forks, spoons, saucers, etc.

Returned to Savannah, reaching wharf at 6:45 PM. The weather was perfect and nothing untoward happened.

March 20, 1880—Leta had a luncheon party at Wormsloe. They went by rail relieved by carriages. (Gave the steward of the Wyoming $5.00 for case of butter.)

At the luncheon, Josiah Murray and brother waited. Annie Nuthall, Mathilda and Katherine in the kitchen. Oyster on the shell, boned turkey truffled, sandwiches, crab salad, orange sherbet, cakes, strawberries, oranges, apples, prunes, dried [crystallized] ginger, coffee, burnt almonds, chocolate caramels. Everything cold, but coffee. Wines, even sherry and champagne. Weather charming.

* As quoted in *The Savannah Cook Book*, Harriet Ross Colquitt, 1933.

Chinese became grocers and, later, opened restaurants, making a subtle but not insignificant impact on our eating habits. Take a peek through the doorways of the dozen hole-in-the-wall Chinese takeouts around town and you'll see a clientele that's mostly African American.

Since World War II, more Italians and Greeks have found their way to Savannah, opening restaurants and sharing recipes with their new neighbors. The Vietnam War brought a community of Vietnamese refugees, which at this writing is in its third generation. The contribution of foodways has made is yet to be measured, but it is already changing the way the rest of the community cooks. Today there are Japanese, Thai, Malay, Pakistani, and Indian communities, as well as rapidly growing enclaves of Mexicans and other Latin Americans. They are only beginning to make their culinary presence felt. Some of their foodways will, like the people who bring them, float through and vanish; some will give way to the existing culture that they encounter; a few will take root and become a permanent part of our collective table.

That's enough to give some idea of the diversity and complexity of what is so casually called "Savannah cooking." Other bits of its story are found throughout this book.

About the Recipes

Savannah remains, at heart, a Southern city, and its cuisine shares much with the rest of the South. Much of it differs from that of nearby Charleston, or of far away Houston, Texas, or Charlottesville, Virginia, only in detail. Recipes for buttermilk biscuits, cornbread, boiled peanuts, deviled eggs, fried chicken, macaroni pie, barbecue, pecan pie, and peach cobbler are common in other Southern cookbooks; unless the details of Savannah's version varied in a significant way, or the dish had a deep association with our city, I did not include it here, since those things can easily be found elsewhere.

Despite what you may have heard about "The Sovereign Free–State of Chatham" (a nickname not always meant as a compliment), Savannah is not a separate country, existing in a vacuum cut off from the world. As we've already seen, its population is far from homogenous. Moreover, Savannahians of all walks and ethnic backgrounds subscribe to national and international food magazines and watched the Food Network long before our favorite adopted daughter was its star. Savannahians have always loved to travel and bring home culinary ideas from distant lands. When America discovered pesto, basil appeared in our courtyards; when Southwestern cooking took the country, we bought chipotle chili peppers and added cumin to our black bean soup; when Thai cooking took center stage, fermented fish sauce appeared (or, more accurately, reappeared) in our pantries. In this respect, this city is no different from any other. Needless to say, a recital of recipes from such sources would be superfluous.

And yet, there's a singularity about Savannah's table, elements of which are not found anywhere else. Among them are dishes that have not changed in centuries, others have been adopted from other lands and made uniquely our own,

A Savannah Dinner from the Nineteenth Century
as recalled by Ward McAllister (famed late Victorian raconteur and nephew of Mary Telfair) in Society As I Have Known It. *

"Some features of the everyday Southern dinner were pilau (boiled chicken on a bed of rice with bacon), hopping john, okra soup, shrimp pie, Pompey head (a stuffed fillet of veal), roast quail and snipe during the season, and shad daily, boiled, broiled and baked."

Terrapin Soup and Oyster Soup or Mock Turtle Soup

Soft Shell or Cylindrical Nose Turtle

Boiled Fresh Water Trout (known with us at the North as Chub)

Shad stuffed and baked (We broil it)

Boiled Turkey, Oyster Sauce—a roast pea-hen

Boiled Southern Ham

Escalloped Oysters—Maccaroni and Cheese—Prawn Pie

Crabs stuffed in shell

Roast Ducks—A haunch of Venison

Dessert

Plum Pudding—Mince pies—Trifle—Floating Island

Blanc Mange—Jelly—Ice Cream.

* As quoted in *The Savannah Cook Book*, Harriet Ross Colquitt, 1933.

still others have found their way to our shores with immigrants who have made a home here and adapted their cooking in ways that are unique to our community. That is the cuisine I have tried to capture here—those elusive flavors and aromas that say "ah . . . Savannah"—at least, to me.

A popular joke about this fiercely historical city is that it doesn't know the nineteenth century has ended, yet in the three decades that I have lived here, its steady evolution makes the joke seem downright silly. This book, then, is part of a continuum, just as a portrait captures the fleeting beauty of a woman whose face continues to change. Very likely, the cooking you find here will be as old-fashioned in another generation as Leila Habersham's seems to us now. The inevitability of that change is part of the charm: we do not hold on to anything; we can only enjoy it as it passes.

Savannah Pantry Basics
Provisions, Techniques, Sauces, and Condiments

THE ROMANTIC IMAGES SO OFTEN PAINTED of Savannah—of an isolated, marsh-bound monument to the past, a veritable hot house for inbred eccentricity—may charm visitors and, on some levels, even have a peculiar element of truth about them, but they are also misleading and inaccurate. From its earliest days as a raw Colonial outpost, Savannah has been a major port of America's Eastern Seaboard, a truly international city with a diverse population. Its markets (and, therefore, its pantries) have been far more cosmopolitan than myth-weavers suppose. The earliest Colonial newspapers routinely carried advertisements not only for staples such as coffee, tea, wheat flour, sugar, rum, and salt-cured pork, but almonds, olives, capers, fresh gingerroot, salt-cured anchovies, olive oil, Madeira and other fine wines, and cheeses. That last included not just Gloucester and Cheshire cheeses from England, but significant amounts of cheeses from other countries. Though records were not specific about what kinds they were, they almost certainly would have included real Italian Parmigiano-Reggiano (one of the first hard cheeses to be widely traveled) as well as a few Dutch, French, and perhaps even German cheeses.

As the colony and early republic flourished, wealthy Savannahians demanded the same pantry stores available not only to America's other urban centers, but to the capitols of Europe as well. Many things that we take for granted today as having only been available since the so-called gourmet foodie movements of the late twentieth century were in those days actually commonplace, at least for

Facing: Apple chutney.
Above: Shrimp Boats off
Tybee Island.

The Andrew Low House,
c. 1841, where Juliette
Gordon Low founded the
Girl Scouts. A museum
owned and maintained by
the Colonial Dames, it was
also the site of a popular
tearoom in the 1920s.

wealthy Savannahians. For example, one thing made with those anchovies was a fermented amber-colored elixir called anchovy ketchup, for all intents and purposes the Southeast Asian fish sauce that locals "discovered" when Thai, Vietnamese, and Malaysian cookery recently became fashionable. There were other bottled sauces in their pantries such as mushroom ketchup that in those days was almost ordinary, while today they're considered almost exotic. Some remain commonplace in Savannah's pantries to this day; others are barely more than memories.

Here are some of the essentials of Savannah pantries past and present.

The Holy Trinity of Lowcountry Cooking

FIRST, LET'S BEGIN WITH A FLAVOR BASE that is essential in so much of Savannah's cookery: onions, sweet bell pepper, and garlic. In Louisiana, the practically ubiquitous flavor base of onion, bell pepper, and celery is sometimes called the "Creole Holy Trinity," but it is not limited to Creole kitchens. While garlic often replaces celery, here, our trinity is used in exactly the same way and almost always carries the suggestion of a Gullah, rather than Creole, cook's hand in the pot. Other flavors were often added to enhance and complicate the mix—celery if it could be had, green onions for herbal freshness, and hot peppers for kick. Occasionally, this "trinity" is added to the pot raw, but most of the time it is laid as a foundation, like a soffritto, upon which the other flavors are built.

When the latter is the aim, the onions and peppers are simmered slowly in a little fat to coax out and mellow their flavors. The garlic is added later so that its flavor is more direct and there's no risk of browning it too much and bringing out its bitterness. If green onions are used, they're added later still—sometimes without cooking them at all, so that their bright, fresh flavor remains intact. Unless the recipe tells you otherwise, when sautéing this flavor base use no more than medium heat so that vegetables almost simmer rather than fry. You do not want them to color any deeper than the palest gold.

Savannah's Spice Cabinet

THE LITANY OF HERBS AND SPICES used in Savannah's kitchens is not much different from anywhere else in America. Though our pantry has always been an international one, growing Southeast Asian, Hispanic, and Middle Eastern populations have introduced a stronger demand for some foods and seasonings that have not always been commonplace, making our choice of pantry stores more cosmopolitan than ever. Herbs such as fresh cilantro and flat-leaf parsley, and spices such as fresh gingerroot and daikon radish have become standard stock in our produce markets. Chinese five-spice powder and garam masala share space with powdered mustard and curry powder even on supermarket spice shelves, and, more to the point, on home pantry shelves of Savannahians with no immediate connection to China or India.

It is little known that ethnic markets have a long history here: Chinese-owned groceries have been around for the better part of a century, and no food business is more deeply connected with Savannah than the old Gottlieb's bakery and delicatessen, founded by a family of Russian Jews. In the last thirty years, they've been joined by Indian, Middle Eastern, and Southeast Asian markets. Thai, Vietnamese, Pakistani, Indian, Moroccan, and Lebanese restaurants are today almost taken for granted. Perhaps nothing sums up this international hodge-podge like a downtown pizza shop owned and operated by a lovely Pakistani couple whose Hindu religious beliefs do not stop them from selling all-the-way pizza with Italian sausage and pepperoni.

Here are a few herbs, spices, and spice blends that have a unique place in all of Savannah's cupboards.

BAY LEAVES

For the ancients, bay laurel was a symbol of honor and nobility, and along the colonial coast of Georgia, settlers often planted it in their cemeteries and ornamental gardens. To this day, ancient laurel trees mark the sites of gardens and cemeteries that are long forgotten. But bay was not, of course, merely a symbol: it is the single most commonplace herb in Lowcountry cooking. When using imported leaves, we use the broad, oval Turkish variety. The long, narrow, and intensely fragrant California bay is too strong. If you have no choice, use half the amount called for the in recipe.

Fresh bay leaves are supple and tender, not nearly as coarse as imported dried ones that are available in most markets, and local cooks often chop or julienne them so that more flavor is infused into the food. An essential in which bay is a key ingredient is Seafood Boiling Spice.

SEAFOOD BOILING SPICE

For the last century, seafood boiling spice has been an indispensable ingredient in the pantry of most Savannah cooks, not merely for boiling seafood, but as a key seasoning for any shellfish, poultry, egg, and vegetable dishes. The two most widely used brands are the original, Old Bay Seasoning, and Old Savannah Spice Company's Seafood Seasoning. If you have trouble finding them, both are available online (www.mccormick.com and www.oldsavannahspice.com). Failing that, here's a blend you can mix at home.

2 tablespoons celery seeds
2 tablespoons whole mustard seeds
1 tablespoon whole black peppercorns
2 tablespoons crumbled bay leaves
2 teaspoons whole coriander seeds
1 teaspoon whole allspice

1 tablespoon ground cayenne pepper
1 tablespoon sweet paprika
1 teaspoon powdered mace
1 teaspoon powdered ginger
2 tablespoons salt

1. Put the celery and mustard seeds, peppercorns, bay leaves, coriander, and allspice in a blender or electric spice mill. Grind them to a coarse powder. Add the remaining ingredients and pulse to mix.

2. Store in an airtight tin or jar.

MAKES ABOUT 3/4 CUP

CURRY POWDER

1 tablespoon each whole coriander, white peppercorns, mustard seeds, and allspice

1 teaspoon each whole cumin, cardamom, and fenugreek seeds

1 tablespoon whole turmeric, freshly ground to a powder, or powdered turmeric if the whole spice isn't available

1 tablespoon powdered dried ginger

1. Grind the whole spices to a powder with a mortar and pestle or spice mill. Mix in the powdered turmeric, if using, and ginger.

2. Sift the powdered spices through a wire mesh sieve and store them in a tightly sealed half-pint jar. Shake the jar well before using the powder.

MAKES ABOUT 1/2 CUP

Never mind that there is no such thing as "curry powder" in the countries where curry originated. This adaptive blend was developed in India for the English and American spice trade and was very popular in English and American markets by the early nineteenth century. By the time of the War Between the States, it was an essential pantry store for most Savannah households and remains so to this day. Many local cooks have long loyalties to one of several brands of Madras curry, but today many have returned to the old practice of making their own blend.

GINGER

This spice's association with Savannah goes back to Colonial days. Importers advertised ginger "for preserving" as early as the 1760s—most likely fresh gingerroot that was home-preserved in syrup, or dried and beaten to a powder with a mortar and pestle. Later, ginger already preserved in syrup was imported as well, packed in beautiful blue and white porcelain jars with domed lids that today are valued antiques.

Since English culture dominated Colonial and early Federal Savannah, ginger was used in essentially English ways—mostly in baked goods and ginger beer, a drink made from fermented gingerroot that was especially popular in hot weather (and can still be found on a couple of local restaurant menus). As trade with Asia increased, it began to be introduced in savory dishes, too. For a time in the twentieth century, fresh gingerroot was hard to come by in Savannah, but today, thanks to a broad spectrum of ethnic communities and a heightened awareness of international cooking, it is standard stock in any local market and commonplace on our collective table.

In a town where traditions run deep, St. John's Episcopal Church on Madison Square is steeped—some Savannahians would say stuck—in them. Each November the parish chapter of the Episcopal Church Women holds a very old-fashioned charity bazaar of the sort that is rarely seen anymore. There is a chili and soup luncheon in the historic parish house, a craft booth, a white elephant sale, and a used book room that often looks like a fully stocked bookstore. Of course, there are also home-baked cakes and pastries, frozen entrées, and a selection of conserves made by a hardworking team of canners during the sultry dog days of July, August, and September. Especially popular are the array of chutneys, from orange-scented cranberry and apple to traditional mango. While working on my second cookbook, I joined the canners as a helper in exchange for recipe testing, and it quickly became the highlight of my summers. I've been doing it every summer since and feel lucky to count the women who do this labor of love as among my closest friends.

ST. JOHN'S MANGO, PEACH, or PEAR CHUTNEY

This gorgeous recipe is used not only for mangoes, but also for peaches and pears.

8 to 10 green mangoes (12 cups, when cut), or about 2 dozen under-ripe peaches or pears

3/4 cup peeled and finely chopped fresh gingerroot

6 small red hot chile peppers, split, seeded, and chopped

4 large cloves garlic, peeled and minced

3 cups golden raisins

1 large yellow onion, split, peeled, and chopped

2 tablespoons whole mustard seeds

1 tablespoon pickling or kosher salt

3 cups cider vinegar

7 cups sugar

1. Peel the fruit, cut the flesh from the pit or core, and then cut it into small dice until you have 12 cups (the exact number of mangoes, peaches, or pears will vary, depending on their size). Mix in the ginger, hot peppers, garlic, raisins, onion, mustard seed, and salt.

2. Put the vinegar and sugar in a stainless steel or enamel-lined kettle that will comfortably hold all the ingredients and stir until the sugar is mostly dissolved. Bring it to a boil over medium-high heat and cook 5 minutes.

3. Add the mango mixture, stir well, and bring it back to the boiling point. Reduce the heat to a steady simmer and simmer until the fruit is just tender and the chutney is thick. How long will depend on the kind of fruit and its state of ripeness. Don't overcook it or the fruit can get mushy. Pack the chutney in sterilized pint or half-pint jars, leaving 1/4 inch of headroom in each. Seal with sterilized new lids and process the jars in a boiling water bath for 5 minutes.

MAKES 7 TO 7-1/2 PINTS

ST. JOHN'S GOLDEN APPLE CHUTNEY

When the canners make this chutney early in October, the warm smells of Christmas fill the parish kitchen, helping us to hope beyond hope that cooler weather is on the way, even though it may not come before Thanksgiving. Because I am not fond of cloves, when I can persuade the canners to do so or when I make this at home, I leave out the cloves altogether and up the cinnamon and nutmeg.

Facing: St. John's Chutneys. Above: St. John's Episcopal Church, founded in 1841. The building dates from 1853.

3 pounds (6 cups) sugar

1-1/2 cups water

1 cup cider vinegar

12 cups (3 quarts) peeled, cored, and diced tart firm apples

1-1/2 cups diced, seeded oranges (including rind, about 2 small oranges)

1 pound seedless golden raisins

1/2 teaspoon cinnamon

1/2 teaspoon freshly grated nutmeg

1/4 teaspoon ground cloves

About 1 cup apple cider, if needed

1 cup roughly chopped pecans

1. Stir together the sugar, water, and vinegar in a large stainless steel or enamel-lined pot, and bring it to a boil over medium heat.

2. Add the apples, oranges, raisins, and spices. Stir and bring to a simmer. Cook, stirring occasionally, until the apples are tender and transparent but still firm, about 10 to 20 minutes. It should be very juicy; if too dry, add a cup of apple cider.

3. Turn off the heat and stir in the pecans. Ladle into sterilized jars, seal with new lids, and process in a boiling water bath for 5 minutes.

MAKES 10 HALF-PINT JARS

BIRD'S EYE PEPPERS

This diminutive member of the capsicum family is a real deceiver. Small but powerful, it packs more punch than cayenne. The origins of the name are lost in time. The most plausible explanation is that the tiny round peppers resemble birds' eyes—though there are several varieties, one of which is not even round, but elongated and pointed. Another rather silly legend holds that they are so named because the seeds won't germinate until they've passed through a bird's digestive system.

Into my living memory, bird's eye peppers were so commonplace in Savannah that travelers and food writers wrote of seeing potted pepper plants "on every front stoop and courtyard." Yet today they've all but vanished. When I began this project, I couldn't find a single plant growing anywhere in town. Fortunately, they're still available from nurseries and seed catalogs, and my friend Carol Titley in Texas supplied enough peppers to test and photograph the recipes included here. While the peppers came from Texas, they still have a Savannah connection, as Carol was inspired to grow them by Harriet Ross Colquitt's essay about the ritual of the bird's eye peppers in *The Savannah Cook Book*. Thankfully, local master gardener Ashby Angell has revived the growing of this fiery little piece of Savannah's table lore with seeds from Carol's plant and from plants nurtured at Thomas Jefferson's Monticello.

Bird's eye peppers rarely made their way into the kitchen but were mainly used at table as a condiment. The ritual that inspired Carol occurred at the soup course. A bowl of green (under-ripe) peppers was passed before the soup. Each diner took one onto his soup plate, crushed it on the bottom with his spoon, and then took it out. You didn't want to get a whole pepper in your mouth, and the trace of juice that remained in the bowl was hot enough to spice an entire serving.

When fresh peppers weren't available, many families used to make Pepper Sherry, a fragrant condiment made by steeping a handful of the peppers in amontillado sherry. It is delicately fragrant but powerful stuff: only a few drops of it are needed for each serving. Here is how it is made.

Bird's Eye Peppers and Pepper Sherry.

Pepper Sherry and two kinds of Pepper Vinegar.

PEPPER SHERRY

This suave condiment has all but disappeared from Savannah sideboards, yet once it was practically ubiquitous, and it deserves to be so again. It is not unique to Savannah, of course, but was common in many of the British Colonies, including the West Indies and South Africa. In Savannah, it was used at table to season soups, especially turtle, creamy crab, and Savannah's unique variation of okra soup. It was so commonplace that it was never mentioned in any old Savannah cookbooks, but while many old-time Savannahians remembered it, no one could quite recall the proportions. It looked as if the recipe had been lost to time when Ashby Angell unearthed a jar, given to her more than twenty years ago by her mother's friend Campbell Stovall. It was still delicious and, more to the point, virtually unused, so it contained what amounted to a recipe in a jar.

1/3 cup bird's eye peppers or 1/2 cup other small hot peppers

1 cup medium dry sherry (amontillado)

1. Rinse the peppers in cold water, drain, and put them in a heatproof bowl. Bring 1 cup of water to a rolling boil and pour it over the peppers. Let stand 1 minute and drain.

2. Put the peppers in a clean cruet, jar, or bottle that will hold at least 1-1/2 cups. Pour the sherry over them, stop or seal it well, and steep for at least 24 hours before using. I find it helps distribute the peppery oils if you gently shake the cruet after 24 hours.

MAKES 1 CUP

VARIATION: PEPPER VINEGAR

Substitute sherry, cider, or white wine vinegar for the wine. Rinse the peppers and put them in a sterilized heatproof jar or bottle, bring the vinegar to a simmer, and pour it over the peppers. If you are using peppers other than bird's eyes, up the amount to between 1/2 and 2/3 tightly packed cup, depending on how strong the peppers are. Seal and steep for at least 2 weeks before using. Each type of vinegar lends a different flavor; sherry and some white wine vinegars are sweeter and more fragrant than cider or distilled vinegar. Experiment with them all until you find the one you like best.

VANILLA

You would never know that this spice, which is the seedpod of an orchid, was ever a rare commodity in Savannah—or anywhere else in America—so commonplace is it in our pantries today. But once it was expensive and very rare. It was not, therefore, used as prodigally as it is today. Good vanilla beans are still expensive, but a single bean can be reused several times, and making your own extract from them stretches their goodness even further.

HOMEMADE BOURBON VANILLA

A note on the whiskey. While recently visiting my friend and mentor Nathalie Dupree, I walked into her kitchen to see a bottle of premium small-batch bourbon stuffed with vanilla beans. It was the loveliest extract I've ever smelled—and also the most extravagant. Nathalie doesn't drink alcohol at all, so that extravagance was completely lost on her. Like a wine for cooking, you don't want to use a bourbon you wouldn't drink, but save the premium stuff for sipping.

I've been making my own vanilla extract ever since I first came to live in Savannah, and it is deeply associated with my culinary experience here. The advantages of making your own are several: it's by far more flavorful than most commercial extracts, lacking the harshness that they can often have, assures consistent quality, and while the initial investment may not seem like it, is by far more economical in the long run. Some cooks swear by vodka, brandy, or pure grain alcohol, but I love the smooth, mellow flavor that bourbon brings to it and never make it with anything else. It multiplies easily; just allow a whole bean for every 2 ounces (1/4 cup) of alcohol.

2 whole, imported vanilla beans   4 ounces (1/2 cup) bourbon

1. Lightly bruise the beans and, with a sharp knife, split them in half lengthwise, and then cut them crosswise into three equal pieces. Reserve any seeds that fall out; they're important to the flavor.

2. Put the beans and any stray seeds in a glass jar fitted with a tight lid. Pour the bourbon over them, tightly seal it, and shake well. Set it aside in a cool, dark pantry or cupboard that you use often and shake it well every day for 2 weeks before using it. As you use it, replenish it with an equal amount of bourbon until you can tell the aroma and flavor begin to wane, then use it up. Mine is three years old at this writing and will probably last another year or two. Before your old batch is used up, start a new one with fresh beans so that it will be ready when you need it.

MAKES 4 OUNCES (1/2 CUP)

Techniques and Methods

MOST OF THE TECHNIQUES AND METHODS required in Savannah cookery are no different from anywhere else, but here are a few that are useful for the recipes for this book.

TO PEEL TOMATOES BY BLANCHING:

When the tomatoes will undergo further cooking, this is the simplest technique to use for peeling them; it's not for tomatoes that will be used in salads or sandwiches. Rinse the tomatoes under cold running water, drain, and lightly cut an X in the skin at the blossom end (opposite the stem). Put them in a heatproof bowl with enough headroom for the tomatoes to be submerged in water by at least 1 inch. Bring a teakettle of water to a full, rolling boil. Pour it over the tomatoes and let them stand for one minute. Drain, cut out the stem core, and slip off the skins.

TO PURÉE TOMATOES WITH A FOOD MILL:

This is the easiest way to prepare fresh tomatoes for sauce, since they don't have to be peeled or seeded—the food mill catches and removes both in the process. Blanch the tomatoes as directed in *To Peel Tomatoes by Blanching.* Cut them in quarters and fit the food mill with the disk with holes just slightly smaller than the tomato seeds. Set the mill over a bowl and purée the tomatoes through it.

TO PEEL AND MINCE GARLIC:

Garlic is to Savannah's table what eccentricity is to its society: there's always a little of it around. However, we love both our crazy people and our garlic in small doses. The secret is to handle the garlic with care and use restraint in throwing it around in the pots. The more garlic is mangled, the more directly its flavoring oils are released, so when the flavor needs to be distinct but subtle (which in Savannah is most of the time), don't use a garlic press. Lay the flat side of a knife blade over the garlic. Give the blade a firm tap with your fist, just enough to lightly crush the garlic and loosen the peel. Cut off the root end, pull away and discard the peel, and then chop with a sharp knife until it is the texture needed—leave it whole (to be removed before serving) for the subtlest flavor, coarsely chop it for a milder flavor, and finely mince it for the boldest flavor.

Dealing with Shellfish

To keep the crab from going into shock when dropped into the boiling water, causing it to drop off its claws, local seafood vendor Charlie Russo numbs them by chilling them in the freezer. When the water is seasoned with seafood boiling spice, he also lets them boil for 8 minutes, then turns off the heat and lets them soak for 8 minutes to absorb the seasonings.

TO COOK AND PICK CRABS:

Though cooked, picked crabmeat is readily available, today most of it is required by law to be pasteurized before it can be sold commercially and it is not nearly as flavorful as freshly caught and cooked crab. In Savannah, seafood markets sell good-quality whole cooked crab, but even they are not as good as crab you've caught and cooked on your own. It's a lot of work but well worth it.

To determine the gender of a live crab, look to the pincer tips of the claws: a female's has reddish tips, a male's doesn't. This distinction disappears when the crab is cooked (the whole animal turns red), but there are other distinguishing features. The apron of the underbelly on a female is broad and triangular; a male's is pointed and roughly shaped like a T.

If you are using the crab in another recipe, add only salt as given here, but if they're to be picked and eaten on the spot, you may add Seafood Boiling Spice (page 6) to taste.

Salt
12 live blue crabs

1. Bring 4 quarts of water to a boil in a large, covered pot. Add a small handful of salt. Drop in crabs, cover, and bring back to a boil. Simmer until they're bright red, about 15 minutes. Immediately drain and rinse in cold water to arrest the cooking.

2. To pick the crab you'll need a sharp, heavy-handled knife, claw crackers, and some patience. Twist off the claws, legs, and swimmer fins. Flip the crab over onto its back. Grasp the belly shell at the mouth and pull it away from the back shell. Remove the gills (locally called "dead man's fingers") and with the knife cut off the knuckle joints where the legs join the body shell. This will get a lot of the cartilage out of your way. Break the body in half and gently squeeze from the back out. The lump meat will come out in large pieces.

3. Finally, crack the claw shell with a cracker or by tapping it round and round with the knife handle. Skilled crab pickers can break the shell in a way that leaves the pincer shells attached to make a natural handle for dipping the whole claw meat in sauce. There is not much meat in the remaining legs, but many locals like to suck out what little there is.

SERVES 4 TO 6 OR YIELDS ABOUT 1 POUND PICKED MEAT

To shuck oysters:

Our local oysters grow in clusters, and their shells are rough and rather intimidating, but the critter inside is sweet and wonderfully briny. The trouble with shucking them is this: you want to get in; the oyster wants to keep you out. But armed with a good oyster knife and thick, cut-resistant glove, you can win the battle. Wear a glove on your passive hand. Grasp the oyster in this hand with the narrow hinge end pointed out. There will be a cleft between the two halves of the shell at this end. Insert the tip of an oyster knife into it until it is wedged in place and twist until the hinge pops. Run the knife under the shell and scrape loose the large muscle that is attached to the top (shallow) shell. Pull the top shell off and scrape the muscle loose from the bottom shell. If you are shucking them to eat on the spot, drink off the liquor along with the oyster. If the oysters are to be cooked, drain but reserve as much of the liquor as you can.

One of the many oyster beds along the banks of Savannah's tidal creeks and rivers.

To dress shrimp:

Shrimp are at their best when cooked whole, with the head and shells still attached to the succulent tail meat. To dress shrimp to cook whole (head-on), you may trim away the long, fine tentacles from the head with a pair of kitchen shears to keep them from getting tangled in the cooking. (If you're poaching them, this isn't necessary.) If you're sautéing them, trim the tentacles and peel the tails as follows, but leave the head attached. If they're to be poached, as in a Lowcountry Boil (page 106), don't peel them, but there are times when they need to be peeled before they're cooked or served. The method for dressing the tails is the same for both raw and cooked shrimp:

If the head is still attached and you need to remove it, snap it at the base, bending the tail toward the back, then pull the tail away. Most of the time this will remove what is called the "vein," which isn't really a vein but a part of the digestive tract.

Bend back the flipper fins and sharp, pointed tip of the tail until you feel them snap. Gently tug each flipper at its tip until the meat within it pulls away.

Grasp the "legs" or swimmer fins and pull them away, loosening the segmented tail shell. Pull them away. If the vein is dark and grainy and has not come off with the head, you can remove it by cutting a channel in the back with a sharp knife, but unless it looks especially gritty, most local cooks don't bother, and some (including me) think it ruins the shape of the shrimp and affects its flavor.

*Whole, head-on shrimp
ready for poaching.*

POACHED SHRIMP

For salads, seafood cocktail, and some prepared dishes. If the shrimp will undergo further cooking, make sure that they are just barely done when you take them up.

4 quarts water
4 pounds whole, head-on shrimp or 5 pounds headed shrimp

1. Bring the water to a full rolling boil in an 8-quart pot. Add the shrimp, cover, and count 2 minutes. Lift shrimp from the pot with a frying basket or skimmer, allowing all liquid to drain back into the pot.

2. For use in other recipes, head and peel shrimp, reserving the shells and heads. Cover and refrigerate the tail meat until you're ready to serve it.

3. Use the heads, shells, and poaching liquid to make Shellfish Broth (page 58).

MAKES 2 QUARTS

Standard and Store Sauces

STORE SAUCES ARE NOT SAUCES bought at a store, but homemade ones that are put up for prolonged keeping. Here are a few that are standards in most Savannah kitchens, ones that we either keep on hand or always have the ingredients so they can be whipped up at a moments notice. I've also included a couple of old ones that used to be commonplace, and ought to be again.

SAVANNAH SEAFOOD COCKTAIL SAUCE

Indispensable for boiled shrimp and crab, or for raw or roasted oysters, this spicy red sauce is also well loved with fried shellfish and as a piquant dipping sauce for French fries.

3/4 cup tomato ketchup or chili sauce

1/2 cup prepared horseradish

2 tablespoons freshly squeezed lemon juice

Hot sauce such as Tabasco

About 1/2 teaspoon freshly ground black pepper

1. Stir together the ketchup, horseradish, and lemon juice. Add several dashes of hot sauce, to taste, and the pepper. Stir well and let stand 30 minutes.

2. Taste and adjust the seasonings and chill at least 1 hour before serving.

MAKES ABOUT 1-1/4 CUPS

VARIATION: SEAFOOD COCKTAIL SAUCE LIPPITT

Anita Lippitt Clay prefers this subtler version of cocktail sauce for shrimp and crab. For about 1-1/4 cups, dissolve 1 teaspoon of anchovy paste in 1 tablespoon of Worcestershire sauce in a small mixing bowl. Stir in 1 cup of mayonnaise, 1 tablespoon of tomato ketchup, and season to taste with salt, freshly ground black pepper, and sweet paprika. Chill well before serving.

A trio of cocktail sauces (clockwise from the bottom): Savannah Seafood Cocktail Sauce (this page), Bonnie's Wow Now Sauce (page 20), and Bonnie's White Crab Cocktail Sauce (page 20).

BONNIE'S WHITE CRAB COCKTAIL SAUCE

For a big cocktail party, Bonnie Gaster mounds fresh lump crabmeat on a long, narrow platter and drizzles one side with the usual red cocktail sauce and the other side with this sauce. You could also put them in squeeze bottles and drizzle them crisscrossed down the entire mound.

1/3 cup sour cream

Juice of 2 lemons

1/4 cup dry mustard or prepared spicy stone-ground mustard

1/2 to 3/4 cup mayonnaise

1 tablespoon freshly ground white or black pepper

1. Thoroughly mix together the sour cream, lemon juice, and mustard. Fold in the mayonnaise (use 3/4 cup if using dry mustard, 1/2 cup if using prepared mustard) and pepper.

2. Let the sauce sit for at least half an hour before serving.

MAKES ABOUT 1-1/2 CUPS

BONNIE'S WOW NOW SAUCE

The invention of this zesty dipping sauce was entirely accidental. After a small, impromptu summer party, Bonnie dumped together the leftover cocktail sauces because there wasn't any room left in her crowded fridge to store them in separate containers. It was so good that now she does it on purpose. To the preceding recipe, add 1 recipe of Seafood Cocktail Sauce or 3/4 cup chili sauce, 3 tablespoons of prepared horseradish, and the juice of half a lemon.

ANITA'S SAUCE MIGNONETTE

Anita Lippitt Clay's family roots run deep in Savannah. A lifelong member of Christ Church on Johnson Square (the mother church of Georgia), a vital member of the Crabettes, an all-female band that specializes in golden oldies, and the driving force behind half the city's old social clubs, she is also heir to some of the most inquisitive culinary minds in the city's history and has never been afraid of bucking the culinary status quo. This suave sauce is her preferred one for oysters on the half-shell. It's subtler than the boldly flavored horseradish and ketchup–based cocktail sauce (page 19) usually served at oyster roasts, seafood boils, and with fried shellfish, and is an ideal accompaniment for raw or roasted oysters, cold steamed or poached shrimp, or crab claws. It also makes a tart, refreshing dressing for ice-cold sliced cucumbers.

1/2 cup white wine vinegar

1/2 teaspoon grated onion

1/2 teaspoon freshly squeezed lemon juice

2 teaspoons minced shallots

2 teaspoons minced chives

2 teaspoons minced flat-leaf parsley

2 teaspoons freshly ground black pepper

Salt

1. Combine all the ingredients and salt to taste in a jar with a tight-fitting lid. Shake vigorously to combine.

2. Chill for at least 2 hours before serving in small individual ramekins as a dipping sauce for Broiled Oysters (page 39), raw or roasted oysters, or for cold, steamed shrimp or crab claws.

MAKES 2/3 CUP, SERVING 4

HOMEMADE MAYONNAISE

If you got a roomful of Savannah cooks together today and tossed the word "salad" into the middle of them, there would soon be a vigorous argument going over which brand of mayonnaise was the "only" one to use. A dwindling few would stand to the side, shaking their heads and remembering a time when no self-respecting Savannah hostess would have let a jar of store-bought mayonnaise within a mile of her kitchen. Many traditional cooks still make it from scratch, even when concerns about using raw eggs made many almost as afraid of homemade mayonnaise as of a burned entrée. Now that we have food processors to make short work of the job and pasteurized eggs to take care of those health concerns, there's no reason not to rediscover the luscious delights of good homemade mayonnaise.

2 large egg yolks (hand method) or 1 whole large egg (processor method)

1 teaspoon dry mustard or 1 tablespoon Dijon-type mustard

Salt and cayenne pepper

1 cup olive, peanut, or other vegetable oil, or 1/4 cup extra virgin olive oil and 3/4 cup peanut or vegetable oil

2 tablespoons freshly squeezed lemon juice or wine vinegar

HAND METHOD:

1. For this method, use only the yolks. Whisk them together in a mixing bowl with the mustard, a healthy pinch of salt, and a tiny one of cayenne until smooth.

2. Put the oil in a container that has a good pouring spout. Whisk a teaspoon of it into the egg until smooth. Whisk in half the remaining oil a few drops at a time, beating well after each addition until it's emulsified.

3. Add a few drops of lemon juice or vinegar and whisk it in, then alternate between the vinegar and oil until both are completely incorporated and the mayonnaise is thick and smooth. Taste and adjust the seasonings and beat them in. Keep it, well covered, in the refrigerator until you are ready to serve it.

FOOD PROCESSOR METHOD:

1. Use only whole egg for this method: the yolks are too delicate to withstand the speed and heat of the processor's blade. Put the egg in the work bowl of a food processor fitted with a steel blade. Add the mustard, a healthy pinch of salt, a tiny one of cayenne, and the lemon juice or vinegar. Process until smooth, about 1 minute.

2. With the motor running, add the oil in a thin, steady stream, which will take between 1 and 2 minutes. When the oil is incorporated, let the machine run for a few seconds more, then stop it, taste and adjust the seasonings, and pulse it a couple of times to mix them in. Keep it, well covered, in the refrigerator until you are ready to serve it.

ONION MAYONNAISE:

Considered indispensable for tomato sandwiches (page 32) by many old Savannah hostesses, the delicate onion flavor also makes it ideal for BLTs, cucumber sandwiches, and shrimp or chicken salad. To make it, just fold 2 tablespoons grated onion into the finished mayonnaise. Let it rest, refrigerated, for at least an hour before using.

HERB MAYONNAISE:

Use the food processor method and add 1 small clove garlic, crushed and peeled, and 1 rounded tablespoon each minced green onion, roughly chopped basil or mint, and rosemary to the work bowl at the beginning of step 1. Do not use dried herbs.

MAKES 1-1/2 CUPS

Parties & Receptions

Appetizers, First Courses, Finger Food, and Beverages

IN EVERYTHING THAT HAS BEEN WRITTEN about Savannah society, a common theme runs consistent and sure: no one else can throw a party the way we do. That reputation has engendered both praise and notoriety. Known for the kind of elegant and gracious welcome that earned the name The Hostess City from European nobility, presidents, and such towering literary figures as William Thackery and Oscar Wilde, Savannah is also host to a St. Patrick's Day celebration that has been described as the largest and most unbridled outdoor cocktail party outside of Mardi Gras in New Orleans.

Part of the Savannah party reputation stems from a unique and wonderful array of food that is delicious, bountiful, and, though elegantly presented, unpretentious. Hosts who don't actually do the cooking themselves will make sure that they've hired the best caterer they can afford. As is true anywhere else in America, Savannahians are not immune to fashion, and there will always be something new and trendy on the menu, yet the sensible core of the food will be tried and true recipes that have been passed down for generations.

Another part of the equation is the almost mythical graciousness of the hosts themselves. It takes a lot for us to be rude to someone under our roof. Most would die rather than make a guest—even one they do not like—uncomfortable. More than one brash newcomer has been marked off a Savannah guest list without a clue it was happening because the hostess smiled and called them sugar right up to the moment that she closed the front door on them for the last time. As a

Facing: Shad Roe Caviar with Mini Buttermilk Hoecakes (page 102) and traditional condiments. Above: City Hall (1902) and the Savannah River.

25

Butter Roasted Pecans.

friend put it so well, Southerners are people who will be polite right up to (and including) the moment they take aim with the pistol.

But the main reason that Savannah parties are so memorable has less to do with the food or any innate graciousness on the part of the hosts. You do not have to serve Lucille Wright's legendary tomato sandwiches; you do not need imported caviar and champagne or a fully stocked bar rivaling the Oak Room at the Plaza Hotel. In the aftermath of the War Between the States, refreshments at many a fashionable ball were little more than water and cold biscuits. No, the secret to our parties lies in this simple fact: Savannahians give parties not out of a sense of social or professional obligation, to pay back debts, impress neighbors, or make headway with a taciturn boss or client, but because they like giving them, and because they invite people they really care about rather than people they think they ought to. Yes, just like everywhere else there are social climbers who come here and throw showy gatherings with guest lists made up by status rather than compatibility. Such parties always cause a stir, and a few of them have entered into local legend, but in the end, they are not the ones that have built Savannah's reputation as The Hostess City.

In short, the reason you have a good time at a Savannah party is because the host is having a good time. And that, my friends, is the whole secret.

BUTTER ROASTED PECANS

Most recipes call for a high temperature roasting, but former *Savannah Morning News* food editor Martha Giddens Nesbit long ago gave us the secret to consistent perfection: slow roasting at a much lower temperature.

1 pound shelled whole pecans   Salt
2 tablespoons unsalted butter

1. Position a rack in the center of the oven and preheat it to 200 degrees F. Put the pecans into a deep-rimmed pan (a 9 x 13-inch sheet cake pan is ideal) and shake the pan to level them. Cut the butter into teaspoon-size bits and scatter it over the pecans.

2. Put the pecans into the center of the oven and toast until the butter is melted, about 15 minutes. Take them out and toss until the pecans are well coated. Roast about 45 minutes longer, stirring every 15 minutes. The pecans continue to cook after they come out of the oven, so don't let them get too dark. To test them for doneness, cool a pecan slightly and break it in half. The center should be a delicate but distinct beige.

3. While the pecans are hot, salt them generously and toss until they are well coated. Serve warm or at room temperature. Once the pecans are completely cooled, store them in an airtight tin box or plastic container.

SERVES 4 TO 6 AS HORS D'OEUVRES

VARIATION: DAMON LEE'S ROSEMARY ROASTED PECANS
During the last 5 minutes of roasting, I toss the pecans with 2 tablespoons of chopped fresh rosemary.

We begin where almost all Savannah hosts begin—after, of course, stocking the bar—with the quintessential party snack: Georgia pecans slow roasted in good butter and tossed with plenty of salt. Though pecans are enjoyed throughout the South, Georgia is America's leading producer of this truly American delicacy, and so it is not surprising that we Savannahians make great use of them in our cooking. Of all the culinary creations they've inspired, however, nothing equals the exquisite simplicity of the season's first fat, sweet pecans simply roasted in butter. Since the harvest parallels the beginning of the old social season, a Savannah party just isn't a party without them.

CHEESE STRAWS (OR BISCUITS)

In nineteenth-century Savannah manuscripts and community cookbooks, these appeared under the name "biscuit," but they're not to be confused with the cheese-flecked baking powder bread popular today. Like the Parmesan Wafers that follow it here, biscuit was being used in its older, original meaning to describe a crisp wafer cracker or cookie.

Today cheese straws are standard fare for any reception or cocktail party in Savannah, but a few traditional hosts still serve them in the old-fashioned way, as a crisp, savory accompaniment to soups and salads.

The secret to good cheese straws is, of course, good cheese. While the original may have been made with Parmesan, an old, super-sharp cheddar has long been the local standard. We use the orange kind, often mixed with a little Parmesan for sass, though white cheddar can, of course, be substituted if you prefer it; just use the oldest, sharpest cheese you can get your hands on.

3/4 pound (12 ounces) well-aged, extra-sharp cheddar, finely grated

1/4 pound (4 ounces) Parmigiano-Reggiano, finely grated

1/2 cup or 1 stick unsalted butter, softened

1 generous teaspoon ground cayenne pepper, or more, to taste

1/2 teaspoon salt

10 ounces (about 2 cups) Southern soft wheat flour or all-purpose flour

1. In a food processor fitted with a steel blade or with a mixer, cream the cheese and butter until fluffy and smooth.

2. Add the cayenne, salt, and flour and work it into the dough until smooth. Gather it into a ball, wrap well in plastic wrap or wax paper, and chill it for at least half an hour. Don't let it chill hard. If you make the dough ahead, let it soften at room temperature so that it's pliable.

3. Position a rack in the center of the oven and preheat to 325 degrees F. Put the dough in a cookie press fitted with the star die (or a pastry bag fitted with a star tip) and press it out onto an ungreased baking sheet into narrow 2-1/2-inch straws, about 1/2 inch apart. It can also be rolled out on a lightly floured work surface about 1/4 inch thick and cut with a sharp knife or a zigzag pastry wheel into 1/2 x 2-1/2-inch strips. It's a nice touch to roll them out about 1/8-inch thick and gently twist each straw into a spiral. We also use cookie cutters to cut the dough into seasonal shapes—autumn leaves, Christmas stars, Valentine hearts, and, of course, St. Patrick's shamrocks.

4. Bake for about 16 to 18 minutes, being careful not to let them brown. The bottoms should be golden, but the tops and sides should not color. Cool on the pan or on wire racks before transferring them to an airtight storage container.

MAKES ABOUT 10 DOZEN

Cheese Straws.

PARMESAN WAFERS (BISCUITS)

The recipe from which this is adapted called for equal weights of butter, Parmesan, and flour, with no mention of added moisture, but Parmigiano has a much lower moisture content than cheddar and isn't moist enough to hold the dough together. Surely, the author took for granted that the reader knew to add just enough cold water to make the dough workable. It makes a firmer, crisper wafer, ideal for accompanying a soup or salad, drinks before dinner, or a glass of Madeira after.

1/2 cup or 1 stick unsalted butter, softened

8 ounces Parmigiano-Reggiano cheese

8 ounces (about 1-1/2 cups) Southern soft wheat flour or pastry flour

1/2 teaspoon cayenne pepper, more or less, to taste

Salt

1/3 to 1/2 cup ice water

1. Using a mixer or food processor fitted with a steel blade, cream the butter and cheese until light and fluffy. Sift or whisk together the flour, cayenne, and a small pinch of salt. Work the flour into the creamed butter and cheese until smooth, then work in ice water a tablespoon at a time until it is just holding together (you may not need all of it). Gather it into a flat disk, wrap it well with plastic wrap, and refrigerate for about 20 minutes.

2. Position a rack in the center of the oven and preheat it to 325 degrees F. Lightly flour a work surface and rolling pin and roll out the dough to the thickness of a standard piecrust (about 1/8-inch).

3. Using a small (1-1/2-inch) biscuit cutter or decorative cookie cutters, cut it into rounds or fanciful shapes. The scraps can be carefully reworked. Gather them into a smooth ball, wrap well, and refrigerate for 20 minutes before re-rolling and cutting. Transfer them to an ungreased baking sheet using a thin flexible spatula, spacing about 1/2-inch apart, and bake until colored a pale gold, about 16 to 18 minutes. Cool on wire racks.

MAKES ABOUT 4 DOZEN

Like cheese straws, these are biscuits in the older, British sense of the word. This is the older version of the previous recipe, which became popular in Savannah during the last half of the nineteenth century. Though any hard cheese can be used to make them, and today cheddar is the most common, Parmesan was probably the original and seems to have been preferred by many traditional cooks.

Parmesan Wafers.

BENNE COCKTAIL BITS

Introduced into the Lowcountry by the West African slave trade, benne (sesame seeds) have become an indelible part of the region's cookery. While more commonly found in sweets and confections, they occasionally turn up in savory dishes, most notably this fiery little cocktail nibble. This is my own version, flavored with a touch of garlic, lemon zest, and rosemary.

1/2 cup white (hulled) sesame seeds

5 ounces (about 1 cup) unbleached all-purpose flour

1/2 teaspoon salt, plus more for sprinkling

1/4 teaspoon freshly ground black pepper

About 1/4 teaspoon (or more, to taste) ground cayenne pepper

8 tablespoons unsalted butter, 4 of them cut into 1/4-inch bits

Grated zest of 1 lemon

1 generously rounded tablespoon chopped fresh rosemary (do not use dried)

2 tablespoons freshly squeezed lemon juice

2 to 3 tablespoons ice water

2 cloves garlic, crushed and peeled but left whole

1. Position a rack in the center of the oven and preheat it to 350 degrees F. Spread the sesame seeds on a metal pie plate or cake pan and toast them in the center of the oven to a pale gold, stirring frequently. Let them cool completely.

2. Whisk or sift together the flour, salt, pepper, and cayenne in a mixing bowl. Work in the butter cut into bits with your fingers until the flour resembles coarse meal. Add the sesame seeds, lemon zest, and rosemary and toss to mix. Sprinkle in the lemon juice and a tablespoon of ice water and work it into a dough that just clumps together and holds its shape, adding water by drops as needed. Gather it into a smooth ball, cover well with plastic wrap, and refrigerate for 30 minutes. Meanwhile, heat the remaining butter and garlic in a small saucepan over medium heat, stirring and mashing on the garlic until it is golden. Turn off the heat.

3. Sprinkle a work surface with flour and roll the dough out slightly thicker than a pie crust—just over 1/8-inch thick. Cut the dough into rounds with a 1-inch round or decorative cookie cutter. Transfer them to an ungreased baking sheet with a spatula and bake in the center of the oven until just beginning to color, about 10 minutes. Remove and brush them with the garlic butter, lightly sprinkle with salt, and return them to the oven. Bake until golden brown, about 3 to 6 minutes longer. Cool on the baking sheet and store in an airtight tin.

MAKES ABOUT 4 DOZEN

Angel Wings with a tall, cold Maharaja's Burra Peg.

ANGEL WINGS

1 teaspoon butter, melted
1/4 teaspoon salt
1 tablespoon sugar
1 large egg, at room temperature
1 tablespoon heavy cream

1 teaspoon brandy or bourbon
5 ounces (about 1 cup)
    all-purpose flour
Lard or peanut oil, for frying

1. Beat together the butter, salt, sugar, and egg. Stir in the cream and brandy, then work in the flour until the dough is the firm consistency of a cookie dough. Cover and refrigerate it for half an hour. Pinch off the dough into 1-inch-diameter pieces.

2. Put enough lard or oil into a deep skillet or heavy-bottomed Dutch oven to cover the bottom by at least an inch but to come no more than halfway up the sides. Heat it to 365 degrees F. Meanwhile, on a floured work surface roll out 3 pieces of dough into the thinnest possible wafers. Make 3 slashes on one side of each and carefully transfer them to the fat. Fry until the bottoms are golden brown, about 1 to 2 minutes, and turn carefully. Fry until uniformly golden, about a minute longer. They are ready to take up when they stop sizzling. Carefully remove them with tongs and drain on absorbent paper. Sprinkle lightly with salt while they're hot and repeat with the remaining dough.

MAKES ABOUT 12 TO 14

While Savannahians love big parties, their favorite way of entertaining is a small, intimate dinner party—ideally for six, and not more than eight, people. These delicate wafers are tailor-made for just such a gathering, the perfect accompaniment for drinks before an intimate, leisurely dinner. Though labor intensive, they are certainly worth it—and, besides, can be made entirely ahead and stored in an airtight tin. The recipe is credited in an old community cookbook to Mrs. Asa Medlin.

Sunday coffee hour at historic St. John's Episcopal Church has changed very little in the last half century. Set in the refined elegance of the church's parish house, the Gothic-Revival Green-Meldrim House (1853), it's an old-fashioned silver and lace affair, where coffee and hot tea are dispensed from Victorian silver urns into real china cups and tables are laden with an assortment of homemade baked goods and tea sandwiches. About the only real change of substance is that the ladies who pour are no longer required to wear hats and gloves—and that has been more recently than you probably think.

An indispensable element of these receptions is, of course, tomato sandwiches, made indescribably delicious by housekeeper Shirley Cannon. No matter what kind of sermon about charity the congregation has just heard, the sandwiches are greedily snatched up and gone in 5 minutes, leaving only depressingly empty, mayonnaise-stained doilies for latecomers and choir members. Shirley's secret is bacon and lots of it. Need I say more?

The Ultimate Tomato Sandwich

FROM JUNE UNTIL THE FIRST SEVERE COLD SNAP in late November or December, tomato sandwiches are expected at any Savannah party or reception. Over the years, local caterers have become legendary for The Ultimate Tomato Sandwich—from departed geniuses like Daisy Redman, Lucile Wright, Sally Sullivan, and Marjory Mingledorff to living legends like Susan Mason and Shirley Cannon. The older versions were made with delicate onion mayonnaise, but contemporary caterers use herb mayonnaise fragrant with basil or bump the flavor up with seasoned salt. Underneath this culinary window-dressing, however, they are all pretty similar, and their real success depends not on what is done to the tomatoes and mayonnaise, but on how good they are to begin with. If the tomatoes are those boiled Styrofoam, out-of-season, artificially ripened types, and the mayonnaise is an indifferent commercial one, well, the sandwich just doesn't have a prayer and that's all there is to it.

SHIRLEY'S TOMATO SANDWICHES

About 5 to 6 medium ripe tomatoes
Salt
60 thin slices firm home-style white bread

About 1 cup mayonnaise, preferably Homemade Mayonnaise (page 22)
8 slices bacon, cooked crisp and finely crumbled
McCormick's Seasoning Salt

1. Cut out the stem end of the tomatoes, and, if you like, peel them with a vegetable peeler (a serrated soft fruit peeler works best). Cut them into 30 even slices. Spread the tomatoes on a platter and sprinkle lightly with salt. Let them stand 15 minutes, drain well, and pat dry. Cut each slice of bread into rounds with a large (2-1/4-inch) biscuit cutter.

2. Blend together the mayonnaise and bacon bits, and mix in seasoning salt to taste. Spread on one side of each round of bread. Lay 1 tomato slice over half the bread rounds, top with remaining bread, spread-side-down. Cut each sandwich in half.

3. Line two 12-inch round trays with paper lace doilies. Arrange the sandwiches on the trays by standing them up on the flat cut side in concentric circles. Serve immediately.

MAKES 30 ROUND OR 60 HALF-MOON SANDWICHES

Shirley's Tomato Sandwiches.

VARIATIONS

For a traditional old-style Savannah tomato sandwich, omit the bacon and seasoning salt and substitute Onion Mayonnaise (page 23). Contemporary celebrity caterer Susan Mason omits the bacon and uses Lawry's Seasoned Salt instead of McCormick's and garnishes each sandwich with bits of fresh basil. The legendary Lucille Wright, whose tomato sandwiches were immortalized in *Midnight in the Garden of Good and Evil*, also used Lawry's Seasoned Salt with onion mayonnaise and made up the sandwiches with thin-sliced white and rye bread—one on each side. My own version omits bacon and seasoning salt and uses Herb Mayonnaise (page 23), made with basil and mint.

CRAB AND PECAN–STUFFED MUSHROOMS

Nothing shows Savannah's indifference to fashion like a cocktail buffet. Passing fads inevitably make an appearance, but some things remain standard no matter what their status with the foodie crowd. Bite-size mushroom caps piled generously with savory fillings are one such perennial favorite. Like the little girl with the curl, when they are good, they are very, very good, and when they are bad—well, you know the rest. This savory crab filling is very good indeed.

Led by stellar cook and master party-planner Jeannie Knight, the Parent Teacher organization of St. Andrews School put together the award-winning cookbook, *First Come, First Served . . . In Savannah.* Not only is it one of the best community cookbooks anywhere, the ladies who put it together know how to throw a party and bring that expertise to the pages of their book with style. In fact, they love parties so much that they'll use just about any excuse to throw one, including a newspaper interview. After suggesting that they might cook a couple of recipes for the photos, our team arrived to find a party ready and waiting to happen. The table was covered end to end with food, wine flowed freely, and as husbands began drifting in, the interview summarily was forgotten.

24 large crimini or small portobello mushrooms
Salt and whole black pepper in a peppermill
4 tablespoons unsalted butter, divided
1 large clove garlic, lightly crushed, peeled, and minced
1 (8-ounce) package cream cheese, softened

1 tablespoon milk
6 ounces (about 1 cup) crabmeat
1/2 cup chopped pecans
2 tablespoons minced green onion
1/2 teaspoon horseradish
1 teaspoon Worcestershire sauce
1/2 cup fine dry breadcrumbs

1. Position a rack in the upper third of the oven and preheat it to 350 degrees F. Wipe the mushrooms thoroughly with a dry cloth or paper towels. Remove the stems and chop them. Put the caps top-down in one layer in a shallow baking dish. Season well with salt and pepper.

2. Melt 2 tablespoons of butter in a sauté pan over medium high heat. Add the chopped stems and sauté, tossing, until firm and opaque, about 4 minutes. Add the garlic and sauté until fragrant, about half a minute. Scrape it into a mixing bowl and add the cream cheese, milk, crab, pecans, green onion, horseradish, and Worcestershire sauce. Season with salt and pepper and mix well.

3. Wipe out the sauté pan and put in the remaining 2 tablespoons of butter. Melt it over low heat and add the crumbs, mixing until the butter is evenly absorbed. Turn off the heat. Spoon the crab filling into the mushroom caps and sprinkle the tops evenly with buttered crumbs. Bake until browned on top and bubbly, about 12 to 15 minutes.

SERVES 6 AS A FIRST COURSE, 8 TO 10 AS HORS D'OEUVRES

JOAN'S CRAB TASSIES

1/2 cup or 1 stick unsalted butter, softened

3 ounces cream cheese, softened

4 ounces (1 light cup) all-purpose flour

1 pound claw crabmeat

1/4 teaspoon salt

1/2 teaspoon seasoning salt

1/2 cup mayonnaise

1 tablespoon freshly squeezed lemon juice

1/2 cup grated Swiss cheese

1/4 cup fresh dill weed, chopped

1/4 cup minced flat-leaf parsley

2 medium green onions, minced

1/2 teaspoon Worcestershire sauce

Dash Tabasco sauce

1 teaspoon sherry

Sweet paprika

Tassies are little cream cheese pastry tartlets. Usually they're filled with a rich, golden pecan custard, but here the pastry encases a savory and highly addictive filling of crabmeat, herbs, and cheese. The recipe is from the files of Joan Levy, a wonderful cook, gracious hostess, and good friend.

1. Cream the butter and cream cheese together until light and very fluffy. Stir in the flour and shape the dough into 24 equal balls. Chill for 1 hour, then press into the cups of a non-stick or lightly buttered mini muffin pan to form shells.

2. Position a rack in the center of the oven and preheat it to 350 degrees F. Pick over the crabmeat for bits of shell and mix it with the remaining ingredients except the paprika. Divide the filling among the prepared pastries, mounding it in the center, and sprinkle lightly with paprika. Bake until golden brown, about 30 minutes. Let cool somewhat before taking them from the pan. They can be made ahead, covered, and refrigerated or frozen. Reheat on an ungreased baking sheet at 350 degrees F.

MAKES 24

Baked Crabs, or Hot Crab Casserole or Dip.

BAKED CRABS, OR
HOT CRAB CASSEROLE OR DIP

This lovely old recipe is very versatile; served as it originally was, in the back shells, it makes an elegant dinner first course or luncheon main dish on the most refined table. When baked in a casserole, it satisfies more casual family suppers but can also do duty as a hot dip, with crackers or toast cups, on the cocktail buffet. In some manuscripts, this recipe is attributed to Savannah's nineteenth-century culinary legend, Leila Habersham.

1 dozen whole boiled crabs (page 16), picked clean, 6 back shells reserved or 1 pound (2 cups) cooked crab-meat

6 large hard-cooked eggs, whites and yolks separated

1 cup fine cracker crumbs, divided

1/4 teaspoon dry mustard powder

Juice of 1 lemon

1/4 cup grated onion

2 cups heavy cream

1/4 cup dry sherry

Salt and whole white pepper in a pep-permill

Whole nutmeg in a grater

1 tablespoon butter

1. Position a rack in the upper third of the oven and preheat it to 375 degrees F. Pick over the crab for bits of shell and cartilage and put it in a mixing bowl. Roughly chop the egg whites and toss them together with the crab. If you are stuffing individual back shells, add half the cracker crumbs to the bowl.

2. Press the yolks through a sieve into a separate bowl. Add the mustard, the lemon juice and onion and mix until smooth. Gradually mix in the cream and then the sherry. Season with salt, white pepper, and nutmeg. Add to the crabmeat mixture and mix well.

3. Put the reserved back shells on a rimmed baking sheet or butter a shallow 2-quart casserole. Spoon the crabmeat into the shells or casserole. Melt the butter in a small pan over medium heat. Stir in the remaining crumbs and stir until evenly coated. Sprinkle the crumbs over the crab and bake until golden brown and bubbly, about 30 minutes.

SERVES 6 AS A FIRST COURSE

CHAFING DISH OYSTERS

Creamed oysters, enriched with bourbon and sherry and served from a silver chafing dish, were once a standard for any autumn or winter party in Savannah. Old-fashioned hostesses still provide baskets of crisp, buttery toast cups for guests to help themselves; others use purchased pastry shells, though they don't hold up nearly as well as the toast cups.

1 pint shucked oysters
3 tablespoons unsalted butter
1/2 cup finely minced shallots
2 tablespoons flour
1 cup heavy cream (minimum 36% milk fat)
1 tablespoon bourbon

2 tablespoons dry sherry
2 teaspoons Worcestershire sauce
Salt and whole black pepper in a peppermill
Toast Cups (below) or bite-size pastry shells

1. Drain the oysters in a sieve set over a bowl. Heat the butter in a sauté pan over medium heat. When it is hot and foaming, add the shallots and sauté, tossing frequently, until they are golden but not browned. Add the flour and stir until smooth.

2. Slowly stir in the drained oyster liquor and bring it to a simmer, stirring constantly. Cook until the sauce is thickened, and then slowly stir in the cream. Bring it to a simmer, stirring constantly, and cook until it is again thickened, about 4 minutes.

3. Add the oysters, bourbon, sherry, and Worcestershire and cook just long enough for their gills to curl. Taste and season well with salt and pepper. Pour into the chafing dish and serve with toast cups or pastry shells.

SERVES 10 TO 12 AS HORS D'OEUVRES

TOAST CUPS

36 extra-thin sandwich slices white bread

About 6 tablespoons salted butter, melted, optional

1. Position a rack in the center of the oven and preheat to 325 degrees F. Trim the crusts from the bread and brush each lightly on both sides with melted butter (you may omit the butter for lighter cups). Gently pinch the centers of each side inward and put the bread into the wells of a mini muffin pan, then press them carefully into the sides and bottom, allowing the four corners to point up and out like tulip petals.

2. Bake until golden brown and crisp, about 20 minutes. Let them cool and air dry until crisp, then store in an airtight tin until needed. They will keep for up to a week if buttered, a month if toasted plain.

MAKES 3 DOZEN

BROILED OYSTERS SAVANNAH-STYLE

The oysters from the tidal creeks and riverbeds around Savannah are more intense and briny than those from other parts of the country. When broiling them in the shell, local restaurants top the oysters with everything from garlic butter and Parmesan cheese to elaborate mixtures of peppers, onions, and lots of bacon. But home cooks know that when the oysters are really good, it is always wisest to err on the side of simplicity. They'll just top them with a square of bacon or a dollop of plain or garlic butter to keep them moist. This version is a little dressier but still in line with those ideas of simplicity.

24 live oysters in shell
1/2 cup finely chopped bacon (about 2 slices)
1/4 cup finely chopped shallots or green onions
2 large cloves garlic, lightly crushed, peeled, and minced
1/2 cup saltine cracker crumbs
Whole black pepper in a peppermill
Anita's Sauce Mignonette (page 21)

1. Position a rack 4 to 6 inches from the heat source and preheat the broiler for at least 15 minutes. Shuck the oysters and cut them loose from the shell, but leave them in the deep halves. Discard the shallow top shells. Spread a 1/2-inch-thick layer of rock salt on a rimmed baking sheet roasting pan. Press the oysters in the shells into the salt until they are level.

2. Mix together the bacon, onion, garlic, crumbs, and a generous grinding of pepper. Sprinkle evenly over each oyster.

3. Broil the oysters until the bacon-crumb topping is golden brown and the gills are lightly curled, about 4 minutes. Quickly arrange the oysters 3 or 4 to a plate (preferably on oyster plates) and put small cups of sauce in the center of each. Garnish with lemon and serve immediately.

SERVES 6 TO 8 AS A FIRST COURSE

Pickled Shrimp.

PICKLED SHRIMP

Historically, shrimp were pickled in spicy marinades as a kind of conserve, but today they are relished more for their flavor than shelf life. At receptions and cocktail parties, Savannah hosts serve them from heirloom silver bowls imbedded in crushed ice. They're also enjoyed on beds of crisp lettuce as a first course for sit-down dinners and as a refreshing summer luncheon or supper entrée.

4 tablespoons Seafood Boiling Spice (page 6), divided

2 large bay leaves, crumbled if dried, chopped if fresh, divided

6 large garlic cloves, lightly crushed and peeled, divided

1 large rib celery, including the leafy top, thinly sliced

Salt

2 pounds small to medium shrimp

1 cup white wine vinegar

1/2 cup minced shallots or Vidalia sweet onions

2 large lemons, zest removed from 1 in strips with a zester, 1 thinly sliced

2 to 3 tablespoons extra virgin olive oil, optional

4 to 6 fresh lettuce leaves

2 tablespoons chopped flat-leaf parsley

1. Put 3 quarts of water in a large stainless steel or enameled pot. Add half the boiling spice, 1 bay leaf, 3 garlic cloves, the sliced celery, and a small handful of salt. Bring to a boil over medium-high heat, reduce the heat to medium, and simmer 10 minutes. Raise the heat, add the shrimp, cover, and count 2 minutes. Drain well, rinse under cold running water, and then peel and devein the shrimp.

2. Bring the vinegar, onions, and remaining bay leaf, spices, and garlic to a full boil in a saucepan over medium high heat, reduce the heat to low, and simmer 5 minutes. Turn off the heat. Let it cool slightly and pour it over the shrimp. Mix in the lemon zest and juice the lemon into it through a strainer. Toss well and let cool completely. Cover and marinate, refrigerated, for at least 4 hours and as long as 24 hours. They will actually keep for up to 2 weeks, refrigerated.

3. To serve, lift the shrimp from the marinade. If you like, you may dress them lightly with a few spoonfuls of olive oil to taste. Line a platter or shallow serving bowl with lettuce leaves. Mound the shrimp on top of them and garnish with sliced lemon and parsley.

SERVES 8 TO 12

RENCE'S SHRIMP MOUSSE

Rence Smyth may have been born and raised in Connecticut, but she's been in Savannah for so long that she drawls with the best of us, and people actually repeat rude Yankee jokes to her, forgetting that she—at least technically—actually is one. More to the point, she is also a wonderful and exuberant cook. Her shrimp mousse has become an institution at St. John's choir parties and at just about any gathering in her Ardsley Park neighborhood. She probably gets tired of making it, but we never get tired of eating it. In fact, she claims that any leftover mousse is good on toast for breakfast, though I'm not really sure how she knows—since the platter almost always goes home scraped clean.

1 bay leaf
1 inch or more peeled lemon rind
1 sprig parsley
1/2 teaspoon dried thyme
4 to 6 whole black peppercorns
1 bottle beer
1 pound (headless weight) raw shrimp
2 envelopes unflavored gelatin
1/2 cup cold water
8 ounces cream cheese, softened

5 tablespoons chili sauce
3/4 cup finely chopped celery
1/4 cup finely chopped scallions
1 tablespoon Worcestershire sauce
1 teaspoon freshly squeezed lemon juice, or to taste
1 teaspoon hot sauce
1 cup mayonnaise
Salt and whole black pepper in a peppermill

1. Half fill a 4-quart pot with water and add the bay leaf, lemon rind, parsley, thyme, and peppercorns. Bring to a boil over high heat and slowly add the beer (it will foam up). Let it return to a boil and add the shrimp. Cook until they just turn pink, about 3 to 5 minutes, depending upon size. Drain well and rinse with cold water to arrest the cooking. Peel and devein the shrimp and transfer put them to in a food processor fitted with a steel blade. Pulse until they are minced fine but not puréed.

2. Sprinkle the gelatin over the cold water and let it soften 10 minutes. Meanwhile, gently heat the cream cheese and chili sauce in a small saucepan over the very lowest possible heat, stirring occasionally until smooth and heated through. Add the gelatin and cook, stirring, until it is dissolved. Remove from heat and let cool. When it is merely lukewarm, add it to the food processor and pulse until fairly well mixed.

3. Add the celery, scallion, Worcestershire sauce, lemon juice, and hot sauce and pulse until evenly mixed, but don't overdo it; they should still have plenty of texture. Fold in the mayonnaise by pulsing until it is mixed, season with salt and pepper, and pulse again. Rinse out a 5-1/2-cup mold with cold water and pour in the mousse. Cover loosely with plastic wrap and refrigerate for at least 4 hours or overnight.

4. When ready to serve, run a thin, sharp knife around the edges of the mousse and dip the mold (without submerging it) in very hot water long enough to loosen the mousse. Invert onto a serving platter and lift the mold away. Garnish with parsley, cress, or other greenery and serve with crackers.

MAKES ABOUT 5-1/2 CUPS, SERVING 15 TO 20 AS COCKTAIL HORS D'OEUVRES

Tybee Shrimp and Crab Cocktail.

TYBEE SHRIMP AND CRAB COCKTAIL

Tybee Island native Bonnie Gaster is always doing something for someone, and her house has a steady stream of impromptu company at cocktail hour. During shrimp and crab season, she'll just put out a large platter of freshly picked lump crabmeat drizzled with two contrasting cocktail sauces, baskets of saltine crackers, and an extra bowl of sauce for dipping perfectly poached, ice-cold inlet shrimp. Here is a dressed-up version.

1 pound lump crabmeat

1 recipe Savannah Seafood Cocktail Sauce (page 19) and Bonnie's White Crab Cocktail Sauce (page 20), or Bonnie's Wow Now Cocktail Sauce (page 20)

2 tablespoons chopped fresh chives or green onion tops

30 large cooked shrimp (See Poached Shrimp, page 18), peeled and deveined

1 lemon or lime, cut into 6 wedges

1. Make sure everything is thoroughly chilled. Chill 6 stemmed cocktail glasses or footed compotes. Divide the crabmeat among the glasses.

2. Drizzle the sauce generously over the crabmeat, sprinkle it with chives, and hang 5 shrimp and 1 lemon wedge around the rim of each glass. Serve immediately.

SERVES 6

Savannah Seafood Cocktails

Shrimp cocktails, that quintessential steak house appetizer of the 1940s and 50s, fell out of favor with the gourmet foodie crowd in the 80s and all but disappeared from restaurant menus and private dinner parties—everywhere, that is, except Savannah. Cold seafood—not only shrimp, but freshly picked lump crabmeat, cracked crab claws, and raw or steamed oysters—accompanied by plenty of spicy horseradish sauce for dipping—remains a popular appetizer here. At parties where real cocktails are served, the seafood is simply piled onto a chilled platter with bowls of cocktail sauce and crackers nearby so that guests can help themselves. The fastidious provide toothpicks, but as the drink flows, even the most formally dressed eventually abandon daintiness and use their fingers.

SHAD CAVIAR

During shad season, locals relish the rich, golden roe mainly as a seasonal breakfast and supper treat, but it is also delicious served just like a fine caviar—and, needless to say, at a fraction of the costs of sturgeon roe. Its assertive flavor stands up very well to martinis, whiskey, and to those infamous Savannah cocktail concoctions.

1 set shad roe

Juice of 2 lemons

Salt

About 1/2 cup minced green or yellow onion

1 hard-cooked egg, pressed through a sieve

About 1/2 cup sour cream

Lemon wedges

Cornbread Madeleines or Mini Hoecakes for Caviar (see Buttermilk Hoecakes, page 102), or crackers, melba toast rounds, or blinis, for serving

1. Rinse the roe under cold water and put it in a covered, close-fitting pan. Add the lemon juice, cover, and bring to a simmer over medium heat. Reduce the heat to medium low and cook till firm, about 20 minutes. Drain. Cool, scrape the roe from its membrane, and season well with salt. Chill well.

2. Serve in a bowl set in crushed ice, with the onion, egg, sour cream, and lemon in separate iced bowls and warmed Cornbread Madeleines or Mini Hoecakes (or crackers or toast) in a napkin-lined basket.

SERVES 6 TO 8 AS HORS D'OEUVRES

GEORGIA STURGEON CAVIAR

Real sturgeon caviar is harvested and cured off the Georgia and Carolina coast. While it's regulated and expensive, it's a fraction of the cost of Beluga caviar and, when harvested and cured properly, rivals it for quality and flavor. Serve it as for Shad Caviar, above. Omit the shad roe, lemon juice, and salt and step 1, using 1 cup caviar.

Shad Caviar (this page) on Mini Buttermilk Hoecakes (page 102).

Beverages

Madeira and Savannah

Madeira, the legendary wine named for the island off the coast of Morocco from which it comes, has a long association with Savannah. Imported since Colonial times—as early as the 1760s it was advertised in Georgia's first newspaper—Madeira owes a large portion of its enormous success in the nineteenth century to our city. By the 1820s, it had become so popular with the elite that the city was a major player in the import trade. Wealthy collectors acquired entire cellars of it that are legendary among connoisseurs (the last of which was auctioned off by Sotheby's), and Madeira parties were common entertainments. Held after dinner at 5 o'clock (until living memory, dinner in many Savannah homes was served mid-afternoon), these informal gatherings were occasions for the host to share and show off those prized Madeira cellars. The parties occurred after a meal by design: the only food served was olives and toasted nuts, more as palate cleansers than refreshment, because this wine is best enjoyed alone. A really fine dessert Madeira is meant to be drunk as the dessert, not *with* it.

Madeira and Toasted Pecans on a late eighteenth century French refreshment table.

A whisper of Savannah's Madeira culture lingers in the venerable Madeira Club, which has been active for more than sixty years. Its all-male member-ship has included such distinguished men as philanthropist banker Mills B. Lane, whose famous cellar of Madeira was stored in a vault at Citizens and Southern Bank, famed writer Arthur Gordon, and The Hon. Judge Alexander Lawrence, who ordered the desegregation of Chatham County's public schools. Members gather in black tie formality to enjoy good food, lively debates, and, of course, fine Madeira. Their letterhead is—what else—the execution of the Duke of Clarence, who in 1478 chose his own manner of death: drowning in a vat of Madeira.

Like port and sherry, Madeira is a "fortified" wine. Brandy is added after the initial fermentation so that the yeast doesn't consume all the sugars, re-sulting in a sweeter, richer, and more potent wine. Historically, it was rather ordinary until distributors discovered quite by accident that it was actually improved after shipping through the tropics—to places like Savannah.

Continued on page 46

Exposure to heat, air, and agitation—things that would ruin most wines—gave Madeira a character it had been lacking before. Some experts also believe that the partial pasteurization of this process is why the wine is practically ageless—there are rare two hundred year old Madeiras that are not only still drinkable, but exceptional.

Most Madeiras sold today are blends of several vintages, and common label wines are mostly made from tinta negra mole grapes. However, four historic varieties of grapes account for most of the classic vintage Madeiras, and it is from these grapes that the four classic styles of Madeira are named: Sercial, pale gold and moderately dry, from grapes grown at the highest elevation on the island; Verdelho, sweeter and richer than Sercial, is deep gold to amber and made from grapes grown right at sea level; Bual, a rich, sweet wine with a correspondingly rich, deep color, is from grapes that grow a few hundred feet above sea level; and Malmsey (or Malvazia), the richest and sweetest of them all. The other style you're likely to see on the label is "Rainwater." One of the most popular Madeiras in the U.S., this Verdelho- or Bual-style wine supposedly got its name when its casks accidentally absorbed rainwater, thus diluting the wine and making it less potent.

All of that is to help you choose Madeira for drinking. To choose one for the pot, use the same judgment as with any other wine: not one you can't drink, only one you might not care to. Most of the recipes herein call for medium-dry Sercial-style, but a moderately priced Rainwater Madeira will also work fine. Save that fine vintage for sipping after dinner or as an aperitif.

CHATHAM ARTILLERY PUNCH

Savannah's infamous signature drink, this innocent-tasting but lethal concoction is supposed to have been created just before the War Between the States by the Chatham Artillery in honor of its rival, the Republican Blues.

1/2 pound green tea leaves
14 large lemons, divided
2 pounds light brown sugar
1 gallon dark rum

1 gallon brandy
1 gallon rye or bourbon whiskey
1 case (12 bottles) champagne

1. In a large container, soak the tea leaves 8 hours or overnight in a gallon of cold water. Strain the liquid from the leaves into a large tub that will hold all the spirits. Juice 12 lemons through a strainer into the tea and add the sugar, stirring until it is dissolved.

2. Stir in the rum, brandy, and whiskey, cover, and let stand at room temperature for at least 8 hours or for up to a week. It's pretty well indestructible at this point.

3. When ready to serve the punch, thinly slice 2 lemons. To serve the punch, allow 6 cups of the base for every bottle of champagne. First pour the brew over an ice ring or large block of ice in a punch bowl. Add the sliced lemon and swirl in the champagne, being careful not to disturb its effervescence. Serve with caution.

MAKES 100 SERVINGS

Notes: The oldest recipes that I've found do not include candied cherries, but most Savannah hosts include them today. If it appeals to you, allow a 6-ounce jar, and—what the heck—throw in the juice, too. A lot of locals do. Gin is often included in modern recipes, but it is not traditional, and merciful heavens—there's already enough alcohol in here to lay an army low as it is. You really don't want to go there.

VARIATION: CHAMPAGNE PUNCH

Lighter and more refreshing than Chatham Artillery Punch—and also much less lethal—this simple punch remains popular for wedding receptions and Christmas parties to this day. Some hosts add 4 to 5 ounces of Curaçao, or Cointreau and a few shots of bitters to the final mix, and float fresh strawberries in the bowl. To serve 25, add the zest (cut in large pieces) and juice of 2 lemons to 2 cups of Simple Syrup (page 51). Add 1 pint brandy and chill thoroughly. Strain, and just before serving, add two thinly sliced lemons and swirl in 2 bottles champagne.

Far be it from me to mess with Savannah legends, but Chatham Artillery bears more than passing resemblance to a punch popular in the household of Britain's George IV, who governed as Prince Regent during the last years of his father's reign. Called, obviously, "Regent's Punch" it became quite popular all along the Eastern seaboard of America, and recipes for it began appearing at least a decade before this punch is supposed to have been created. What's more, suggestively similar concoctions turn up elsewhere—fish house punch in the northeast, for example. Legend holds that the original was mixed in horse-watering tubs. If that offends your modern ideas about sanitation, well, all I can say is you've never experienced Chatham Artillery Punch first hand: no self-respecting germ would live through a dose of this stuff.

SHERRY COBBLER

The name of this very old punch seems curious to modern Americans since, today, a "cobbler" is a deep-dish pie. It's basically a sherry-spiked lemon- or orangeade, milder and easier on your company (not to mention breakable valuables) than Chatham Artillery Punch. This is an old Savannah variation, adapted from a 1913 cookbook published by First Baptist Church—yes, First Baptist. Temperance came late to the Baptist church and even later to the ones here. In those days they didn't have to pretend not to recognize one another in the liquor store.

2 small oranges

2 lemons

1/2 cup sugar, more or less, to taste

1 cup thinly sliced fresh pineapple (do not use canned)

4 cups cold water

1-1/2 cups medium dry sherry, or to taste

Mint sprigs, for garnish

1. Thinly slice 1 orange and 1 lemon and juice the remaining ones. Put the sliced orange in a 2-quart glass pitcher. Sprinkle with sugar and cover with a 1/2-inch layer of finely crushed ice. Next add the sliced lemon, again sprinkle lightly with sugar, and cover with a second layer of ice. Finally add the pineapple, sprinkle with sugar, and top with a third layer of ice. Pour the orange and lemon juice over it and let stand for 30 minutes.

2. Stir in the water and sherry. Taste and adjust the sugar and sherry to suit, then fill the pitcher with crushed ice. Serve in tall glasses with straws, garnishing each serving with mint.

SERVES 8 TO 12

Sherry Cobbler.

Rum and Savannah

In early Colonial Savannah, rum was frowned on by General Oglethorpe and outright forbidden by the Trustees in their original charter, but these had little effect on the drinking habits of Savannahians; both were conveniently and routinely ignored, pretty much the way a similar ban was largely ignored in the 1920s. As historian Carl Weeks put it so well in his book *Savannah in the Time of Peter Tondee*, rum was money—"an investment that readily converted to cash and high profits"—and settlers who could afford it bought it, more than a few sold it on the quiet, and, by all accounts, still more imbibed as often as they could. Eventually, the Trustees recognized the futility of the ban and rescinded it. Today, whiskey probably eclipses rum in most home bars, but it is an essential ingredient in Chatham Artillery Punch and remains a large part of Savannah's party legends.

MILK OF A WILD COW
(MILK RUM PUNCH)

Milk rum punch is an old, old specialty of the Carolinas and Georgia, dating to colonial times. Bowls of this punch were almost certainly shared by the Sons of Liberty at Peter Tondee's tavern. Though served ice cold, it is equally refreshing in cold weather as well as hot, and, at any rate, winter was the only time in Colonial Savannah that it could have been chilled. Variations are legion; this is the one made by the late Max Lippitt, which he dubbed with the peculiarly appropriate moniker "milk of a wild cow." His daughters, Ashby Angell and Anita Clay, still make it, though sometimes Mrs. Angell substitutes bourbon for the rum. A woman after my heart.

18 ounces (2-1/4 cups) light rum

6 ounces (3/4 cup) Jamaican dark rum

12 ounces Simple Syrup (facing)

9 cups (2-1/4 quarts) ice-cold whole milk

1. Combine the rums and syrup the day before, cover, and refrigerate overnight.

2. To serve it, put 3 ounces in each tall glass and fill with 6 ounces (3/4 cup) milk and stir well. You may also mix the rum with the milk in a large punch bowl. Keep cold.

SERVES 12

SIMPLE SYRUP
(FOR DRINKS AND FRUIT)

A basic for the bar because it instantly dissolves in the cold liquids of chilled cocktails and punches, simple syrup's usefulness is not limited to cocktail hour. It's the perfect solution for families' differing tastes in iced tea, and is also useful in the kitchen for fresh fruit desserts and any other sweet in which granulated sugar does not dissolve easily.

2 cups granulated sugar   1 cup water

1. Bring the water and sugar to a simmer in a heavy-bottomed saucepan over medium heat, stirring occasionally. Reduce the heat to medium low and let simmer 5 minutes.

2. Let the syrup cool and decant it into a pint bottle or jar. Seal and refrigerate until chilled.

MAKES 2 CUPS

MAHARAJA'S BURRA PEG

"Peg" is the old English term for a jigger, but in British Colonial India it also named cocktails made with a "peg" of whiskey or brandy—like this one. While researching his Time-Life Foods of the World series book, *American Cooking: Southern-Style*, Eugene Walter was served this lovely drink by Mrs. Henrietta Waring, widow of Dr. Antonio Waring, a leading Savannah pediatrician in the middle of the last century. Champagne punches and cocktails have always been popular with Savannah's *dolce vita* set, and Mrs. Waring believed the concoction to be her father's invention. Most likely, he had a copy of Charles Baker's *The Gentleman's Companion* (1937) in his library, wherein Baker described this as being to "the ordinary champagne cocktail what Helen of Troy was to a local shepherd's maiden." Regardless of its provenance, it has deep Savannah roots, being a variation of the Champagne Punch (page 47) that had long been popular. Anita Lippitt Clay recalls a cocktail made by her father, called a King's Peg, which is essentially the same.

"Burra" is Hindustani for "big," and the original was two jiggers of cognac and nearly twice as much champagne. This is pared down for a standard champagne flute.

1 lime
4 sugar cubes
Angostura bitters

4 jiggers of cognac or single-barrel bourbon, chilled
Ice-cold medium dry champagne

1. Peel 4 long, thin curls of zest from the lime with the large curling blade on the side of a zester. Put the sugar cubes on a saucer and sprinkle them with droplets of bitters until they are saturated but not falling apart. Put a sugar cube in each of 4 champagne flutes.

2. Add a jigger of cognac to each flute and fill it with champagne. Garnish with lime zest, either hanging on the rim or floating in the cocktail, and serve at once.

SERVES 4

VARIATION: KING'S PEG

Omit the lime and bitters and garnish the cocktail with a twist of lemon zest. Mr. Lippitt omitted the sugar when the champagne was not very dry.

SAVANNAH EGGNOG

This is a lusciously thick eggnog, the sort that, as more than one Savannah hostess has remarked of her grandmother's Christmas morning brew, "you had to eat with a spoon."

12 large eggs, separated
1-3/4 cups sugar
1 fifth bourbon or dark rum, or 1 pint of each

1 quart heavy cream (minimum 36% milk fat)
Whole nutmeg in a grater

1. Beat the egg yolks until smooth. Add the sugar and beat until it is light and ribbons when dropped from the spoon or whisk. Stir in the liquor, cover, and refrigerate at least 8 hours.

2. When you are ready to serve, pour the yolk-liquor base into a punch bowl. Separately whip the egg whites and cream to soft peaks. Gently fold first the egg whites into the base, then the cream. Dust the top with nutmeg and serve immediately.

SERVES ABOUT 25

There are two—no, make that three—camps among Savannahians when it comes to eggnog. Some insist that rum is the only proper spirit to use, some adhere to bourbon, and others, in a true spirit of ecumenism, unabashedly use both. Some add a dash of vanilla extract or powdered cinnamon (or, again, both). Some, who like things completely over the top, fold in softened vanilla ice cream.

HOT BOURBON TODDY

When a bad cold strikes during a blistering midwinter Nor'easter, Savannahians know that nothing soothes like this warming, potent drink. For that matter, when a Nor'easter blows in, there's nothing more soothing even if you *don't* have a cold. Some make this with dark rum instead of bourbon. I don't know why, but they do.

1 jigger good bourbon
Local honey
1 slice lemon

6 ounces (3/4 cup) strong-brewed hot tea
Freshly squeezed lemon juice

1. Scald a ceramic or pewter mug with boiling-hot water. Put in the whiskey and a heaping teaspoon of honey and mix well.

2. Add the lemon and fill the mug with hot tea, pouring it directly over the lemon. Stir, taste, and add more honey and lemon juice to suit your taste.

SERVES 1

Soups, Seafood Stews, & Gumbos

IN ALMOST EVERY SAVANNAH COOKBOOK from the first half of the twentieth century, one name stands larger than life: Eliza Mackay Elliott (Mrs. Fred) Habersham (1831–1901), known to her family and friends as Leila. Though born to privilege and married into one of Savannah's oldest and most prominent families, the desperate days of the War Between the States left her widowed and impoverished with three young children to raise. Since she was already known for her cooking (she paid her children's school tuition by making and selling whole preserved oranges), she did the only thing she knew how to do: she moved home to live with her mother and opened a cooking school. Over the ensuing thirty years, nearly every society matron gathered at one time or another with notebook and pen in the kitchen of the old Elliott house at the corner of State and Abercorn to learn how to make Miss Leila's famous turtle soup, crab stew, and a handful of other dishes.

Facing: Bonnie's Ham and Crab Gumbo.
Above: Ferryboat.

Something of Leila Habersham's lovely character survives in a beautifully written memoir that she wrote about her husband, Fred, in the desperately sad days after his death in 1863 so that her children would know something of their father. It survives in beautiful condition and has been transcribed with supplemental letters and commentary by Habersham descendent Anna Wright Smith. Unfortunately, all that survives of Miss Leila's legendary cooking are the notes of her students, some of whom paid better attention than others. If she kept a notebook, it has not survived. We do know, however, that her kitchen bible was *Mrs. Hill's New Cook Book* (1867), by Georgia's own Annabella P. Hill.

Eighteenth-century bronze cannon on Madison Square, laid out in the late 1830s near the site of the Revolutionary War Battle of Savannah, October 1779.

In the nineteenth century, Turtle Soup was considered the very height of elegance. No formal dinner was complete unless it began with it, and dozens of recipes for mock turtle soup and stew hint at how prized it must have been. It goes without saying, then, that turtle soups and stews were Miss Leila's most famous recipes, with her mock turtle stew running them a close second. From the student notebooks that survive, we know that these soups and stews took two days to make. The first day of class began with detailed instructions on butchering, bleeding, and cooking the turtle. On the second day the stewed meat, reserved eggs, and rich, jellied broth were used to make soup and two different kinds of stew—brown and white. Turtle soup very much like the one Miss Leila taught remained popular in Savannah well into the twentieth century (it was a specialty of the famous DeSoto Hotel's dining room), and there are many who remember hunting for turtles and digging for their eggs on the long beaches of the barrier islands that form Georgia's coastline.

Today, of course, sea turtles are protected, and while farmed turtle meat is available frozen and canned, in Savannah the soup is little more than a memory. Turtle meat is a strong flavor that most locals are no longer accustomed to. Creamy Crab Soup, Oyster or Shrimp Bisque, and silky Bouillon have taken the place of turtle soup at formal dinner tables, and winter meals are warmed by Black Turtle Bean Soup, Chicken and Corn Chowder, and hearty gumbos rather than thick egg-enriched turtle stew.

BASIC MEAT OR CHICKEN BROTH

5 pounds meat scraps and bones (beef, veal, or pork, or a mixture of all, or a 5-pound stewing hen or chicken or turkey scraps)

3 large yellow onions (2 for chicken or turkey), 2 peeled and thinly sliced, 1 peeled but left whole and stuck with 4 whole cloves

1 large carrot (2 for chicken or turkey), peeled and thickly sliced

1 large rib celery (2 for chicken or turkey), including the leafy top

1 large leek, split, thoroughly washed, and sliced (including the green top)

3 to 4 large cloves garlic, lightly crushed and peeled but left whole

1 quarter-size slice fresh gingerroot

1 large, leafy sprig parsley (at least 3 inches of leafy stalk)

2 large, leafy sprigs fresh thyme (at least 3 inches long), or 1 teaspoon dried thyme tied up in a cheesecloth or stainless-steel tea ball (or sage for chicken or turkey)

2 bay leaves

1 teaspoon whole black peppercorns

5 quarts water

Salt

1. Put all the ingredients into an 8- to 10-quart stockpot, adding a small handful of salt. Turn on the heat to low, cover loosely, and bring the broth slowly to a simmer. This could take from 30 to 45 minutes.

2. Adjust the heat so that the liquid simmers very slowly, the bubbles not quite breaking the surface of the broth. With the lid askew, let it simmer for a minimum of 2 hours; 3 or 4 will only improve it. If you use a whole bird, you may take it up after it is tender (about 1-1/2 to 2 hours), skin and bone it, and return the bones, skin, back and neck to the pot. Let it simmer at least an hour longer.

3. Turn off the heat and let the broth settle for 30 minutes. Strain it carefully through a wire mesh strainer and let it cool completely. Cover and refrigerate until the broth is very cold and the fat on the surface is congealed. Lift off the fat and discard. The broth will keep for up to a week in the refrigerator, or for up to 6 months if frozen in small portions.

MAKES ABOUT 4 QUARTS

Many soup and stew recipes can be made with canned broth or reconstituted bouillon, but there are times when there is no substitute for homemade broth. Happily, broth is easy to make, fills the house with the most sublime perfume imaginable, and is best made from inexpensive meat scraps and trimmings. You can freeze your own trimmings until you have enough for the stockpot, but make sure they are well wrapped and use them within 3 months: freezer-burned scraps will result in a broth that tastes freezer-burned. When using fatty scraps, don't trim off the fat because it will help flavor the broth. The fat itself will be easily removed when the broth has been strained and chilled.

Chicken broth is, of course, made in exactly the same way as meat broth, but the ingredients are designed to complement poultry. You may also use turkey or any other poultry scraps that you may have on hand for this recipe.

SHELLFISH BROTH

Many old coastal fish and seafood soups are founded on the distinctive flavor and rosy-orange color of broth made from shrimp, crab, or crawfish shells. Always buy whole shellfish when you can: they are so much tastier when cooked in their shells, and the shells and heads can later be put to good use to make this important flavor base.

6 cups shrimp, crawfish, or crab shells, including the heads, if possible

3 quarts water

1 medium onion, thickly sliced

3 to 4 cloves garlic, peeled but left whole

2 leafy celery tops

2 large sprigs parsley

1 teaspoon peppercorns

1 whole fresh or dried pod hot red pepper such as cayenne

Salt

1. Put all the ingredients into a 6-quart stockpot with a healthy pinch of salt. Bring it almost to a boil over medium high heat. When it is almost boiling and foam begins to form on the top, reduce the heat to medium low and simmer, uncovered, for an hour.

2. Raise the heat to medium-high and reduce the liquid to about 2 quarts, skimming off any foam that rises to keep it from boiling over. Turn off the heat, allow the broth to settle, and strain it, discarding the solids. Cool, cover, and refrigerate or freeze promptly. It will keep for 3 or 4 days in the refrigerator, or up to 6 months in the freezer.

MAKES ABOUT 2 QUARTS (8 CUPS)

BOULLION

1 (3-pound) chicken

2 pounds meaty beef shank bones

2 ounces country ham or prosciutto, in one slice

4 quarts water

1 tablespoon salt

1 teaspoon peppercorns

2 tablespoons bacon drippings or unsalted butter

1 large onion, trimmed, split lengthwise, peeled, and thinly sliced

1 small carrot, peeled and thinly sliced

1 small parsnip, peeled and thinly sliced

1 small rib celery heart, including the leafy top

1 large sprig parsley

3 whole cloves

2 large egg whites and shells

Optional, for serving:

About 1/4 to 1/2 cup medium-dry (Sercial) Madeira

1 lemon, thinly sliced or cut into eight wedges

1/4 cup thinly sliced chives or green onion tops

Bouillon is an especially rich clear broth that can be served hot, with a slice of lemon on each serving, or jellied, with the lemon cut into wedges. One of my earliest exposures to elegant Savannah entertaining was a luncheon that began with a jellied bouillon generously laced with Madeira. This particular version is an old family recipe shared by Emma Morel Adler. It was served in their family both as bouillon and as the base for Shallot Soup (page 71).

1. Rinse the chicken well and cut it up as for frying. Put it in a large stockpot with the beef, ham, and water. Add the salt and peppercorns and bring to a simmer over medium-low heat. Simmer gently, the bubbles never quite breaking the surface, for 3 to 5 hours—the longer, the better.

2. Warm the drippings in a skillet over medium heat, add the onion, and sauté until golden brown. Add the onion, carrot, parsnip, celery, parsley, and cloves to the bouillon and simmer an hour longer. Turn off the heat. Strain the broth into a large bowl, let it cool completely, and refrigerate overnight, or until the fat is congealed.

3. Remove and discard the layer of fat. Ladle the jelly into a pot, being careful not to take up any of the dregs at the bottom. Heat until it is just melted. Beat the egg whites lightly and then add their crushed shells. Stir this into the bouillon and bring to a boil over medium heat. Boil half a minute and remove from the heat. Carefully skim off the scum and egg white.

4. Ladle it through a jelly bag or a wire mesh sieve lined with a piece of clean muslin set over a large bowl. Let it drip through.

5. Serve bouillon hot in bouillon cups, adding a spoonful of Madeira to each, and garnished with a slice of lemon and sprinkle of chives. Or, stir 1/4 cup Madeira into the bouillon, chill until jellied, and serve cold, with wedges of lemon passed separately.

SERVES 8

Hot Bouillon.

OKRA SOUP

There is probably no other dish that is more characteristically Old Savannah than this simple, hearty mélange of beef and ham broth, tomatoes, and okra. Each family—indeed, each cook, has its own version. Often other vegetables are added to the pot—a heaping cup each of butterbeans, diced yellow summer squash, and freshly cut corn are the most frequent—but the essential core is a homemade trio of broth, fresh tomatoes, and okra. Many cooks today make it with canned tomatoes, but it is at its best when it can be made with fragrant, sweet vine-ripened tomatoes. Though this recipe is based on several old manuscripts, its core is from Leonora Candler, whose cooking, in the early to mid-twentieth century, was legendary among her family and friends.

A large spoonful of rice is always added to each serving, and when it is the main course, cornbread is usually passed. Once upon a time, bird's eye peppers and/or Pepper Sherry were always offered as condiments.

The passing of whole bird's eye peppers with okra soup was once quite a ritual. The fiery peppers were passed in a small bowl, and each guest took a single pepper to crush in the bottom of his soup plate. The pepper was then removed before the soup was ladled in; you did not want to run the risk of biting down on the whole thing.

2 pounds meaty beef shank (soup) bone, or 2 quarts Basic Meat or Chicken Broth (made with beef, see page 57); do not use canned broth

1 smoked ham hock, about 3/4 pound

2 medium white onions, trimmed, split lengthwise, peeled, and chopped

1-1/2 pounds small, tender okra (about 8 cups), trimmed and thinly sliced

3 pounds ripe tomatoes, scalded, peeled, seeded (page 15), and roughly chopped

Salt and whole black pepper in a peppermill

Pepper Sherry (page 13), Pepper Vinegar (page 13), or fresh Bird's Eye Peppers (page 10)

1-1/2 cups hot Lowcountry Steamed Rice (page 78)

1. If using beef shank bones, put them with the ham hock in a heavy-bottomed soup kettle or Dutch oven with 3 quarts of water. Bring to a boil over medium heat. Reduce the heat to medium low and simmer until the liquid is reduced to 2 quarts, at least 2 hours. If using meat broth instead, bring the broth and ham hock to a simmer over medium high heat, reduce the heat to medium low, and simmer, loosely covered, for at least an hour. Skim off the excess fat, add the onion, and simmer slowly until it is tender, about 20

minutes. You may make the broth a day ahead up to this point, cool, cover, and refrigerate. Remove the solidified fat from the top before bringing the broth back to a simmer over medium heat.

2. Stir in the okra and tomatoes, loosely cover, and let it come back to a simmer. Uncover, reduce the heat, and simmer gently for about 20 minutes.

3. Taste and season the soup with salt and pepper. Simmer, uncovered, until the okra and tomatoes are very tender and the soup is quite thick, at least an hour more—longer won't hurt it. Remove the bones and hock from the pot. Some cooks cut up any meat on the bone and add it back to the soup. Discard the bones.

4. Pour the soup into a heated tureen or divide it among heated soup plates. If offering fresh bird's eye peppers, allow guests to crush a single pepper in their bowls and remove it before the soup is ladled in. If not passing fresh peppers, pass Pepper Sherry or Pepper Vinegar separately. Put 1/4 cup of rice in the center of each serving, or pass it separately.

Notes on additions: For most traditional cooks, okra soup is a 2-day operation. The broth is made one day, chilled and degreased, and then the soup is finished the second day. Other vegetables may be added, the most common additions being butterbeans and corn. Add a generous cup each of fresh, small green butterbeans and freshly cut white corn for the last 40 minutes of simmering.

SERVES 6

SAVANNAH BLACK TURTLE BEAN SOUP

Nowadays we would hardly think of black bean soup as anything but hearty family supper fare, but Savannah hostesses of the past had different ideas. No one would have been embarrassed to begin her most elegant dinner with what was often called "turtle" bean soup. Considered nearly as elegant as real turtle soup, this subtle and delicious purée is a revelation in what humble ingredients can do when given the chance. Unfortunately, it rarely gets that chance today: though once popular, it is now rarely seen except on traditional family tables and has been displaced in our restaurants by a more prosaic version heavy with cumin, garlic, and hot pepper. Tasting more of the Caribbean or Southwest than old Chatham, it shares only one flavor (other than beans) with the classic—garlic. While it wasn't always included in the old manuscript recipes, where an old black cook ran the kitchen, you can bet it was in the pot.

In the old recipes, the entire soup was puréed to suave velvety smoothness, but that's never done today. Most cooks like to leave at least a few beans whole, as the contrasting texture makes a more interesting soup. In many old recipes, the eggs were merely sliced and laid on the bottom of the tureen or soup plate before the hot soup was added. A handsome accompaniment is Savannah Flatbread (page 103), which was once traditional with turtle and other thick soups.

1 pound dried black beans

1/2 pound lean salt-cured pork, in one piece, or 1/4 pound if presliced

6 cups Basic Meat or Chicken Broth (page 57)

1 large or 2 medium white onions, trimmed, split lengthwise, peeled and chopped

1 large or 2 small cloves garlic, lightly crushed, peeled, and minced

1 large carrot, peeled and diced small

1 small turnip, scrubbed, peeled, and diced small

2 ribs celery, washed, strung, and diced small

2 medium ripe tomatoes, scalded, peeled, seeded, and chopped (see page 15)

1 bay leaf

2 large sprigs of parsley

6 whole cloves, powdered with a mortar and pestle or spice mill

Salt and whole black pepper in a peppermill

Ground cayenne pepper

1 tablespoon Worcestershire sauce

2 large hard-cooked eggs, peeled

6 to 8 tablespoons sherry (1 tablespoon per serving)

2 lemons, thinly sliced

Pepper Sherry (page 13), optional

1. Rinse the beans under cold running water, sort through and discard any damaged or discolored ones, and put them in a large, heavy-bottomed pot. Add enough water to cover them by 2 inches. Beans cook better in soft water: If your water, like Savannah's, is hard, use bottled or filtered water. Bring the beans slowly to a boiling point over medium heat. Turn off the heat and soak until the beans have doubled in volume, about an hour.

2. Replenish the water with enough to cover the beans by 1 inch. Put the pot back over medium heat and bring it to a simmer again, skimming away any scum that rises. Reduce the heat to a slow simmer and cook until the beans are tender, about an hour.

3. Drain, reserving the cooking liquid, and return the beans to the pot with 2 cups of cooking liquid, the salt pork, and meat broth. Raise the heat to

*Savannah Black Turtle Bean
Soup.*

medium and bring it back to a boil. Add the onion, garlic, carrot, turnip, celery, and tomatoes, let it return to a boil, skimming off any scum that rises, then put in the bay leaf and parsley, powdered cloves, a pinch or so of salt (going easy; you can correct it later), a liberal grinding of pepper, a small pinch of cayenne, and the Worcestershire. Reduce the heat to a slow simmer, cover, and cook until the vegetables are very tender, about 2 hours.

4. Take up 1 heaping cup of beans and put them aside. Purée the remainder through a food mill or with a stick blender or food processor. If it's too thick, thin it with some of the reserved bean cooking liquid. Stir in the reserved beans and heat it through. Taste and adjust the seasonings, and let it heat for 2 to 3 minutes to meld.

5. Force the eggs through a coarse wire sieve. Add a tablespoon of sherry to each bowl, and ladle in the soup. Float a slice of lemon and sprinkling of egg on top of each bowl and serve at once, passing Pepper Sherry separately, if you like.

SERVES 8 AS A FIRST COURSE AT DINNER OR 6 AS A MAIN COURSE AT LUNCH OR SUPPER

Soups, Seafood Stews, & Gumbos   63

CHICKEN AND CORN CHOWDER

Corn chowder is a rich, simple soup that has been a fixture in Savannah for at least a century, turning up in community cookbooks from the early 1900s forward. Its variations are legion: in summer during the height of corn season it is sometimes made with shrimp or crab and Shellfish Broth, but it is also a popular cold weather supper when made with frozen corn and crab or oysters. Many Savannahians buy extra Silver Queen corn while it is in season and brave the heat to put it up in the freezer just for this chowder.

4 to 6 ears sweet white corn such as Silver Queen

4 slices thick-cut bacon, diced

1 large yellow onion, trimmed, split lengthwise, peeled, and diced small

2 large ribs celery, strung and diced small

2 cups Basic Meat or Chicken Broth (page 57) or 1 cup canned broth mixed with 1 cup water, even if label says not to dilute

2 cups whole milk

Salt and whole black pepper in a pepper-mill

Ground cayenne pepper

Whole nutmeg in a grater

1/2 cup heavy cream

1/2 cup fine soft white breadcrumbs, firmly packed

2 cups small-diced cooked chicken

1/4 cup thinly sliced green onion tops

2 tablespoons chopped parsley

1. Shuck, silk, and wash the corn. Cut enough kernels from the cob to make 3 cups.

2. Sauté the bacon in a heavy-bottomed 4-quart pot over medium heat until it is golden brown and its fat is rendered. Add the onion and celery, and sauté until translucent and softened but not colored, about 5 minutes. Add the broth and the corn. Bring it to a simmer and cook, stirring often, until the vegetables are tender, about 10 minutes. Add the milk and season well with salt, pepper, cayenne, and nutmeg. Let it come back to a simmer.

3. Add the cream, breadcrumbs, and chicken and simmer, stirring often, until the crumbs dissolve completely and the chowder is thick, about 10 minutes more. Taste and adjust the seasonings, ladle into warmed bowls, and sprinkle with green onions and parsley.

SERVES 6 AS A FIRST COURSE, 4 AS A MAIN DISH

VARIATION: SEAFOOD CORN CHOWDER

Substitute Shellfish Broth (page 58) for the Basic Meat or Chicken Broth and 8 ounces (1 tightly packed cup) of picked crabmeat and 2 dozen small peeled and deveined shrimp for the chicken. Some cooks also add a cup of our small but big-flavored local oysters.

Chicken and Corn Chowder in the Historic
Green Meldrim House (1851-53).

CRAB SOUP WITH TOMATOES

This classic soup, attributed in some household notebooks to Leila Habersham, departs from the usual regional crab soups in that it has a tomato rather than milk or cream base. The old recipes cooked the crabmeat in the soup at a long, slow simmer—great for flavor, but, unfortunately, not good for the crab. To get the same deep flavor without that drawback, I've used a stock made from the shells, a step rarely suggested in the old recipes. If you don't have whole blue crabs at your disposal, substitute a pound of packed crabmeat, omitting the first two steps, and use 4 cups of Shellfish Broth (page 58).

1 dozen medium blue crabs

1 pound crawfish or shrimp heads (optional)

6 medium ripe tomatoes or 1 (28-ounce) can crushed tomatoes

2 tablespoons butter

1 large onion, split lengthwise, trimmed, peeled, and chopped

1 clove garlic, lightly crushed, peeled, and minced

1 bouquet garni made of a large sprig each of parsley, marjoram, and thyme

Salt, ground cayenne pepper, and whole black pepper in a peppermill

2 lemons, divided

2 tablespoons finely powdered cracker crumbs

1. Bring 3 quarts water to a boil in an 8-quart pot. Add the crab, cover tightly, and cook until they are bright red. Lift the crabs from the pot with tongs or a skimmer, reserving the cooking water. Cool and pick them (page 16), reserving the shells. Cover and refrigerate the crabmeat if you aren't finishing the soup right away.

2. Return the shells to the pot and add the crawfish or shrimp heads. Bring it to a boil, carefully skimming, and reduce the heat to a slow simmer. Loosely cover and simmer for at least an hour, or until the liquid is reduced to 1 quart (4 cups). Strain the broth through a fine wire sieve, discarding the shells, and return it to the pot. Meanwhile, if using fresh tomatoes, scald, core, and quarter them and put them through a food mill (page 15).

3. Put the butter and onion in a large pot over medium heat. Sauté until softened and colored pale gold, about 5 minutes. Add the garlic and sauté until fragrant, about a minute more. Add the tomatoes and simmer for about 5 minutes.

4. Add the broth, bouquet garni, and season well with salt, cayenne, and black pepper. Pare the zest from 1 lemon in large pieces with a vegetable peeler.

Crab Soup with Tomatoes.

Halve the lemon and juice one of the halves into the soup. Blanch the zest by bringing it to a boil in enough water to completely cover it and let it boil 2 to 3 minutes. Drain and add zest to the soup.

5. Cover, reduce the heat to low, and simmer half an hour, stirring occasionally. Remove and discard the lemon zest. The soup can be made a day ahead through this step. Cool, cover, and refrigerate. When you are ready to serve it, reheat gently over medium heat.

6. Stir in the crumbs, cover, and simmer for another 15 minutes. Add the crab and simmer for about 5 minutes—just enough to let the crab heat through. Meanwhile, slice the other lemon as thinly as possible. Taste and adjust the seasonings, remove and discard the herbs, and ladle the soup into heated soup plates, floating a slice of lemon on each serving.

SERVES 6 AS A FIRST COURSE, OR 4 AS A MAIN COURSE

When Blanche Rhett, wife of South Carolina Governor Goodwyn Rhett, asked her butler William Deas to dress up his crab soup, by legend for a dinner honoring President Taft, he made this simple bisque into a legend simply by stirring in crab roe. She-Crab Soup, as it came to be called, became Deas' trademark when he later cooked at Everett's Restaurant and has since been indelibly associated with Charleston. Though overshadowed by Mr. Deas' famous adaptation, the simple, elegant soup that inspired him is still delicious. Sometimes appearing in manuscripts under the titles of crab stew or crab soup, it was a standard on dinner and supper tables throughout the Lowcountry, most notably in Savannah. Now that harvesting of female crabs is more vigorously regulated, the roe is not as easy to come by, and the original soup has regained some of its old footing.

CREAM OF CRAB SOUP

8 ounces (1/2 pound or 1 cup tightly packed) cooked and picked crabmeat

2 tablespoons unsalted butter

1/4 cup finely minced or grated shallots or yellow onion

2 teaspoons all-purpose flour

2 cups whole milk

1 cup heavy cream

Salt

Ground cayenne pepper

Dry mustard

About 1 large blade mace, large pinch powdered mace, or whole nutmeg in a grater

1/4 cup dry sherry

4 very thin slices lemon

1. Carefully pick through the crabmeat for bits of shell. Put the butter and onion in a heavy-bottomed saucepan over medium low heat. Simmer until the onion is soft, but not colored, about 5 minutes. Stir in the flour and simmer, stirring constantly, about 2 minutes.

2. Gradually whisk in the milk and cream. Season with a large pinch of salt, a small one each of cayenne and mustard, and the mace or nutmeg to taste and heat, stirring constantly, until thickened, about 5 to 8 minutes.

3. Stir in the crabmeat and let it heat through, stirring frequently, about 5 minutes more. Taste and adjust the seasonings and simmer 1 minute. Turn off the heat, stir in the sherry and immediately ladle it into heated soup plates. Float a thin slice of lemon on each serving.

SERVES 4

SHRIMP BISQUE

This sumptuous soup is a Savannah specialty throughout shrimp season despite the fact that it is always served warm and shrimp season peaks during the hottest months of the year. It used to be common in local restaurants until so-called She-Crab Soup made from a packaged base pretty much edged it out. Now it is rarely seen except on home dinner tables. It can serve as an elegant first course for a formal dinner or, with rolls and a salad, as a main dish for lunch or a family supper.

Many local cooks grind up the shrimp with a meat grinder or in the food processor, but I like to leave at least some of them in bite-size chunks so that they add texture and interest to the soup.

4 cups Shellfish Broth (page 58, only if using headed shrimp)

2 pounds whole shrimp (head-on weight), or 1 pound (headless weight) small to medium shrimp

3 tablespoons unsalted butter

1 medium shallot or yellow onion, finely minced

1 rounded tablespoon all-purpose flour

2 cups whole milk

1 cup heavy cream (minimum 36% milk fat)

Salt and ground cayenne pepper

6 tablespoons dry sherry, and/or Pepper Sherry (page 13) in a cruet

1 lemon, thinly sliced

Paprika, optional (see step 3)

1. Bring 4 cups of water or, if using headed shrimp, Shellfish Broth, to a boil in a lidded 3-quart pot over medium-high heat. Add the shrimp, cover, and count 2 minutes. Lift the shrimp out of the cooking liquid and rinse under cold water. Shell, head, and devein the shrimp and cut them into small dice. Finely mince half of them with a knife or in a food processor fitted with a steel blade. Cover and refrigerate until needed. Return the shells (and heads, if any) to the cooking liquid. Bring it back to a boil over medium high heat and cook until it is reduced to 2 cups. Strain the broth, discarding the shells.

2. Wipe out the pot and put in the butter and shallot. Sauté over medium heat, tossing frequently, until softened, about 5 minutes. Stir in the flour and cook, stirring, until smooth. Slowly stir in the broth, milk, and cream. Season well with salt and cayenne. Bring to a simmer, stirring constantly, and reduce the heat to medium low. Simmer, stirring frequently, for about 20 minutes.

3. Add the shrimp and cook until they are just heated through, about 1 to 2 minutes longer. Taste and adjust the seasonings and turn off the heat. Serve at once, adding a tablespoon of sherry to each serving, if liked, and pass Pepper Sherry separately. Garnish each serving with a slice of lemon and light sprinkling of cayenne (only if not using Pepper Sherry) or paprika.

SERVES 6 AS A FIRST COURSE SOUP, 4 AS A MAIN COURSE

OYSTER BISQUE

From Leila Habersham to popular late-twentieth-century caterer Lucile Wright, Savannah hostesses have gilded special dinners with oyster bisque. The historical recipes seem wildly extravagant to modern cooks, since they call for twice as many oysters as end up in the tureen, but that did not phase cooks who were surrounded by abundant oyster beds. Today those beds are not quite so plentiful, and no one would waste good oysters making broth. We use the liquor from the shucked oysters, which in those days was discarded. Its real secret is that the oysters that do end up in the bowl are lightly poached and chopped fine, thus lending every spoonful a good portion of rich oyster flavor.

Lucile Wright's tomato sandwiches were immortalized in a certain famous book, but it was her oyster bisque that locals recall the most wistfully. She never wrote it down, yet there have been at least three attempts to reproduce it in print. It was not my privilege to know her—I only met the two brothers who helped her in her business—so this is my own recipe, based on the several versions of hers. Here goes nothing.

2 pints of shucked oysters, with their liquor

1 small yellow onion, trimmed, split lengthwise, and minced

2 large ribs celery, strung and minced

1 blade of mace or whole nutmeg in a grater

Salt and whole black pepper in a peppermill

Ground cayenne pepper

4 cups whole milk

2 cups heavy cream

2 tablespoons unsalted butter

3 tablespoons all-purpose flour

2 teaspoons Worcestershire sauce

8 thin slices of lemon

2 tablespoons chopped fresh parsley

8 tablespoons medium dry (amontillado) sherry or (Sercial) Madeira, or Pepper Sherry (page 13)

1 cup buttered croutons

1. Pick over the oysters for bits of shell. Strain their liquor and put it in a large saucepan with the onion, celery, mace or a generous grating of nutmeg, a little salt, a generous grinding of pepper, and a pinch of cayenne. Bring it to a simmer over medium heat and cook until the onion and celery are softened, about 8 to 10 minutes. Add the oysters and cook, stirring occasionally, just until the gills begin to curl, about 2 to 4 minutes. Lift out the oysters and vegetables with a slotted spoon and transfer them to a colander set over a bowl. Strain their broth and return it to the pot. When the oysters are cool enough to handle, mince them fine. Add any broth that has drained from them to the liquid in the pot.

2. Bring the broth back to a simmer over medium heat. Add the milk and cream and let it come back to a simmer, stirring frequently to prevent scorching. Melt the butter in a small pan over medium heat and stir in the flour. Cook, stirring often, until it is bubbly and smooth, about 2 minutes. Gradually whisk in 2 cups of the broth and milk and cook, stirring constantly, until it is quite thick. Gradually stir it into the remaining broth and milk and bring it to a simmer, stirring constantly. Cook until thick, about 5 minutes.

3. Add the chopped oysters and vegetables and Worcestershire sauce, taste and adjust the seasonings, and let it heat through. Serve at once, with a slice of lemon and sprinkling of parsley over each serving, passing sherry, Madeira, or Pepper Sherry, and croutons separately.

SERVES 8

SHALLOT SOUP

Once upon a time, spring gardens across Georgia produced a rare and coveted treat: young, tender shallot sprouts. They are never found in the market, and today only cooks with gardening friends can get them. But when they can be had, they are the very essence of spring on the table and are still used in place of scallions in salads, and, on occasion, in such delicacies as this lovely soup from Emma Adler's childhood. When she shared it with me, as she talked of it, her eyes were bright with the wistful hunger of a young girl. It's very rich and is best served in small portions, preferably in little bouillon cups.

1 cup firmly packed green shallot tops cut into 1/2-inch lengths (chives or scallions may be substituted)

3 cups Bouillon (page 59)
3 cups heavy cream
Salt

1. Bring 2 cups water to a boil in a small saucepan over medium heat. Put in the shallot tops, bring it back to a simmer, and then drain off the water.

2. Add the bouillon, bring it back to a simmer, and simmer until the shallot greens are tender, about 4 minutes more. Add the cream, taste and adjust the salt, and let it just heat through. Serve at once in bouillon cups.

SERVES 6

BONNIE'S HAM AND CRAB GUMBO

Most people assume, quite wrongly, that gumbo originated in New Orleans, but its roots are West African (the name even derives from one of the African names for okra), and it can be found in any part of the South where people of West African descent have settled, especially the Carolina and Georgia Lowcountry. In fact, when asked what best characterized old Savannah cooking, many a native said gumbo. The flavors of our versions are not, perhaps, as complex as those of Louisiana, but we think they are cleaner, and they hold their own gastronomically.

Bonnie Gaster grew up barefoot and happy on Tybee Island, Savannah's official beach. No one knows more about choosing and cooking local shellfish than she does, and it has been my privilege not only to call her a dear friend, but to have cooked with her more times than either of us cares to count. One hot, lazy August afternoon, she showed me how to pick crab and make

Continued on next page

For the stock

4-1/2 pounds meaty ham bone (Bonnie uses those from a spiral-cut ham)

6 quarts water

For the gumbo

2 large Vidalia or other sweet onions, trimmed, split lengthwise, peeled, and chopped

3 cups thinly sliced celery

1 medium ripe red bell pepper, stem, core, and membrane removed, diced

1 small green bell pepper, stem, core, and membrane removed, diced

4 large cloves garlic, lightly crushed, peeled, and minced

1 large ripe jalapeño or other hot red pepper, stem, core, and seeds removed, minced

1 large bay leaf

6 cups sliced young, tender okra, trimmed and cut 1/2-inch thick

2 pounds ripe Roma tomatoes, cored, quartered lengthwise, and sliced 1/2 inch thick

1 teaspoon crushed hot red pepper flakes

2 to 3 ribs leafy celery heart

2 generous tablespoons Seafood Boiling Spice (page 6), or Old Bay or Savannah Spice Company seasoning

2 teaspoons salt

2 tablespoons freshly cracked black pepper

1 tablespoon chopped fresh thyme

1/4 cup chopped flat-leaf parsley

5 cups shredded or diced cooked ham (from bones)

3 pounds (6 packed cups) cooked and picked crabmeat

2 cups sliced green onions, divided

8 cups Lowcountry Steamed Rice (page 78)

About 30 cooked, peeled shrimp, for garnish

1. Pick over the ham bones and remove about 5 cups of meat. Put the bones, water, hot pepper flakes, and celery in a large, heavy-bottomed stockpot. Bring it slowly to the boiling point, reduce the heat to a bare simmer, and gently cook for 2 to 3 hours. Bonnie does this in a slow cooker and lets it simmer all day. Let it cool, then strain and degrease it, reserving about 1/4 cup of fat. You may make the stock up to 3 or 4 days ahead. Cover and refrigerate it until needed.

Bonnie's Ham and Crab Gumbo.

2. Warm the reserved fat (or 1/4 cup vegetable oil, if you prefer) in a heavy-bottomed 12-quart stockpot or Dutch oven over medium heat. Add the onions and let them wilt, about 2 minutes, and then add the celery and let it simmer until translucent, about 2 minutes. Add both red and green peppers and let wilt, about a minute. Stir in the garlic, jalapeño, and bay leaf and cook until fragrant, about a minute longer. Add the okra, and toss until it's bright green; then add the tomatoes and let them heat through.

3. Add 12 cups of ham stock, the Seafood Boiling Spice, salt, cracked pepper, thyme, and parsley. Let it come to a simmer and cook until the okra and tomatoes are just tender, about 10 to 15 minutes.

4. Add the ham, let it heat through, and then add the crab and 1 cup of the green onions and let it come back to a simmer. Taste and adjust the seasonings and simmer another minute to let the flavors meld. Remove the bay leaf. Serve with about 1/4 cup of rice in the bottom of each bowl, garnishing each serving with a whole shrimp and the remaining green onions.

SERVES ABOUT 30

one of the most perfectly balanced gumbos you will ever taste. No one flavor dominates, but all—the ham, crab, tomatoes, and okra—are allowed to shine at their best. One secret is that the broth is allowed to simmer for a long time, but the gumbo is not; so the crab, tomatoes and okra are tender but still fresh and sweet tasting.

Sometimes she makes this same recipe Louisiana-style, with a roux. It is actually more of a traditional Lowcountry gumbo without the roux (and, to my palate, better) but here's how to add it: use 1/2 cup vegetable oil instead of the ham fat and work in 3/4 cup flour. Cook it over medium high heat, stirring constantly, until it is pecan colored (it should smell pleasantly toasty, not scorched), then add the onions, celery, peppers, garlic, and remaining ingredients in the order given.

The Essential Grains

Rice, Grits, Noodles, and Bread

THOUGH THE COTTON GIN WAS PERFECTED in Savannah by Eli Whitney (with the help, by the way, of his hostess, Kate Green, widow of Revolutionary War hero Gen. Nathaniel Green), cotton was not the only thing to make Savannah's fortunes. During the eighteenth and early nineteenth centuries, many a fortune was made by rice, the legendary Carolina Gold that thrived in the marshy flatlands of the Carolina and Georgia Lowcountry. This grain was a major money crop for many of Savannah's surrounding plantations, and the city's port became an important processing and export center.

Rice culture was not, however, to last: dealt a major blow by the War Between the States and Emancipation, it faltered during the last decades of the nineteenth century and collapsed altogether in the early twentieth century when machine cultivation and harvesting began to replace hand labor. The marshy Lowcountry land was too soft for these machines, and rice cultivation began to migrate west to Louisiana and Texas.

Today, rice culture has almost vanished from the face of Savannah—the Habersham family's famous rice mill that once stood tall by the river, the vast plantations that once lined that same river's banks to the west, and the powerful merchant banks are little more than memory. All that remains of the culture today are a few proud houses, a strong genetic and cultural imprint left by the West African slaves who tended those vast rice fields, and the fragrant traces of a unique rice-based cuisine that these slaves introduced and nurtured.

Facing: Sour Cream Rice Muffins.
Above: The ancient oak avenue leading into Bethesda Home for Boys, founded in 1740, the oldest orphanage in America. The first buildings were completed in 1742.

Carolina Gold is once again growing in the region thanks to the work of a Savannah doctor, Dick Schulz, and his family, who more than twenty years ago rescued seed rice from a national archive and began cultivating it on the old Turnbull Plantation in South Carolina. They have since been joined by other growers, and while rice is not likely to ever be a major factor in South Carolina's agricultural economy, it is at least no longer a mere memory.

To this day, even after the late-twentieth-century rage for pasta, rice remains a staple throughout the region, and fifty- and one-hundred-pound sacks of it are still commonplace in Savannah markets. Most of the rice-cooking techniques and dishes that survive have distinctly West African origins: fluffy, rattle-the-plate, dry steamed rice, aromatic pilaus, stir-fried leftovers, the delicate moist rice breads. Many of them differ from their West African counterparts only in detail. There are other rice cultures that play a part in Savannah's rice cuisine—the Chinese, for one, who have been here since the 1880s—and the Vietnamese, Thai, Malay, and Indian immigrants of later years, but West Africa remains the dominant influence.

Like every other place in the South, the other grain that has left a strong culinary imprint is maize, or corn. Like rice, it was a major staple in the diet: in summer, as a fresh vegetable, and year-round as dried fodder for animals, meal for bread, and as the base for grits, that universally famous—some would say infamous—hot cereal of the South. Today grits, especially the whole corn variety milled on water-powered stones by a handful of specialty millers, have become haute cuisine on the dinner tables of Savannah's elite restaurants. But historically they were humble fare, reserved only for breakfast and family supper tables, an indispensable accompaniment for crisp-fried fresh-caught whiting or quail, butter-braised crab or shrimp, fried chicken, or eggs, ham, and bacon. Occasionally, the supper grits at home might be dressed up—molded into cakes, rolled in crumbs and fried, or baked with garlic and cheese, or folded into spoonbread. But you can be sure of one thing: no self-respecting Savannahian would ever subject grits to any of the truffle-oiled weirdness that some of the nouvelle restaurant crowd are trying today.

Pasta is enjoyed by more Savannahians than ever before and can almost be said to outstrip rice as a starchy staple. Indeed, its popularity is so raw and new that the uninitiated might think that it was a relative newcomer to our food-ways. But it has actually been around in some form or other since the earliest Colonial days. It just wasn't called "pasta"—it was "noodles" or "macaroni." The

The Forsyth Park Fountain, the centerpiece of the city's largest park since the 1850s and a popular site for concerts, picnics, and weddings.

English and Salzburger Lutherans had their own egg noodles and dumplings that were used to thicken soups, bake in savory and sweet puddings, and eat with stews or as a side dish simply dressed with butter. There was also a smattering of Italians, from Oglethorpe's first landing onward, though in truth they left a minimal culinary imprint until an influx of Sicilian and Neapolitan immigrants came in the early twentieth century. Other ethnic groups brought in their own ways of dressing pasta—the Greek community's Makaronatha, for example, or Chinese lo mein. And wealthy Savannahians who traveled also brought home some of Italy's ways with pasta, included Mrs. Minis' Gnocchi alla Romana on page 94. Each has found its own enriching place in the fabric of Savannah's cookery.

Finally, no Savannah meal is complete without bread, and for many traditional families, that bread was always made at home. Though commercial bakeries existed, homemade rolls, biscuits, and simple cornbread and rice muffins were the most usual accompaniments to family meals. Some of these breads—fluffy buttermilk biscuits and crusty skillet cornbread and muffins, for example—differ from those elsewhere in the South only in detail. To have included them here would be superfluous, but there are many simple home-style breads to share that are unique to Savannah, or at the very least have a special place on our tables, and I've shared as many of those as space allowed.

LOWCOUNTRY STEAMED RICE

1 cup raw, long-grain rice (my own   Salt
preference is real basmati)

1. Put the rice in a large bowl (or the cooking pot) and fill to within an inch
   of the rim with water. Gently rub handfuls of rice between your fingers until
   the water is milky and pour off the water through a large fine-mesh sieve.
   Repeat until the water is nearly clear. Many local cooks also let the rice soak
   for a few minutes. Drain thoroughly.

2. Put the rice and a scant 2 cups of cold water in a heavy-bottomed pot. Add
   a healthy pinch of salt. Stir once to make sure the salt is dissolved. Bring to
   a boil over medium high heat, stir once to make sure that the rice is not
   sticking, and reduce the heat to low. Set the lid askew on top of the pot and
   simmer for 12 to 14 minutes, or until the water is almost completely
   absorbed and clear, dry steam holes form on the surface.

3. Gently fold the top rice under with a fork, close the lid tightly, and heat for
   a minute more to build the steam, and turn off the heat. Move the pot to a
   warm spot (if you have an electric range, leave the pot where it is; the residual
   heat in the burner should be just right). If you don't have a warm spot, put
   the pan in a larger pan of hot water. Let it stand for 12 minutes—longer
   won't hurt it. Fluff the rice with a fork, and turn it out into a serving bowl.

MAKES ABOUT 3 CUPS, SERVING 4 TO 6

NOTES ON USING RICE COOKERS AND STEAMERS

If you are using an electric rice cooker or stovetop rice steamer (often called a
"Charleston" rice steamer), it is especially important to thoroughly wash the
rice and to follow the manufacturer's exact proportion of water to rice. If you're
using an old Charleston rice steamer without directions, put the washed rice
into the upper pot with an equal volume of water (1 cup for every cup of rice),
and put 4 to 5 cups of water in the lower pot. The steamers take longer to cook
the rice, usually about 50 minutes to an hour, but are practically foolproof.

Lowcountry cooks, regardless of pedigree, prefer rice that has distinct, separate grains, and still make it in the way that West Africans introduced more than three hundred years ago. The method is straightforward, but there are a few basic rules that ensure success. Use long-grained rice, always wash it before cooking to remove the excess surface starch, and never stir the pot while it is cooking. Stirring not only breaks the delicate grains but also releases more starch, making the rice gummy and sticky. When it is done, the rice is fluffed by picking it with a fork.

Though the famous Carolina Gold rice is once again available to Savannah cooks, many prefer to use an aromatic Asian rice such as basmati or jasmine. They take beautifully to this treatment and are actually easier to cook than most domestic long grains.

SHRIMP PILAU

4 ounces (about 4 slices) thick-sliced bacon, pancetta, or smoked sausage, diced

1 medium onion, trimmed, split lengthwise, peeled, and chopped

1 medium green bell pepper, stem, seeds, and membranes removed, chopped

1 large rib celery, minced

1 large clove garlic, lightly crushed, peeled, and minced

1 tablespoon chopped parsley

1 cup raw rice, washed and drained (see Lowcountry Steamed Rice, opposite, for the method)

2 cups chopped ripe tomatoes, blanched, peeled, and seeded (page 15), or chopped canned tomatoes with their juices

1 cup Shellfish Broth (page 58)

1 bay leaf

1 pod cayenne or other hot pepper, left whole

Salt and whole black pepper in a peppermill

1-1/4 pounds (headless weight) shrimp

10 to 12 fresh basil leaves

1. Put the bacon in a deep skillet or flameproof casserole over medium heat. Fry until the fat is rendered and the bacon is browned. Spoon off all but 2 tablespoons of fat, add the onion, bell pepper, and celery, and sauté, tossing occasionally, until softened but not browned, about 5 minutes. Add the garlic and parsley and toss until fragrant, about half a minute.

2. Add the rice and stir until evenly coated with fat. Add the tomatoes, broth, bay leaf, and hot pepper pod, and season well with salt and pepper. Stir and let it come back to a boil.

3. Reduce the heat to the lowest possible setting, cover the pan tightly, and simmer for 12 minutes. Carefully fold the top grains of the rice under to the bottom. Don't stir it—fold it. Spread the shrimp over the rice, cover tightly, and let it steam for about 5 minutes more. Turn off the heat and let it sit, tightly covered, until the rice is tender and the shrimp are pink and cooked through, about 8 to 10 minutes. Scatter the basil over it and fluff with a fork, tossing to mix in the shrimp, and serve at once.

SERVES 4

Surrounded as it is by salt marshes teeming with shellfish and by fields of Carolina Gold, it's only natural that shrimp and rice would be staples in Old Savannah kitchens, and this classic combination of the two is a standard local supper dish. Far more so than shrimp and grits, this simple dish distills the very essence of traditional Lowcountry cooking.

Most old recipes called for the shrimp to cook in the rice for the entire time. While this does infuse more flavor, it also makes the shrimp tough. For maximum flavor while preserving the character of the shrimp, many modern cooks prefer to simmer the rice first in Shellfish Broth and add the shrimp at the end, as is done here.

Probably nothing in all of Southern cooking is less understood than this classic pilau. Its origins are indisputably West African, but since its transplanting into Lowcountry cookery, it has acquired touches not found in the bean pilaus of Africa. The origin of the name has likewise been debated among historians, but most agree that it''s probably a corruption of West African or West Indian patois words. The folk tales that it originated with a lame servant are, excuse the expression, pretty lame themselves.

Red peas were the original Hoppin' John pea in Savannah, and many traditional cooks like chef Nita Dixon still use them. But when I said as much in the *Savannah Morning News,* it set off a sharp debate between those who agreed and those who vigorously disagreed and claimed that only black-eyed peas were authentic. Probably the confusion comes from the fact that "cowpea" was once a generic name applied to all field peas, but in some places it meant only black-eyed peas but here in Savannah and in much of Carolina, it meant red peas.

CHATHAM HOPPIN' JOHN

2 cups dried red peas (see sidebar)

1/2 pound lean salt-cured pork or bacon, cut into 1/4-inch dice

1 large onion, trimmed, split lengthwise, peeled, and finely chopped

2 large cloves garlic, lightly crushed, peeled, and minced

1 small pod hot red pepper, stemmed, seeded, and minced, or hot sauce

1 bay leaf

Whole black pepper in a peppermill

Salt

1 cup long-grain rice, washed and drained (see Lowcountry Steamed Rice, page 78, for the method)

1. Wash and drain the peas. Put them in a large pot with about 6 cups water and bring them to a boil over medium heat. Do not add salt. Carefully skim off the scum, reduce the heat to a slow simmer, cover, and simmer half an hour.

2. Meanwhile, put the salt pork or bacon in a sauté pan or skillet over medium heat. Fry until browned and the fat is rendered. Add the onion and sauté until golden, about 5 to 7 minutes. Add the garlic and hot pepper pod and sauté until fragrant. Turn off the heat and add it to the peas along with the bay leaf. Season liberally with pepper, cover loosely, and simmer until the peas are tender, about 45 minutes to 1 hour.

3. Taste the broth and correct for salt, keeping in mind that the broth must be highly seasoned in order to flavor the rice. Drain but reserve the broth, measure it and return 2 cups to the pot. Bring it to a boil over medium heat, add the rice, and let it come back to a boil. Reduce the heat, cover, and simmer gently 14 minutes, until the liquid is absorbed into the rice and distinct steam holes appear. Cover tightly, turn off the heat, and let it steam 12 minutes, or until the grains of rice are tender but still loose and distinct. Fluff with a fork and, if it seems too dry, fold in a little reserved broth.

SERVES 4 TO 6

RED RICE

1/4 pound thick-cut bacon or salt pork, diced small

1 medium onion, trimmed, split lengthwise, peeled, and chopped

1 medium green bell pepper, stemmed, seeded, and chopped

1 cup long-grain rice, washed and drained (see Lowcountry Steamed Rice, page 78, for the method)

1 pound tomatoes, blanched, peeled, and seeded (page 15), or 2 cups Italian canned plum tomatoes, with their juice, chopped

1/2 cup Basic Meat or Chicken Broth (page 57) or water

1 tablespoon Worcestershire sauce

Salt, ground cayenne pepper, and whole black pepper in a peppermill

1. Put the bacon or salt pork in a deep, lidded skillet (preferably cast iron) or Dutch oven and turn on the heat to medium. Fry, uncovered, until the fat is rendered and the bacon is crisp. Spoon off all but 2 tablespoons of fat. Add the onion and bell pepper and sauté until translucent, about 5 minutes.

2. Add the rice and stir until it is well-coated and warmed, about 3 or 4 minutes. Add the tomatoes with their juice, broth, Worcestershire sauce, salt, cayenne, and a liberal grinding of pepper to taste. Bring to a boil, stir, scraping any loose grains that are sticking to the pan.

3. Loosely cover, reduce the heat as low as possible, and let simmer 14 minutes. Uncover and, with a large fork, gently fold the top grains of rice under until the bottom and top rice have exchanged places. Cover and cook at the lowest possible temperature for 12 minutes more, or until the rice is just tender but still distinct and separate. Remove it from the heat and let it steam for 3 to 5 minutes, fluff it with a fork, and serve at once.

SERVES 4

In the middle of the last century, the famed Pirate's House Restaurant added the name "Savannah" to the red rice on its menu, beginning a modern food myth that, within little more than twenty years, became deeply imbedded in Southern lore. Actually, red rice did not originate in Savannah and cannot be construed as unique to our area by any stretch of the imagination. It can be found throughout the Carolina and Georgia Lowcountry, and even appears inland as "Spanish" rice. Nonetheless, this spicy pilau has long been a standard on Savannah tables and is always on the menu of local oyster roasts and seafood boils—or, for that matter, just about any outdoor entertainment. Old Savannahians knew it first as tomato pilau, and later as "mulatto" or just "red" rice.

Facing: Chatham Hoppin' John.

DUCK AND OKRA PILAU

Pilaus are a favorite way to cook game birds of all kinds, especially dove, duck, quail, and pheasant. Many modern recipes use only the breast meat, cut up in bite-size pieces, but the whole bird is more traditional, not to mention more flavorful. Here it is paired with okra and that Lowcountry trinity of onions, peppers, and garlic, suggesting that the original pot was almost certainly stirred by the hand of a Gullah cook.

1 young duckling, about 3 to 5 pounds, disjointed and cut up as for frying

Salt and whole black pepper in a peppermill

Ground cayenne pepper

2 tablespoons bacon drippings, unsalted butter, or olive or vegetable oil

1 medium yellow onion, trimmed, split lengthwise, peeled, and chopped fine

1 medium green or red bell pepper, stem, core, seeds, and membrane removed, chopped fine

2 large cloves garlic, lightly crushed, peeled, and finely minced

1 cup raw rice, washed and rinsed (page 78)

2 cups young, tender okra sliced 1/2-inch thick

1-3/4 cups duck broth, made with the back, neck, giblets, and 4 cups water as for Basic Meat or Chicken Broth (page 57) or water

1 pound tomatoes, scalded, peeled, seeded, and chopped, or 1-1/2 cups canned tomatoes, seeded and chopped, with their juices

1 tablespoon chopped fresh, or 1 teaspoon dried, thyme

1 tablespoon chopped fresh, or 1 teaspoon dried, sage

2 bay leaves

1. Rinse the duck and pat dry. Season it well with salt, pepper, and cayenne. Heat the drippings in a wide Dutch oven over medium heat. Add the duck and brown it well on all sides, about 5 minutes. Remove it from the pan and add the onion and bell pepper. Sauté, tossing often, until the onion is golden, about 5 minutes. Add the garlic and sauté until fragrant, about half a minute.

2. Add the rice and sauté, tossing, until it is beginning to color, about 5 minutes. Add the okra and cook, tossing, until it is bright green. Return the duck to the pan along with any juices that have accumulated. Add the broth, tomatoes, and herbs, let it come to a boil, and lower the heat to a simmer.

Duck and Okra Pilau.

Cook until the liquids are absorbed and evaporated, about 15 minutes. Gently fluff the rice with a fork, cover tightly, and let it sit over low heat for 1 minute. Turn off the heat and let it sit 12 minutes longer.

3. Serve the pilau directly from the pot or transfer the duck to a platter, fluff the rice with a fork, and spoon it around the edges of the platter.

SERVES 4

Shrimp Fried Rice.

Fried Rice, A Lowcountry Tradition

SAVANNAH'S CHINESE COMMUNITY goes back to 1889, by legend on the very day that Hogan's fire leveled a big chunk of Broughton Street and gutted Independent Presbyterian Church. Supposedly, young Chinese revolutionary Robert Chung Chan, fleeing retaliation from the Manchu dynasty, arrived just in time to see the church's elegant Wren-style spire in flames, and, taking that as a heavenly sign that he was supposed to join the congregation, settled in Savannah and did just that. He was later joined by several compatriots, and a community that remains a viable part of Savannah's fabric was born.

It would seem obvious, then, that it was by way of this Asian community that Savannah came to have a long-standing tradition of stir-frying leftover rice. But the dish actually predates Mr. Chan by at least two decades and is found in outlying communities on Daufuskie Island and in Sunbury, a fishing village south of Savannah, where there can have been little, if any, direct Chinese influence. The more likely source for our version of fried rice is West Africa, since it first turns up in the household notebooks of matrons who had African American cooks and is consistent with many West African culinary traditions.

SHRIMP FRIED RICE

The deceptively simple elegance of this recipe depends entirely on the quality of its ingredients. When the shrimp are the tiny, intensely sweet creek shrimp, freshly caught just minutes from the pan, this is at its best as a simple trio of shrimp, butter, and leftover rice. Any additions seem superfluous, even intrusive. When the shrimp are not so fresh, however, it helps to boost their flavor by infusing the butter with the essence of their shells and a whisper of shallots and garlic.

2 pounds whole (head on) or 1-1/4 pounds (headless weight) medium inlet shrimp, not peeled

5 tablespoons unsalted butter

1/2 cup finely chopped shallots (about 1 large or 2 medium) or yellow onion

1 large or 2 medium cloves garlic, lightly crushed, peeled, and minced fine

3 cups Lowcountry Steamed Rice (page 78)

Salt and ground cayenne pepper

1. Peel and head the shrimp, reserving both the heads (if any) and shells. Put the butter in a large, deep skillet or sauté pan over medium-high heat. When it is melted, add the shrimp heads (if any) and shells and sauté, tossing constantly, until the shells and butter are bright orange-pink and the butter is deeply infused with the essence of the shrimp. Strain the butter, pressing hard on the shells, discard the shells, and return the butter to the pan.

2. Add the shallots and sauté, tossing frequently, until softened and beginning to color, about 4 minutes. Add the garlic and peeled shrimp tails and sauté, tossing frequently, until they are curled and pink, about 2 minutes. Stir in the rice and cook, tossing constantly, until it is hot through and, as one old recipe puts it, "all buttery and shrimpy." Season it well with salt and cayenne pepper, toss well, and serve at once.

SERVES 4

ADDITIONS AND VARIATIONS

Many old Savannah cooks would not think of making this without bell pepper. Allow 1 medium green bell pepper, stemmed, seeded, and chopped, and add it with the shallots in step 2. Sliced green onions, which in old Savannah were truly spring onions pulled fresh from the garden, add a fresh lift when substituted for the shallots and garlic. When the shrimp are not so fresh, or later in the season when palates become a bit jaded, each local cook makes this dish her own with a number of added seasonings, including Worcestershire sauce, hot pepper sauce, or even a few dashes of soy sauce.

DAUFUSKIE CRAB FRIED RICE

Sallie Ann Robinson is a Daufuskie Island native who has preserved much of her homeland's culinary heritage and lore in two lovely cookbook memoirs, *Gullah Home Cooking The Daufuskie Way* and *Cooking the Gullah Way*. Sallie Ann is one of the most infectiously joyful people I know, and her cooking reflects that exuberance. This is basically her recipe, which she taught me to make in her snug little kitchen one crisp, sunny winter afternoon. Like any Savannah cook, I have since added touches of my own.

4 strips thick-cut bacon, diced

1 medium yellow onion, trimmed, split lengthwise, and chopped

1 medium green bell pepper, stemmed, cored, seeded, and chopped

1 rib celery, strung and chopped

1 large or 2 medium cloves garlic, lightly crushed, peeled, and minced fine

1 pound crabmeat

3 cups Lowcountry Steamed Rice (page 78)

Salt and whole black pepper in a peppermill

1. Put the bacon in a large, deep skillet or sauté pan over medium-high heat. Sauté, tossing frequently, until the fat is rendered and it's golden brown. Add the onion, pepper, and celery and sauté, tossing frequently until it is softened and the onion is golden, about 5 minutes. Add the garlic and crab and sauté, tossing, until the crab is hot through and golden brown, about 5 minutes.

2. Add the rice and toss until it is well coated and the crabmeat is evenly distributed. Season it liberally with salt and pepper, if needed. Toss well, lower the heat to medium low, cover, and let steam gently for about 10 minutes. Taste and adjust the seasonings, toss well, and serve hot.

SERVES 4

NOTES

Like most local African American cooks, Sallie uses garlic powder instead of fresh garlic, and in prodigal quantities. The taste reflects her exuberant personality—bright, forthright, and sunny, but I prefer the more subtle sweetness of fresh garlic and, when the crabmeat is not so fresh, give it added kick with a touch of Worcestershire or soy sauce.

MRS. HABERSHAM'S SAVANNAH JAMBALAYA

4 strips bacon, diced, or 3 tablespoons unsalted butter

1 small onion, trimmed, split lengthwise, peeled, and chopped

1 medium green or red bell pepper, stemmed, cored, seeded, and chopped

1 cup cooked green peas, red peas, or black beans, optional

1 cup diced cooked chicken, turkey, ham, pork, or beef, or 1 cup lump crabmeat, or small shrimp, cooked and peeled

3 cups Lowcountry Steamed Rice (page 78)

1 scant cup tomato sauce

Salt, ground cayenne pepper, and whole black pepper in a peppermill

1. If you're using bacon, put it in a large, deep skillet or sauté pan over medium heat. Sauté, tossing frequently, until the fat is rendered and it is golden brown. If using butter, put it in the pan over medium heat and let it just melt.

2. Add the onion and bell pepper and sauté, tossing, until the onion is softened and translucent and just beginning to color, about 5 minutes. Add the peas and meat or shellfish and heat them through, tossing constantly. Add the rice and toss until it is well coated and warmed, then stir in the tomato sauce and season liberally with salt, cayenne, and black pepper. Sauté, tossing constantly, until the rice is well coated.

3. Reduce the heat, cover, and let steam 3 to 5 minutes. Uncover, toss, and serve hot.

SERVES 4

Jambalaya can be found all over the South, especially in places where rice was a staple of the diet—in Louisiana, the gulf coast of Alabama, and all along the rice-growing coastal plains of South Carolina and Georgia. It is, beneath its Creole skin, the same thing as a Lowcountry pilau. Though today most Savannah Jambalaya resembles the Louisiana version, historically it took two forms. The first, closely resembling Red Rice (page 81), was made with bacon, onions, sweet bell peppers, and tomatoes, and was drier than Louisiana jambalaya. The second was this fried rice supper dish, attributed to legendary cooking teacher Leila Habersham, which was no doubt devised as a means of using up leftovers from midday dinner. The version in Nellie Gordon's recipe book used butter instead of bacon fat and makes wholesale use of leftovers, giving away that most of the old cooks—Miss Leila included—must have improvised wildly.

Grits

Though whole corn grits, ground on antique water-powered millstones by specialty millers and hobbyists, have become fashionable on Savannah restaurant menus and among its "foodie" crowd, most traditional cooks continue to prefer hominy grits, ground from hulled corn that has been treated with lye. They are more pristinely white than whole corn grits and have a completely different flavor. You may use either one: just don't annoy us by comparing them, as some visitors have done, to boiled sand and spackling paste.

Regardless of whether you use whole corn or hominy grits, the rule of thumb ratio of water to raw grits is 4 to 1. Like most rules of thumb, it's never exact. The proportions will vary depending on the grits, their moisture content, the ambient humidity, and the taste of the cook. Since it will never take less than 4 to 1, you can safely begin with that proportion, keeping a teakettle of simmering water on hand to add more as needed. Once the grits begin cooking, never add cold water to the pot.

COOKED GRITS

If you are making large quantities of whole corn or plain hominy grits, a ceramic-lined slow cooker is ideal. Put them on the night before and they'll be perfectly cooked by breakfast time the next morning.

Traditional Savannah cooks always wash their grits before cooking them, just as they do rice, to remove any bits of chaff and ensure that the grits will be creamy smooth and pristinely white. Here is how they do it.

1 cup raw hominy or whole corn grits   Salt
4 cups water

1. Put the grits in a heavy-bottomed 3-quart porcelain enamel or stainless-steel, lined pot. Fill it 2/3 full with water and stir with your hand until it's milky. Let the grits settle to the bottom and carefully pour off the water. Repeat at least once more, drain well, and add 4 cups cold water.

2. Put the pan over medium heat and bring it slowly to a simmer, stirring constantly. Keep stirring until the grits are beginning to thicken, loosely cover, and reduce the heat to medium low. Cook, stirring frequently at first and then occasionally as the grits thicken, until thick and creamy, about an hour for whole corn grits or regular hominy grits, and at least 30 minutes for quick grits. Add salt to taste and simmer for a few minutes longer. Taste and adjust the salt and serve hot.

TO COOK GRITS WITHOUT RINSING THEM

Lowcountry cooks who adhere to washing frown on this method, but it sure is simpler and I can't tell the difference.

1. Bring the water to a boil over medium heat. Slowly stir in the grits, pouring them in a thin, steady stream. Bring it back to a boil, stirring constantly.

2. Reduce the heat to a slow simmer, loosely cover, and cook, stirring frequently at first and then occasionally as the grits thicken, until thick and creamy, about an hour for whole corn grits or regular hominy grits and at least 30 minutes for quick grits. Add salt to taste and simmer for a few minutes longer. Taste and adjust the salt and serve hot.

SERVES 4

BREAKFAST SHRIMP

This simple triad of shrimp, butter, and creamy grits is richer, for times when the cook was flush and had a bit of butter on hand, but it's no less reverent. The recipe calls for raw shrimp, but some traditional cooks poach them first. With care, precooked shrimp will work well, and it does make an excellent way to get rid of leftovers from a party tray, especially if you have shells to infuse the butter with shrimpy essence as is done in step 2. But whether you use precooked or raw shrimp, be sure they are at room temperature when you start and don't overcook them.

2 pounds whole small raw shrimp (head-on weight) or 1-1/4 pounds (headless weight)

8 tablespoons unsalted butter

Salt and whole black pepper in a peppermill

4 cups hot Cooked Grits (facing)

1. Head and peel the shrimp and set the tails aside. You may do this ahead and refrigerate, covered, overnight, but allow them to sit at room temperature for 30 minutes before cooking.

2. Over medium heat, melt the butter in a large sauté pan or skillet. When it begins to bubble, put in the shrimp heads and shells and sauté, tossing, until bright pink—about 5 minutes. Remove them from the heat and strain the butter through a coarse wire sieve. Discard the shells. The butter can be made ahead.

3. When you're ready to serve the shrimp, put the butter in a large sauté pan or skillet and turn on the heat to medium high. When it's hot, add the shrimp and sauté, tossing constantly, until pink, curled, and just cooked through, about 2 to 3 minutes. Remove from the heat, season with salt to taste, and continue tossing to arrest further cooking. If you're using cooked shrimp, toss until just heated through, less than 2 minutes.

4. Quickly divide the grits among four warm plates. Spoon on the shrimp and butter and serve immediately.

SERVES 4

Breakfast shrimp, or "Shrimp and Grits" as it is more widely known on the menus of nouvelle Southern restaurants, is today a popular elegant first course, but originally, it was simple subsistence food. If you had a shrimp net and grits in your pantry, in season a hearty breakfast or supper was yours for the taking. Nouvelle restaurant versions are inevitably complexly layered, but the old recipes were simple almost to the point of austerity. When the shrimp are the tiny creek shrimp from our inlet waters, such restraint is actually the better part of wisdom. One of the most reverently simple and exquisite recipes I know of calls for freshly caught shrimp to be carefully poached in sea water, peeled, piled into a pale green bowl (the color was specific), and passed with a separate bowl of hot grits.

DOWNTOWN BREAKFAST SHRIMP

This slightly upscale version, while not quite as simple as the previous recipe, still maintains the same level of respect for the natural flavors of the shrimp and is how local cooks coax that fresh-caught sweetness from shrimp that have been frozen or are not quite as fresh from the net as they'd like. It also works wonders with the large white shrimp that have come from deeper waters. At supper, this same dish was also served over cooked rice, sometimes (in the fall when their seasons overlap) with a few oysters added at the end.

2 pounds (head-on weight) or 1-1/4 pounds (headless weight) small to medium shrimp

1/4 pound bacon, diced

1 medium yellow onion, trimmed, split, peeled, and cut into 1/2-inch dice

2 large or 3 medium cloves garlic, lightly crushed, peeled, and minced

2 tablespoons all-purpose flour

Salt and ground cayenne pepper

4 cups hot Cooked Grits (page 88) or Lowcountry Steamed Rice (page 78)

1. Head and peel the shrimp, reserving the heads and shells; cover and set aside (refrigerate if not finishing it immediately). Put the heads and shells and 2 cups of water in a stainless or enameled pot. Bring to a boil over medium-high heat, being careful not to let it boil over. Reduce the heat to medium and simmer until the liquid is reduced to 1 cup. Turn off the heat, strain the broth into a stainless steel or glass bowl. Discard the heads and shells. If you are not proceeding right away, cool the broth completely, and then cover and refrigerate it.

2. When you are ready to serve it, put the bacon in a large sauté pan or skillet that will hold the shrimp in one layer. Turn on the heat to medium and sauté, tossing occasionally, until it is browned but not crisp. Spoon off all but 2 tablespoons of fat and add the onion. Raise the heat to medium high and sauté, tossing frequently, until the onion is pale gold, about 4 or 5 minutes. Add the garlic and sauté until fragrant but not colored. Sprinkle in the flour and cook, stirring constantly, until it is browned, about 2 minutes more.

3. Add the shrimp and sauté, tossing constantly, until they begin to turn pink, about a minute. Season lightly with salt and cayenne. Slowly stir in the shrimp broth and bring it to a boil, stirring constantly. Simmer, stirring occasionally, until lightly thickened and the shrimp are just cooked through, about 2 minutes. If the gravy is too thin when the shrimp are done, lift them from the pan with a slotted spoon and cook until the gravy is lightly thickened, then return the shrimp to the pan and turn off the heat. Taste and adjust the seasonings and serve at once over hot grits or rice.

SERVES 4

Downtown Breakfast Shrimp.

VARIATION: DAISY REDMAN'S LOWCOUNTRY SHRIMP AND OYSTERS

Daisy Redman, a celebrated caterer in Savannah for three decades, was one of four African American Georgians featured in the classic *Four Great Southern Cooks* (1980). Her version of the previous recipe included half a cup of chopped green bell pepper, sautéed with the onion in step 2. She sometimes added freshly shucked oysters as well: omit half the shrimp broth and allow 1 cup shucked oysters, drained but with the liquor reserved. Add them when you add the shrimp. Simmer until the shrimp are curled and pink and the oysters are plump and their gills have curled, about 3 minutes. The oysters will throw off a good bit of juice, but you may need to thin it with some of the reserved oyster liquor if it is still too thick when the shellfish are done.

CRAB AND GRITS

Close kin to the more universally known shrimp and grits, this simple yet delicious way of serving crabmeat was once common on local breakfast or supper tables and was so taken for granted that it was almost never written down. In her classic, *The Savannah Cook Book*, Harriett Ross Colquitt described it in a very off-hand way without giving a real recipe, implying that everyone knew how to make it.

When the crabmeat is very good and fresh, it will need absolutely nothing but a little salt and cayenne pepper—if that. When it is not so fresh, however, or has been pasteurized, it can be enlivened by sautéing about 1/4 cup of finely minced onion and a clove of garlic in the butter before adding the crabmeat. Waken the flavors further with a dash of Worcestershire sauce or pinch of Seafood Boiling Spice (page 6).

1 pound (2 cups) picked cooked lump crabmeat, in large pieces
5 tablespoons unsalted butter

Salt and ground cayenne pepper
4 cups hot Cooked Grits (page 88)

1. If you're using commercially packed meat, pick over it for bits of shell. Put the butter in a sauté pan over medium heat. When it is melted and hot, add the crab and toss until hot through and butter has absorbed some of the crab flavor. Season to taste with salt and cayenne and let it warm another half a minute to let the seasonings settle in.

2. Divide the grits among 4 warm serving plates, spoon the crab and butter evenly over it, and serve at once.

SERVES 4

GARLIC AND CHEESE GRITS

These grits are sometimes served, especially in restaurants, with Breakfast Shrimp, but I think that is unnecessarily gilding the lily. They're best served as a supper side dish, especially for fried fish, or when you want to dress up the breakfast grits for a brunch. Often they are passed in thick Styrofoam bowls on the morning of the St. Patrick's Day parade when families will stake out their favorite picnic spots along the parade route literally at the crack of dawn.

3 cups whole milk

1 cup water

1 cup quick-cooking grits

Salt

2 ounces (4 tablespoons) unsalted butter

3 large or 5 small cloves garlic, lightly crushed, peeled, and finely minced

8 ounces very sharp cheddar, grated, divided

1 tablespoon Worcestershire sauce

Ground cayenne pepper

Sweet paprika

1. Position a rack in the center of the oven and preheat it to 375 degrees F. Bring the milk and water to a simmer over medium heat. Slowly stir in the grits, adding them in a thin, steady stream. Let it come back to a simmer, stirring constantly, and reduce the heat to medium low. Loosely cover and simmer until the grits are very thick and each grain is tender, about 30 minutes. Season well with salt and let simmer 1 to 2 minutes longer.

2. Melt the butter in a small skillet over medium heat. Add the garlic and sauté, tossing often, until it is fragrant and just beginning to color. Pour the butter and garlic into the grits and mix well. Add all but 1 cup of the cheese, Worcestershire, and a pinch or so of cayenne, to taste. Stir well. Lightly butter a 2-quart casserole or soufflé dish and pour in the grits. Smooth the top and sprinkle with the remaining cheese and dust lightly with paprika. Bake in the center of the oven until lightly browned and bubbly, about 30 minutes.

SERVES 4 TO 6

Garlic Cheese Grits.

GNOCCHI ALLA ROMANA

What, you may well ask, is this classic recipe of the Roman Jewish community doing here? The simple answer is that it has a deep connection with Savannah. Contributed by Mrs. J. F. Minis, a member of the socially and economically prominent Jewish family, to *Favorite Recipes From Savannah Homes*, a cookbook published in 1904 by the Ladies of the Bishop Beckwith Society, it is absolutely classic, down to the last detail. Yet its wording is purely Southern, not only calling for the semolina paste to be cut "into biscuits," but forthrightly referred to the gnocchi as "biscuits" throughout the remainder of the recipe. Clearly it was a dish that was both used in the Minis household and shared with friends of all faiths in the community.

4 scant cups milk

8 tablespoons or 1 stick unsalted butter, divided

Salt

Whole nutmeg in a grater

5-1/2 ounces (about 1 cup) semolina

5 large egg yolks

1-1/2 cups (about 4 ounces) freshly grated Parmigiano-Reggiano cheese, divided

1. Bring the milk, 6 tablespoons of butter, a large pinch of salt, and a generous grating of nutmeg to a boil in a heavy-bottomed saucepan. Slowly add the semolina in a thin, steady stream, whisking constantly to prevent lumps. Return to a boil, reduce the heat to low, and simmer for about 15 to 20 minutes, until it is a very thick.

2. Remove it from the heat, let it cool slightly, and then beat in the egg yolks and about half the grated Parmigiano. Pour the semolina paste onto a dampened rimmed baking sheet or large baking dish. It should be about 1 inch thick. Let it cool, then cover and refrigerate until it is firm, about 2 hours.

3. Position a rack in the center of the oven and preheat the oven to 375 degrees F. Lightly butter an 8 x 12-inch baking dish. Melt the remaining butter. Remove the paste from the refrigerator and, with a 2-inch biscuit cutter dipped in cold water, cut it into round dumplings. Arrange the dumplings, overlapping slightly, in the prepared baking dish, sprinkling each layer sparingly with melted butter and generously with the remaining cheese. Bake until bubbly and the top is golden brown, about half an hour.

SERVES 6

Bread and Gottlieb's Bakery

LIKE MANY OTHER SOUTHERN HOMEMAKERS, Savannah housewives of the past took pride in making bread for their family's tables. A little known but telling detail of that favorite Southern title "Lady" is that it originally meant "the bread giver." Not surprisingly, home baking figures prominently in the Savannah homemaker's repertory. That said, there have been public bakeries in Savannah almost from its founding in 1733. The first, probably located on Ellis Square (the city's original open market), had a dual function. In the early days of the colony, private ovens were rare, so while they baked bread to sell, like the bakeries the settlers had known in Europe, they also provided communal ovens, where housewives could bake their homemade loaves as well as the family joint of beef, mutton, or pork wrapped in a hard pastry. As the city prospered and home ovens became more commonplace, public bakeries settled into the role that they fill today.

One of Savannah's most famous bakeries was Gottlieb's, founded in 1884 by Russian-born Isadore Gottlieb in a humble basement shop on the corner of York and Jefferson Streets. The business knew several locations, first at Bryan and Montgomery Streets, and later on Oglethorpe, Broughton Street, and, finally Bull and 32nd Streets, near Sacred Heart Church and the old Benedictine Academy. It remained in the family until Isser and Ava Gottlieb closed its doors in 1994. More than a decade later its reputation remains lively in Savannahians' memories, and the family name is still deeply rooted in Savannah's food community through Isser and Ava's three sons, Richard, Laurence, and Michael, who briefly revived the family business as an elegant white cloth restaurant on Broughton Street.

GOTTLIEB'S CHALLAH

This enriched egg bread is traditionally served with Friday night Sabbath dinners, and Gottlieb's always had baked up a goodly supply because customers of all religious persuasions loved it. The dough is essentially a brioche made without butter—a necessary for Kosher meals when meat is served—and it can be shaped and baked in the same top-knotted roll or coiled in a muffin tin like Olde Pink House Tea Room French Rolls (page 97). The Gottliebs also layer this dough with butter to make their signature Butter Rolls, detailed in the variation at the end of the recipe. (Recipe continued on next page.)

1 envelope active dry yeast or 1/2 ounce cake compressed fresh yeast

1/2 cup sugar

1-1/2 cups water warmed to 110 to 115 degrees F (not hot tap water)

1/2 cup vegetable oil

3 large eggs, at room temperature, divided

1 tablespoon salt

5 to 6 cups (about 1-1/2 pounds) unbleached all-purpose flour, divided

1. Dissolve the yeast and sugar in the water and proof 10 minutes. With a mixer fitted with a paddle or a wooden spoon, beat in the oil, 2 eggs, salt, and 2 cups of flour. Beat in the remaining flour a cup at a time, holding back 1 cup. Turn it out onto a well-floured surface and knead until elastic and smooth, adding more flour as needed, about 8 to 10 minutes.

2. Shape it into a ball and put it in a well-oiled bowl. Cover with a double-folded damp linen towel or plastic wrap and let it rise until doubled, about 4 to 6 hours.

3. Punch the dough down and turn it out onto a lightly floured work surface. Divide it into 4 or 6 equal pieces and roll each out in a long sausage-like cylinder about 1 inch in diameter. Pinch them together at one end and braid them, always crossing them to the middle, and place on a buttered baking sheet. Cover loosely with a damp cloth and let it double, about an hour.

4. Position a rack in the center of the oven and preheat it to 375 degrees F. Beat the remaining egg with 1 tablespoon of water and brush it generously over the bread. Bake in the center of the oven until golden brown and hollow sounding when tapped, about 30 minutes.

MAKES 1 LARGE BRAIDED LOAF OR 24 SMALL BRIOCHE ROLLS

GOTTLIEB'S BUTTER ROLLS

For 1 recipe Challah dough, allow 6 ounces (1-1/2 sticks or 3/4 cup) softened butter. Roll the dough out into a rectangle. With an icing spatula, spread the softened butter over two-thirds of the dough. Fold the unbuttered third over toward the center until it covers half the buttered side, then fold the remaining buttered third over the top, like folding a letter. Roll it out and fold the dough again, without buttering it. Cut the dough with a pizza wheel or sharp knife into small squares. Butter the wells of two 24-well mini muffin pans and stand a square of the dough in each well. Brush with egg wash and bake until golden brown, about 18 minutes.

OLDE PINK HOUSE TEA ROOM
FRENCH ROLLS

1 teaspoon active dry yeast or 1/2 ounce
cake compressed fresh yeast

1 cup water

1 cup whole milk

1/2 cup sugar

40 ounces (about 8 cups) bread flour or
unbleached all-purpose flour, including 1/4 cup whole-wheat pastry flour

2 teaspoons salt

4 large eggs, lightly beaten

1 cup or 2 sticks unsalted butter, softened, plus 4 tablespoons melted

1. Dissolve the yeast in the water and let it proof for 10 minutes. Meanwhile, scald the milk in a heavy-bottomed saucepan over medium heat. Remove it from the heat and stir in the sugar until it is dissolved. Let it cool to 110 degrees F and stir in the dissolved yeast.

2. Whisk or sift together the flour and salt in a large mixing bowl and make a well in the center. Beat together the eggs, milk, and yeast. Pour it into the well and, by hand or with a mixer fitted with a paddle, gradually mix in the flour until it becomes almost too stiff to stir. Work the rest of the flour in by hand. The dough should be almost too soft to handle.

3. Work the softened butter into the dough by hand or with a mixer fitted with a dough hook. Knead until it is elastic and smooth, about 8 minutes. Rub a clean bowl with 2 tablespoons melted butter and put in the dough, turning it until it is coated on the outside, cover with plastic wrap and leave it in a warm spot to rise until it is doubled, about 4 to 6 hours. Refrigerate the dough until it is chilled.

4. Lightly flour your hands and a work surface. Roll the chilled dough out into a long sausage shape about 1-1/2 inches round. Lightly butter three 12-well standard muffin tins. Pinch off lumps of the dough and roll them out into 1/2-inch-diameter by 6-inch-long sausage shapes. Coil them into the cups of the muffin tin, forming a spiral with the center sticking up slightly. Loosely cover with damp linen towels.

5. Position a rack in the center of the oven and preheat the oven to 350 degrees F. Melt the remaining 2 tablespoons of butter in a small pan over low heat. Uncover the rolls and lightly brush the tops with the melted butter. Bake them in the center of the oven until they are risen and golden brown on top, about 18 to 20 minutes.

MAKES 3 DOZEN ROLLS

In nineteenth-century English and American cooking, bread enriched with egg and milk was often called "French" even though it had nothing to do with France, possibly because the dough bore more than a passing resemblance to brioche. At any rate, one such roll was the signature bread of the Olde Pink House Tea Room, in the historic James Habersham House on Reynolds Square. One of the oldest continuously operating dining rooms in the historic district, it later became a white cloth restaurant known for its new take on traditional Southern cooking. The tearoom's fare is only a memory, but native Savannahians wistfully remember this delicious bread.

SAVANNAH CREAM ROLLS

In her 1933 *Savannah Cook Book*, Harriet Ross Colquitt wrote that these rich rolls were "for high state occasions," but they are enough by themselves to turn any occasion into a high state one. They have been doing so in Savannah for at least a hundred and fifty years.

1/4 teaspoon active dry yeast or
   1/2-ounce cake compressed fresh yeast
2 cups heavy cream, scalded and
   cooled to 90 degrees F

2 large eggs
25 ounces (about 5 cups) unbleached
   all-purpose flour
1 teaspoon salt

1. Dissolve the yeast into the cream and let it proof 10 minutes. Break the eggs into a bowl, beat them lightly, and then stir in the cream and yeast.

2. Whisk together the flour and salt in a large mixing bowl. Make a well in its center and pour in the liquids. Gradually work it into a smooth dough. Turn the dough out onto a lightly floured surface and give it a light kneading, about 5 to 7 minutes. Gather it into a smooth ball. Wipe out the bowl and return the dough to it. Cover with a damp linen kitchen towel folded double, or plastic wrap, and set it aside to rise in a warm spot, about 4 to 6 hours, or in a cool spot overnight or while you are at work.

3. Punch the dough down and knead lightly for 1 to 2 minutes. Lightly butter two 12-well muffin pans. Dust the dough with flour and divide it into 24 equal balls. Put each one into a muffin well, cover the pan with a damp towel, and let it rise until the rolls are doubled, about 1 to 2 hours depending on the warmth of the room.

4. Position a rack in the center of the oven and preheat it to 400 degrees F. Bake until golden, about 20 minutes. Immediately remove from the pans and serve hot.

MAKES 2 DOZEN ROLLS

Savannah Cream Rolls.

SOUR CREAM RICE MUFFINS

2 cups rice flour (available at Asian markets and health food stores)

2 teaspoons baking powder

1 teaspoon salt

1 cup Lowcountry Steamed Rice (page 78)

1 cup sour cream or more (see step 2)

2 large eggs, beaten

Throughout the two centuries that rice was the staple money crop of the Carolina and Georgia Lowcountry, rice flour was a common ingredient in regional bread—either mixed with wheat or corn flour or replacing them both altogether. While rice has lingered as a staple in the diet of the region, rice flour had all but disappeared from Lowcountry larders by the middle of the last century. These rich, simple muffins are typical of the kinds of rice flour breads that once graced our tables. They make fine breakfast bread and are very good with luncheon or suppertime soups and stews. Leftovers hold up beautifully and are very good warmed over the next day in a 425-degrees-F oven.

1. Position a rack in the upper third of the oven and preheat the oven to 425 degrees F. Lightly butter the wells of a 12-well standard muffin tin. Whisk together the rice flour, baking powder, and salt in a large mixing bowl. Add the rice and toss until it is evenly mixed.

2. In a separate bowl, beat the sour cream and eggs well. Make a well in the center of the dry ingredients and pour in the liquids. Quickly stir them together. The batter should be very thick—stiffer than cornbread batter but softer than biscuit dough. If it's too dry, add a few more spoonfuls sour cream or milk. Divide the batter among the muffin wells and bake in the upper third of the oven until golden brown, about 25 minutes.

MAKES 12 MUFFINS

NOTES

A similar muffin is still made in Savannah using plain, all-purpose wheat flour rather than rice flour. We prefer an all-purpose soft-wheat flour such as White Lily or King Arthur Pastry Flour for quick breads like this, but unbleached all-purpose flour works fine. Rice flour doesn't fluff with air the way wheat flour will, so its volume measures are fairly consistent. Wheat flour, however, is best measured by weight in all baking recipes. Allow 10 ounces for this recipe. If you measure by volume, that's about 2 cups measured by scooping the flour and sweeping off the excess.

SAVANNAH RICE WAFFLES

2 tablespoons unsalted butter

1 cup hot Lowcountry Steamed Rice (page 78)

10 ounces (about 2 cups) unbleached all-purpose flour

2 teaspoons baking powder

1/2 teaspoon baking soda

1 teaspoon salt

2 large eggs, separated

1-3/4 cups whole-milk buttermilk or plain, whole-milk yogurt thinned to buttermilk consistency with milk

Melted butter or oil, for greasing the waffle iron

1. Stir the butter into the hot rice until melted and incorporated, then let it cool to room temperature.

2. Meanwhile, whisk or sift together the flour, baking powder, baking soda, and salt in a mixing bowl and make a well in the center. Beat the egg yolks and buttermilk together and pour them into the flour. Quickly mix the wet and dry ingredients together and stir in the rice.

3. Prepare a waffle iron and preheat at medium heat. In a separate bowl, beat the egg whites until they form soft peaks. When the iron is ready, fold the egg whites into the batter, brush the iron well with fat, and spoon some of the batter evenly over it, leaving room at the edges for it to spread as it cooks. Close the iron and bake until the steam stops rising from it and the waffle smells toasty and is golden brown, about 5 to 8 minutes. Serve the waffles as soon they come off the iron and repeat with the remaining batter.

MAKES ABOUT 6 LARGE OR 10 TO 12 SMALL WAFFLES

NOTES ON THE ART OF MAKING WAFFLES

It is always hard to judge just the right amount of batter to use in order to fill the waffle iron without having the excess ooze out the sides, so your first few waffles may not be picture perfect—but so what? They'll still taste good. The waffles are usually done when the steam stops rising from the edges of the iron, but if it begins to smell scorched before the steam stops completely, check it to be sure it hasn't browned too much. Waffles are, of course, best eaten hot from the iron, but they can be made ahead and reheated in a toaster or on a rack in an oven preheated to 400 degrees F. To store leftover waffles, let them get completely cold, put them in ziplock plastic freezer bags, and freeze them until needed.

Though today they are but rarely made at home, rice waffles were once a specialty of Savannah's best cooks and a fixture on the best breakfast and supper tables. They were served as any waffle might be today, with butter and syrup, honey, fresh fruit, and perhaps whipped cream, but they might also turn up at either meal topped with poached eggs and ham or with creamed chicken, seafood, or turkey.

The aim of every cook in the old days was to produce a waffle so crisp and light that it could be picked up with a dress pin. I don't know anyone, however, who actually tried to prove the point.

Facing: Sour Cream Rice Muffins.

BUTTERMILK HOECAKES

The original hoecakes were very simple griddle breads, consisting of little more than cornmeal, water, and salt. Whether or not it was actually baked on the blade of a hoe is lost in time. Today, it is griddle baked, and in the Savannah restaurants that have made it popular, its batter is generally enriched with milk, eggs, and melted fat.

Hoecakes are served as a bread with meat-and-three meals and at breakfast, but they are also good substituted for Holland rusk or English muffins in Eggs Benedict, or as a carrier for creamed chicken or seafood.

1 cup stone-ground white cornmeal
1/2 teaspoon baking soda
1/2 teaspoon salt
2 tablespoons sugar
1 large egg, lightly beaten

About 1-1/4 cups whole-milk buttermilk or plain, whole-milk yogurt thinned with milk to buttermilk consistency
Melted bacon drippings, butter, or vegetable oil, for greasing the griddle

1. Position a rack in the center of the oven, place a large baking sheet on it, and preheat to 170 degrees F (the warm setting). Whisk together the cornmeal, baking soda, salt, and sugar in a large mixing bowl. In a separate bowl, beat together the egg and buttermilk. Make a well in the center of the dry ingredients, pour in the liquids, and quickly stir them together. It should be moderately thick but should still pour easily from a spoon: if it doesn't, add a little more milk.

2. Place a griddle or wide, shallow skillet over medium-high heat, or heat an electric griddle to 325 degrees F. The griddle should be hot enough for a drop of water to "dance" on the surface, but not so hot that the batter browns too quickly. Brush with fat—just enough to coat it. Pour the batter in about a 2-tablespoon-size portion from the end of a large spoon—enough for cakes about 3 inches in diameter. The edges will sizzle and form lacy air bubbles. Cook until golden brown on the bottom, turn, and cook until uniformly golden, about 2 to 3 minutes per side. Transfer to the baking sheet in the oven as they are finished and repeat with the remaining batter until it is all cooked. Serve hot.

MAKES ABOUT 12, SERVING 4 TO 6

VARIATION: CORNBREAD MADELEINES (OR MINI HOECAKES) FOR CAVIAR

Seasoned Savannah host, the late Dean Owens, gave caviar a deliciously Deep South twist by serving it with cornbread baked in mini madeleine molds instead of blinis or toast points. I used mini hoecakes. For about 60 mini madeleines or hoecakes—serving 10 to 20—add 1/4 teaspoon freshly ground white pepper, 1 teaspoon baking powder, 2 tablespoons minced scallion or other green onions (green part only) and the grated zest from 1 lemon. Use about 3/4 cup whole milk buttermilk and bake the batter in two lightly greased mini madeleine pans or drop it on greased baking sheets, spacing them 1/2 inch apart. Bake at 400 degrees F until golden brown, about 10 minutes. These can be made ahead and reheated in a 200-degrees-F oven.

SAVANNAH FLATBREAD

1 rounded tablespoon sugar

1/2 cup buttermilk

2 cups Southern soft-wheat flour, pastry flour, or all-purpose flour

1 teaspoon salt

1/2 teaspoon baking soda

1/2 cup or 1 stick unsalted butter, cut into bits

1 tablespoon lard or shortening, cut into bits

1. Position a rack in the center of the oven and preheat it to 400 degrees F. Stir together the sugar and buttermilk until dissolved.

2. Whisk or sift together the flour, salt, and baking soda. Cut the butter and lard or shortening into the flour until it resembles coarse meal. Make a well in the center and pour in the buttermilk. Quickly mix together into a soft dough, turn it out onto a lightly floured work surface and lightly work until the dough is uniform, about two or three turns.

3. Pinch off six 1-inch-diameter balls of dough and, on a lightly floured surface, roll them wafer thin (about 3-1/2 to 4 inches in diameter). Lay them on an ungreased baking sheet. Bake about 5 to 7 minutes, or until golden brown. The bread crisps as it cools. Meanwhile, roll out six more rounds while the first batch bakes, repeating until all the dough is rolled and baked. Cool the bread completely before storing it in an airtight tin.

MAKES ABOUT 3 DOZEN 3-1/2- TO 4-INCH FLATBREADS

VARIATION

You may also divide the entire dough into six equal portions, roll them out one at a time, and cut each with a knife or zigzag pasta wheel into 3-inch squares or wedges. Bake them in batches as for the round bread.

Modern legend connects this bread back to Savannah's colonial days, when it was purportedly baked on the super-heated floor of wood-fired brick ovens. It's possible that such a bread was made in the ovens of the old bakery on Ellis Square where the disastrous fire of 1795 began, but in Colonial days only a few wealthy Savannahians had such ovens at home, and the earliest recipes I've found date from the mid-nineteenth century. At least one recipe suggestively called it Bread To Serve With Terrapin Soup. The truth is the Colonial connection was popularized during the 1970s when the Desoto Hilton Hotel featured a crisp flatbread under the trademarked name "Brittlebread." Regardless of its provenance, this bland, crisp bread is a perfect foil for any soup or stew. It's also fine for dipping or for slathering with spicy or sweet cocktail party spreads or at teatime.

Fish & Shellfish

CHATHAM COUNTY'S SHARE OF GEORGIA'S relatively short coastline may be small, but the entire county is riddled with marsh creeks and rivers, including the famous Back River that inspired native son Johnny Mercer's best-known song (and Savannah's unofficial anthem), "Moon River." The river has even been renamed in its honor—but I digress. The point is, there is almost more marsh here than solid land, and Savannah is literally surrounded by tidal marshes teeming with blue crabs, shrimp, and oysters. Three things can be said to have shaped Savannah's early table—a dominating English culture, West African cooks in the kitchen, and that plenitude of those three shellfish.

Well into the twentieth century, in living memory of some older Savannahians, this essential triad was supplied mostly by African American street vendors who plied the city's lanes with hand-woven marsh grass baskets of produce and shell-fish balanced on their heads. Today, locals who do not catch their own know to buy from a few select fish markets like Russo's and Matthews' Seafood, or from small shrimpers or fishermen who sell directly from the docks or from the back of a pickup by the roadside on one of the islands.

All three of these shellfish have a season. Though legends have given all kinds of mythical explanations for them, they mostly go back to availability and taste. As the weather cools, shrimp stop feeding close to the surface and retreat to deep waters. Their season runs from May until around December, when the waters begin to cool. Today, the legal shrimp season reflects that

Facing: Baked Shad Stuffed with Roe.
Above: Harvest of the warm months: a local shrimper with his haul of freshly net-ted shrimp.

When the weather turns hot in Savannah, seafood boils are a favorite way to entertain. They commemorate all sorts of rites of passage: birth, birthday, engagement, graduation, rehearsal dinner, retirement, arrival of a new neighbor, or departure of an old one. They have even been known to feed a wake or two. Because this is, of necessity, finger food, the setting is casual and almost always outdoors. The boil is dumped unceremoniously onto a tall table lined with newspapers or, in households that have them, freshly cut banana leaves. There are always bowls of cocktail sauce and butter for dipping, thick wedges of lemon, and sometimes bottles of hot sauce.

Guests literally belly-up to the feast, peeling their own shrimp and eating everything else, including the potatoes, with their fingers, so many hosts sensibly provide terry cloth hand towels for napkins. For larger parties, thick paper plates, knives, and forks may be provided, and other traditional picnic food will be offered—coleslaw, potato salad, red rice, and, of course, lemon meringue pies and homemade peach or buttered-pecan ice cream.

but is designed to protect the shrimp from over-harvesting during spawning. Oysters are seasonal in cold weather—not because they're bad in warm weather or because they spoil too easily as popular myth would have it, but because their texture and flavor aren't good while the water is warm and the oysters are spawning, so their season runs through cooler weather—traditionally in months that have an R in them.

LOWCOUNTRY BOIL

Lowcountry Boil is more of an idea than a specific recipe. I know of no two Lowcountry cooks who make it exactly the same. The least common denominator is shrimp, smoked link sausage, corn, and potatoes, but the permissible additions are legion and the variations practically limitless. One very common addition is whole live blue crab. Add them when you add the corn, allowing a dozen for the quantities given here, and add another 1/2 pound of potatoes and 4 ears of corn. It will up the servings to about 20.

4 tablespoons Seafood Boiling Spice (page 6)

1/2 cup unsalted butter

3 medium Vidalia sweet or yellow onions, trimmed, quartered lengthwise, and peeled

2 pounds smoked link sausage such as kielbasa, cut in 2- to 3-inch pieces

2 pounds new red-skinned potatoes

8 ears fresh sweet corn, preferably Silver Queen, shucked and broken in half

6 pounds whole (head-on) shrimp or 4 pounds if headed

Savannah Seafood Cocktail Sauce (page 19)

1/2 to 1 cup warm clarified butter

4 to 6 lemons, cut into wedges

1. Half fill a 12- to 20-quart stockpot with water. Bring it to a boil over medium-high heat. Reduce the heat to medium and add the boiling spice, butter, onion, and sausage. Let it return to a simmer and simmer 10 to 15 minutes.

2. Add the potatoes and cook 10 minutes, or until they're almost tender. Add the corn and cook 5 minutes longer. Add the shrimp and cook just until they are curled and pink, about 2, and not more than 3, minutes.

3. Drain thoroughly and pour out onto a large platter, lined with banana leaves if you have them, or, outdoors, onto a picnic table lined with newspaper and/or banana leaves. Pass cocktail sauce, butter, and lemons separately.

SERVES 10 TO 12

Lowcountry Boil.

A SAVANNAH OYSTER ROAST

Perhaps nothing better encapsulates casual entertaining during Savannah's winter social season than Oyster Roasts, but actually they were a favorite way of enjoying our area's abundant bivalves long before Oglethorpe landed on the *Anne* in 1733. Gigantic mounds of oyster shells left by Native Americans can still be found on the barrier islands that dot the marshes between Tybee and Savannah's old town center, giving some credence to the legends that the settlers learned to roast oysters in this way from the Yamacraw Indians.

To season melted butter, add a crushed but whole clove of garlic for every 1/2 cup butter when you melt it. Discard the garlic after seasoned butter is ready. Add salt to taste if using unsalted butter. Some also add Worcestershire and hot sauce, both to taste.

The menu for these events has changed over time. We know nothing of what Native Americans may have eaten with their oysters, but in her 1933 *Savannah Cook Book*, Harriet Ross Colquitt wrote that the traditional accompaniments for oyster roasts of the late nineteenth and early twentieth centuries were Hoppin' John (page 80) and hot biscuits, probably buttermilk or Savannah Cream Biscuits. Once upon a time, a country ham, poached to perfection and then baked with a glaze, would always have been found on the picnic table. Today the usual accompaniments are red rice, coleslaw, baked beans, and barbeque or fried chicken.

The menu is not all that has evolved; so has the cooking method. The original, and most flavorful, way of roasting oysters is on a gridiron or corrugated metal sheet over a pit of hardwood coals. The oysters are delivered in burlap sacks, and the sacks are often soaked in water and laid over the oysters, though some cooks prefer not to cover them. While that method survives, today many cooks use a large, propane-fired steamer.

In any case, this is outdoor cooking and eating. Be sure your guests dress casually and are provided with oyster knives specially designed for opening the shells, and thick, cut resistant gloves to protect the hand holding the oyster shells.

16 dozen freshly harvested live oysters, well-scrubbed

Seasoned Melted Butter (sidebar)

Anita's Sauce Mignonette (page 21)

Savannah Seafood Cocktail Sauce (page 19)

3 to 4 lemons, cut into wedges

Saltine crackers

1. Prepare a large grill or pit with enough charcoal to make a thick layer of coals over the entire bottom. Light them and let them burn down to a bright red glow. Position a rack about 6 inches above the coals.

2. Spread as many oysters as will fit in one layer on a rimmed baking sheet and place it on the grill rack. (If you have a round kettle grill, use a pizza pan.) You may cover them with the burlap bags if that's how the oysters came to you, or with kitchen towels soaked with water and wrung out. Grill until the shells are hot and you see them pop open slightly, about 5 to 8 minutes.

3. Immediately pile them in buckets or on a deep-rimmed platter, and serve them at once, with the sauces and crackers passed separately.

SERVES 8

Soft-shelled crabs

LOCAL RESTAURANT CHEFS have devised many ingenious ways of serving this delicacy, but wise home cooks know that the simpler and more reverent the treatment, the better. The following are time-honored recipes that have been enjoyed in Savannah homes for generations.

TO CLEAN SOFT-SHELL CRABS

If they haven't already been cleaned, cut out the eyes, mouth, and sand sack; flip it onto its back, lift the apron, and remove the gills and internal organs. Rinse them well under cold running water.

SAUTEED SOFT-SHELL CRABS WITH SHALLOT BUTTER

When the soft shells are very fresh and sweet, no sensible cook will go beyond step 2 but will omit the shallot and wine and serve the crabs sauced only with the butter in which they have cooked.

4 medium soft-shell crabs	Ground cayenne pepper
8 tablespoons unsalted butter	1/4 cup finely minced shallots
2 large cloves garlic, crushed and peeled but left whole	1/2 cup sherry
Salt	2 lemons, cut into wedges

1. If it has not already been done by the fishmonger, clean the crabs (see above) and pat them dry. Melt the butter in a large, heavy-bottomed skillet over medium heat and put in the garlic. Sauté, tossing occasionally, until the garlic is a light gold. Remove and discard it.

2. Put in the crabs and sauté, turning once, until they are pink and cooked through, about 4 minutes per side. Season well with salt and cayenne and remove them to a warm platter or individual serving plates.

3. Add the shallots to the pan and sauté, tossing frequently, until they are golden and softened, about 3 minutes. Add the wine and bring it to a boil, stirring and scraping to loosen any cooking residue. Simmer until it is slightly reduced, about 2 minutes longer. Pour the sauce over the crabs. Garnish with lemon wedges and serve at once.

SERVES 4 AS A FIRST COURSE OR LIGHT MAIN COURSE, 2 AS A MAIN COURSE IN A SIMPLE MEAL

Like most crustaceans, as blue crabs outgrow their hard outer shells, they shed them and immediately grow a new one. For a few fleeting hours before the new shell hardens, it is delicate and completely edible. They're a much-anticipated local delicacy, found in our markets and restaurants only for a brief time in late spring. While frozen soft-shell crabs are available at other times of the year, they have only a ghost of the rich, sweet flavor and texture of freshly caught ones, and locals would rather do without than settle for second best. If frozen ones are all that you can find, thaw them in salted water and soak them for a few minutes in milk. This helps preserve the texture and flavor, and keeps the shells from being tough.

Deep Fried Soft-Shell Crabs.

DEEP FRIED SOFT-SHELL CRABS

With its delicate, golden crust encasing a sweet, succulent interior, this is by far the most satisfying of all ways to cook soft-shell crabs and the only effective way to cook them once they've been frozen. Many local cooks use a crumb breading, some mix both crumbs and batter, and native-son chefs Michael and Laurence Gottlieb add finely ground pecans to the mix, but I like the delicacy of this thin, elegant fritter batter best.

8 medium soft-shell crabs

2 large eggs

1-1/2 cups whole milk

About 3/4 cup all-purpose flour, divided

Salt and whole white pepper in a peppermill

Ground cayenne pepper

Lard or vegetable oil, for frying

2 lemons, cut into wedges, optional

1 recipe Herb Mayonnaise (pages 23)

8 firm, home-style sandwich buns, split, buttered, and toasted, optional

1. Clean the crabs as directed on page 16 and pat them dry. Beat the eggs together in a large mixing bowl until smooth. Beat in the milk and gradually whisk in about 1/2 cup of flour, sifting it over the top a little at a time, until it forms a thin batter. Season well with salt, pepper, and cayenne. Let it rest for 20 to 30 minutes.

2. Meanwhile, position a rack in the center of the oven and preheat it to 170 to 180 degrees F (the warm setting). Fit a cooling rack over a rimmed baking sheet and have it close to your pan. Put enough oil in a heavy-bottomed Dutch oven, deep skillet, or deep fryer to come no more than halfway up the sides. Heat it over medium heat until it is hot but not smoking and the top "shimmers," 365 degrees F. Spread 1/4 cup of flour in a wide, shallow bowl.

3. Stir the batter, then lightly roll a crab in flour, shake off the excess, and dip it into the batter until it is coated. Lift it out, allowing the excess batter to flow back into the bowl, and slip it into the fat. Repeat with more crab until the pan is full but not crowded. Fry, turning once, until golden and cooked through (they will float when done), about 3 minutes per side. Lift them out with tongs or a frying skimmer, drain well, and put them on the prepared rack. Keep them in the warm oven while you fry the remaining crabs.

4. To serve the crabs as a main or first course, garnish them with lemon and serve with small ramekins of herb mayonnaise. To serve them as a sandwich, generously spread the toasted buns with the mayonnaise and allow 1 crab per sandwich.

SERVES 4 AS A MAIN COURSE, 8 AS A FIRST COURSE OR AS A SANDWICH

Though crab cakes are practically ubiquitous in Savannah's restaurants and many home cooks prize their own version of them, I prefer deviled crab, because they require less breading (that is, almost none at all) and the back shells in which they cook help preserve the moistness and rich-ness of flavor. Virtually every Lowcountry cook has his or her own version of this dish. I am not about to pretend to compete with Daufuskie Islanders, whose deviled crabs are legendary, but I do think my own version is awfully good.

DEVILED CRAB

1/2 cup finely minced yellow onion

1/2 cup finely minced green bell pepper

2 tablespoons olive oil

2 cloves garlic, minced

1 small hot red pepper, stemmed, seeded, and minced, or hot pepper flakes to taste

24 medium blue crabs, cooked and picked, with 8 whole back shells reserved (page 16), or 2 pounds packed crabmeat

1 cup soft breadcrumbs

1 to 2 tablespoons Dijon mustard, to taste

Salt and whole black pepper in a peppermill

Worcestershire sauce

2 tablespoons unsalted butter

1 cup fine cracker crumbs

1. Position a rack in the upper third of the oven and preheat it to 375 degrees F. Put the onion, bell pepper, and olive oil in a sauté pan over medium heat and sauté until it's translucent and softened, about 5 minutes. Add the garlic and hot pepper and sauté until fragrant, about a minute longer.

2. Pick over the crabmeat for bits of shell and put it into a mixing bowl. Add the breadcrumbs, onion, peppers, and garlic. Toss and season to taste with mustard, salt, pepper, and Worcestershire.

3. Divide the filling among reserved back shells (or scallop shells or 6-ounce ramekins), mounding the tops. Wipe out the sauté pan and add the butter. Melt it over low heat and stir in cracker crumbs until the butter is evenly absorbed. Sprinkle evenly over the crab filling.

4. Bake the crabs on a rimmed baking sheet in the upper third of oven until they're just heated through and their tops are nicely browned, about 20 minutes.

SERVES 4 AS A MAIN COURSE, OR 8 AS FIRST COURSE

LOWCOUNTRY CRAB AU GRATIN

1 pound crabmeat
1/4 cup finely minced shallots or yellow onions
2 tablespoons unsalted butter, divided
2 teaspoons all-purpose flour
1 cup light cream
1/4 cup medium dry sherry (amontillado)

2 tablespoons freshly grated Parmigiano-Reggiano cheese
Salt
Ground cayenne pepper
Whole nutmeg in a grater
1/4 cup fine cracker crumbs
1/2 cup (about 2 ounces) grated sharp cheddar cheese

1. Pick over the crab and remove any bits of shell and cartilage.

2. In a heavy-bottomed saucepan, sauté the onion in 1 tablespoon of butter over medium heat, tossing frequently, until softened but not colored, about 4 minutes. Sprinkle in the flour and cook, stirring, for a minute more. Slowly stir in the cream, bring it to a simmer, stirring constantly, and reduce the heat to medium low. Simmer, stirring, until lightly thickened, about 3 minutes. Stir in the sherry, return it to a simmer, and turn off the heat.

3. Position a rack in the upper third of the oven and preheat to 400 degrees F. Lightly butter a 1-1/2-quart casserole or 4 ramekins. Fold the crab and Parmigiano into the cream sauce. Season to taste with salt, cayenne, and nutmeg and pour it into the prepared casserole or ramekins.

4. Melt the remaining butter in a small skillet over low heat. Stir in the crumbs and toss until the butter is evenly absorbed. Sprinkle the cheddar evenly over top of the casserole or ramekins and top with the buttered crumbs. Bake until the filling is bubbly and the cheese is melted, about 15 to 20 minutes. Serve hot.

SERVES 4

Mellow and creamy under its tangy golden blanket of toasted cheese, crab au gratin is one of the best loved of the old-fashioned crab casseroles still found on both home and restaurant tables around Savannah. It is one of the first local seafood dishes that any budding young Lowcountry cook learns to make, but familiarity and simplicity take nothing away from its fine, comforting harmony of flavors.

OYSTERS IN LEEK
AND BOURBON CREAM

Chafing Dish Oysters (page 38), whether ladled right from the pan over homey thick slabs of buttered toast or hoecakes, or from a silver chafing dish into elegantly trimmed toast or puff pastry cups, are a favorite supper and party buffet dish in Savannah. Often they're paired with mushrooms and laced with sherry; here they bathe in a luxurious cream that is spiked with leeks and bourbon. While hoecakes may be the lowliest and humblest of breads, they make the perfect foil for the rich, complex flavors of the sauce.

This is mainly a first course, but it is substantial enough to serve as a main dish for an elegant post-party supper.

1 pint shucked oysters

2 medium (or 1 large) leeks

2 tablespoons unsalted butter

1 large or 2 medium cloves garlic, lightly crushed, peeled, and minced

2 quarter-size slices fresh gingerroot, peeled and minced

2 tablespoons bourbon

1 cup heavy cream

8 small (2-inch diameter) Buttermilk Hoecakes (page 102)

Salt and whole white pepper in a peppermill

1 tablespoon chopped parsley

1. Set a sieve over a stainless-steel or glass bowl and pour the oysters into it. Drain for at least 10 minutes. Reserve the liquor to freeze and use as fish broth. Trim the roots and any yellowed leaves from the leeks and split them in half lengthwise. Holding each half root end up, wash thoroughly under cold, running water, bending back the leaves to get all the dirt from between them. Thinly slice the white and most of the tender greens.

2. Put the butter in a large skillet or sauté pan. Turn on the heat to medium high. When the butter is just melted, add the leeks and sauté, tossing frequently, until wilted, about 3 to 4 minutes. Add the garlic and ginger and continue sautéing until fragrant, about half a minute more. Add the bourbon and let it evaporate, then pour in the cream. Bring the cream to a boil and cook until it is thick, about 2 to 3 minutes. It should be somewhat thicker than a cream sauce, since the oysters will throw off moisture as they cook, diluting it. Turn off the heat. You may prepare it up to this point several hours in advance. Cover and refrigerate the oysters and sauce in separate containers.

3. Half an hour before you are ready to serve the oysters, preheat the oven to 170 degrees F (or the "warm" setting). Put the hoecakes on a baking sheet in a single layer and put them into the warm oven. Turn on the heat under the sauce to medium and bring it to a simmer. Add the oysters, a small pinch of salt (go easy, you can correct the salt later), and a liberal grinding of white pepper. Bring to a simmer and cook until the oysters plump and their gills curl, between 1 and 2 minutes. Turn off the heat, and taste and adjust the seasonings.

4. Put 2 hoecakes per serving onto warmed individual serving plates. Spoon the oysters and sauce over them, and sprinkle with parsley. Serve at once.

SERVES 4 AS A FIRST COURSE, 2 TO 3 AS A MAIN DISH

Oysters in Leek and Bourbon Cream.

HOME-FRIED OYSTERS

The late Marjory Mingledorff was one of those towering Southern dowagers that humorist Florence King described as a "battleship in full sail." One of the very few people capable of holding her own with the late Rev. William Ralston, the beloved but opinionated rector of St. John's Episcopal Church on Madison Square, she guarded the dignity of our historic parish house better than Cerberus could ever have guarded the gates of Hades. Miss Marjory's real gifts, however, were in the kitchen. When Fr. Ralston fell ill with the flu and was brought a medicinal drought of her fragrant chicken soup, the entire staff began to cough hopefully.

Her daughter, Anne, says that you had to be standing over Miss Marjory to know how she cooked anything. Asking how she did it was impossible. Of her consistently perfect fried oysters, Anne recalled all that her mother would give away: "When you asked Mama how she knew when they were ready, she'd just smile and say 'Oh, I just pretend I'm an oyster, and then I know when I'm done.'"

24 large, select oysters, shucked
Lard or peanut or other vegetable oil,
    for frying
2 cups fine saltine cracker crumbs
Whole black pepper in a peppermill

Ground cayenne pepper
2 large eggs, lightly beaten
Salt
1 lemon, cut into 6 to 8 wedges

1. Drain the oysters in a wire mesh sieve set over a bowl, reserving their liquor to use in shellfish soup or shellfish broth. Put at least 1 inch of lard or oil in a deep, heavy-bottomed skillet or Dutch oven (but not more than halfway up the sides). Heat it over medium heat until it is hot but not smoking (about 375 degrees F). Meanwhile, put the crumbs in a wide, shallow bowl and season well with black pepper and cayenne.

2. When the fat is ready, pat the oysters dry with clean linen towels or absorbent paper. Dip them, one at a time, first in the egg and then roll them in the crumbs until they are well coated. When half of them are coated, add them to the fat, a few at a time, and fry, turning once, until they are golden brown on all sides, about 3 minutes.

3. Lift them out of the fat with a wire frying skimmer, blot briefly on absorbent paper, and then transfer to a wire cooling rack set over a rimmed baking sheet and lightly season with salt to taste. Quickly bread, fry, and drain the remaining oysters and serve them at once, garnished with lemon wedges.

SERVES 2 TO 3 AS A MAIN DISH, 6 AS A FIRST COURSE

PANNED OYSTERS

This is a homey, simple supper dish that has a reputation among Savannahians as especially masculine. "All men love this," wrote one matron in a community cookbook, and she is probably right. I don't know one man who doesn't like it, and in some families, it is only the men who make it.

Don't let the simplicity of ingredients fool you here: the point of this is the pure, briny essence of oysters, brought to their fullest flavor with only a minimum of seasonings. Some old Savannah cooks made this by stirring the oysters with a bare finger: when the liquor got too hot to keep their finger in it, the oysters were done. A spoon and a watchful eye will do just as well.

1 pint shucked oysters	Salt
2 tablespoons unsalted butter	4 pieces firm, home-style bread, toasted
Hot sauce	
Worcestershire sauce	1 lemon, cut in wedges
Whole black pepper in a peppermill	8 healthy sprigs watercress

1. Pour the oysters into a strainer set over a bowl. Let them drain at least 15 minutes. Cover and save the strained liquor for fish stock.

2. Melt the butter in a shallow, heavy-bottomed saucepan over medium heat. Add the oysters and cook, stirring constantly, until their gills begin to curl, about 2 minutes. Season generously with a few dashes each of hot sauce and Worcestershire and a liberal grinding of black pepper. Remove the pan from the heat, taste and adjust the seasonings, adding salt if needed. Put the toasted bread on warmed salad plates, spoon the oysters and pan juices evenly over them, and garnish with lemon wedges and watercress. Serve immediately.

SERVES 4

CURRIED SHRIMP

This is still a popular main course for formal luncheons in Savannah, but it can also be served in individual scallop shells as a first course at dinner. The first time I ever had this it was the main dish for an intimate lunch cooked by former *Morning News* food editor Martha Giddens Nesbit, a woman whose cooking is marked by the kindest of hearts and most gracious spirit.

4 tablespoons unsalted butter

1 large (or 2 medium) cloves garlic, crushed and peeled but left whole

1 medium yellow onion, trimmed, split lengthwise, peeled, and chopped fine

2 generous teaspoons curry powder (page 7) or to taste

2 teaspoons all-purpose flour

1-1/2 cups light cream, heated to the boiling point

1-1/2 pounds (headless weight) medium shrimp, peeled and deveined

1/4 cup cream sherry

Salt

4 cups hot Lowcountry Steamed Rice (page 78)

1/4 cup thinly sliced green onion or scallion

1. Simmer the butter and garlic in a large sauté pan over medium heat until the garlic is colored pale gold. Add the onion and sauté, tossing frequently, until golden, about 5 minutes. Stir in the curry and cook until fragrant, about 1 minute, and then stir in the flour and cook until bubbly and smooth. Slowly stir in the cream and cook, stirring, until quite thick, about 2 minutes more. Remove and discard the garlic.

2. Add the shrimp and simmer until they are just pink, about 2 minutes. Do not overcook. Stir in the sherry, let it just warm through, then taste and adjust for salt, and serve immediately over rice with the green onion scattered generously over the top.

SERVES 4

Unlike the bold curries of Southeast Asia that inspired it, the aim in this fragrant old recipe is subtlety. Savannahians have always loved spicy food, but they still know when to leave well enough alone. Local brown shrimp, freshly caught in season from tidal inlets, are intensely sweet and delicate, and are easily overwhelmed by a lot of culinary pyrotechnics. When used with judicious restraint, however, curry spices enhance those delicate flavors and give new life to shrimp that have been previously frozen.

Curried Shrimp

Sherried Shrimp.

This lovely recipe comes from the household recipe book of Elizabeth Malone Smart, whose granddaughter Connie Hartridge is an ardent preservationist and mistress of one of Savannah's finest old homes, the Battersby-Hartridge House on Lafayette Square. The only thing I've added is a touch of seasoning that the manuscript author almost certainly took for granted—salt and cayenne, both of which were usual for shrimp in those days. Its impeccable simplicity is deceptive: because there's nothing to cover up mistakes, success depends entirely on the quality of the shrimp and the carefulness of the cook. If the shrimp are not absolutely fresh, you may bump up the garlic to two cloves, but keep in mind what Mrs. Smart knew—it's shrimp and not garlic that is the star here.

SHERRIED SHRIMP

1 large clove garlic, lightly crushed and peeled but left whole

8 tablespoons unsalted butter

48 large shrimp (about 1-1/2 pounds), peeled

Salt and ground cayenne pepper

1/2 cup dry sherry

3 tablespoons chopped flat-leaf parsley

3 cups Lowcountry Steamed Rice (page 78)

1. Heat the garlic and butter in a large sauté pan over medium heat. Cook until the garlic is golden, about 2 minutes, and then remove and discard the garlic. Add the shrimp and sauté, tossing frequently, until they are curled and pink, about 3 minutes. Season well with salt and cayenne, both to taste (our local shrimp often don't need added salt), and remove them with a slotted spoon to a warm platter.

2. Add the sherry and bring it to a boil, stirring and scraping the pan, and let it boil half a minute. Stir in the parsley and pour it over the shrimp. Serve at once, over rice or with plenty of crusty bread to sop up the sauce.

SERVES 4

SHRIMP AND CORN PUDDING

4 to 6 whole ears of corn (enough for 3 cups when cut from the cob, see step 1 below)

2 tablespoons unsalted butter

4 to 5 medium green onions or scallions, trimmed and thinly sliced

2 tablespoons chopped fresh parsley, preferably flat-leaf

2 large eggs, lightly beaten

1/2 cup light cream or half-and-half

Salt and whole white pepper in a peppermill

Ground cayenne pepper

Whole nutmeg in a grater

1 pound small to medium shrimp, peeled, or large shrimp cut in half

1/4 cup all-purpose flour

1. Position a rack in the lower third of the oven and preheat it to 350 degrees F. Holding the ear of corn stem end up in a wide mixing bowl, cut the kernels from the cob by cutting straight down midway through the thickness of the kernels with a short, sharp paring knife. When all the kernels have been cut, scrape the cob with the dull side of the knife blade until all the juice and remaining kernel solids are removed. You will need 3 cups of kernels.

2. Put the butter and onion in a sauté pan over medium-high heat. Sauté, tossing frequently, until translucent but not colored, about 2 minutes. Stir in the parsley and turn off the heat.

3. Combine the corn, onion, parsley, eggs, and cream in a mixing bowl. Season lightly with salt, white and cayenne pepper, and a generous grating of nutmeg, and mix until thoroughly combined. In a separate bowl, toss the shrimp in the flour and shake off the excess. Fold them into the corn batter.

4. Lightly butter a 2-quart casserole or soufflé dish well and pour in the corn batter. Bake about 1 hour in the center of the oven, until set and lightly browned. Be careful not to overcook, as this makes the shrimp tough and could cause the custard to break. Serve hot.

SERVES 4

VARIATION: CRAB OR SEAFOOD CORN PUDDING

Substitute a pound of cooked, picked crabmeat (preferably both claw and lump meat) for the shrimp, or use a mixture of picked crabmeat, shrimp, small bay scallops, and/or diced fresh flounder or grouper fillets.

In the Carolina and Georgia Lowcountry, corn comes into season just as our tidal creeks and inlets begin to teem with tiny but intensely sweet brown shrimp. Local cooks make wide use of these delectable crustaceans, often pairing them with seasonal garden delicacies—fragrant vine-ripe tomatoes, spicy, snapping-crisp bell peppers, succulent eggplants, and, of course, fresh summer corn. The sweet little shrimp and corn are ideal complements for one another, but for those who cannot get such wonders, it's a comfort to know that corn also adds sweetness and delicacy to the heftier large shrimp, and gives a lift to shrimp that have been frozen.

Dr. Antonio Waring's fanciful version of this pudding was immortalized in *American Cooking: Southern Style*, though the recipe he provided gave was nothing like the dish he described. The pudding was spooned into the reserved, whole corn husks—not unlike tamales—and tied up to look like a whole, unshucked ear of corn—it was an intriguing idea, but in practice, it was honestly a lot of more trouble than it was worth.

SHRIMP IN SAVANNAH
RED PEPPER SAUCE

When nouvelle chefs began using purées as sauce thickeners, they acted as if they had invented something entirely new, but these shrimp, in their elegant red pepper purée, give away that it is a very old idea. It's adapted from a manuscript cookbook that is at least a hundred and fifty years old. Originally served over rice as a main dish, today it also makes a very elegant first course. I sometimes serve it as such mounded in scallop shells.

4 large red bell peppers, or 12 ounces commercially packed roasted peppers

2 tablespoons unsalted butter

1/4 cup minced shallot or yellow onion

1 large clove garlic, mashed, peeled, and minced

1 small red hot pepper, stemmed, seeded, and chopped, or ground cayenne pepper

Salt

1/4 cup Shellfish Broth (page 58)

1-1/2 pounds (headless weight) shrimp, peeled and deveined

2 cups Lowcountry Steamed Rice (page 78), optional

2 tablespoons chopped fresh parsley

1. If you are using commercially packed peppers, drain them and skip to step 2. Position a rack in the upper third of the oven and preheat it to 400 degrees F. Scrub the peppers under cold water, remove any labels, and pat dry. Put them on an ungreased baking sheet and roast in the upper third of the oven, turning occasionally, until the skin is evenly blistered and charred, about half an hour. You may also roast the peppers over a gas flame: insert a carving fork into the stem end and hold it 4 inches above a high flame, turning constantly, until the skin blackens. Put them in a paper bag, close it, and let stand for 10 minutes.

2. Skin, stem, split lengthwise, and seed the peppers and rinse well. Put the butter and shallot in a lidded skillet or sauté pan over medium heat. Sauté, tossing frequently, until softened but not colored, about 5 minutes. Add the garlic and sauté until fragrant, about a minute longer.

3. Add the peppers, a healthy pinch of salt (only if using fresh peppers), a tiny pinch of cayenne, and about 2 tablespoons of broth or water. Bring it to a boil, cover, and reduce the heat to medium low. Simmer until the peppers are tender, about 15 minutes. If the liquid evaporates completely, add a spoonful or so more broth.

4. Purée the sauce with a food mill, blender, or food processor fitted with a steel blade. Taste and correct the seasonings. It can be made a day or so ahead up to this point. Refrigerate in a covered glass or stainless steel container.

5. Take the shrimp from the refrigerator half an hour before cooking them. Gently reheat the sauce over medium-low heat, stirring frequently to prevent it from scorching or sticking. Raise the heat to medium, add the shrimp, and toss until well coated. Cover and cook until the shrimp are pink and cooked through, about 3 minutes. Taste and correct the seasonings. To serve as a main dish, ladle each serving over rice; to serve it as a first course appetizer, omit the rice and divide it among small plates or scallop shells. Either way, sprinkle each serving with parsley.

SERVES 4 AS A MAIN DISH, 6 AS A FIRST COURSE

SEAFOOD-STUFFED TOMATOES

Fresh tomatoes, sweet inlet shrimp, and delicate blue crab are all made for one another, and when they all come together in the same dish, good things are bound to happen. The savory stuffing for these tomatoes is adapted from a couple of very old community cookbooks, but the flavors are fresh and anything but old-fashioned.

4 medium tomatoes

Salt

1/2 pound (headless weight) small shrimp

1/2 pound (1 packed cup) picked crabmeat

3 tablespoons unsalted butter, divided

1/2 cup minced yellow onion (about half a medium onion)

2 large (or 3 medium) cloves garlic, lightly crushed, peeled, and minced

1 rounded tablespoon chopped parsley

1 rounded tablespoon chopped fresh basil

1 cup coarsely crushed cracker crumbs

Whole black pepper in a peppermill

Ground cayenne pepper

Whole nutmeg in a grater

1/4 cup fine cracker crumbs

1. Cut 1/4 inch from the stem end of the tomatoes, scoop out and discard their seeds, and then carefully scoop out the inner pulp with a sharp spoon or melon baller, leaving the outer walls of each tomato intact. Roughly chop the pulp and set it aside. Lightly salt the shells and invert them over a colander.

2. Bring 2 quarts of water to a boil and add a large pinch of salt and the shrimp. Cover, count 2 minutes, and immediately drain them (if it comes back to a boil before 2 minutes, drain it immediately). Rinse the shrimp under cold running water, peel, and if they are not very small, cut them in 2 or 3 pieces. Pick over the crabmeat for bits of shell.

3. Heat 2 tablespoons butter and the onion in a sauté pan over medium heat and sauté, tossing, until it is translucent, about 4 minutes. Add the garlic and sauté until fragrant, about half a minute more, then add the chopped tomato pulp and cook until it is beginning to break down and its juices are thickening, about 4 minutes. Add both herbs and the coarse crumbs and toss well. Off the heat, add the crab and shrimp and toss until evenly mixed. Season it well with salt, pepper, cayenne, and nutmeg.

Seafood-Stuffed Tomatoes.

4. Position a rack in the center of the oven and preheat it to 375 degrees F. Butter a 9-inch square casserole, wipe the inside of the tomato shells dry and put them in it, open side up. Divide the filling among them.

5. Wipe out the pan in which the onion and tomato pulp were cooked and add the remaining butter. Melt it over low heat and add the fine crumbs. Toss until even mixed and sprinkle them over the tops of the tomatoes. Carefully pour boiling water around them until it comes not quite halfway up the sides of the tomatoes. Bake until the shells are barely cooked and the filling is hot through, about 20 minutes.

SERVES 4

Shad Season

WITH THE DAWNING OF EACH NEW YEAR comes an event that is eagerly awaited by Savannahians: Atlantic shad born in the Ogeechee River obey an internal radar as old as time itself and return to their birthplace, where they will make a penultimate run upriver to spawn and then die. Though these fish make this same run up rivers all along the eastern seaboard, the Ogeechee is a major spawning ground, so the roe-fattened fish have always been plentiful. There are even tales of being able to cross the Ogeechee on the backs of the teeming fish. Tall tales aside, shad has long been relished as one of our region's great seasonal delicacies.

The main point of all the fuss is the roe. Local aficionados put it on equal footing with the finest sturgeon caviar and, unlike caviar, it is relatively cheap and is enjoyed in myriad ways. It's broiled with bacon or scrambled with eggs for breakfast or supper. For cocktail hour it can be poached in lemon juice and served like sturgeon caviar (see page 44). At dinner, nothing is more sublime than shad roe sautéed in butter and served on toast as a first course or carefully seasoned and stuffed into a whole or filleted fish.

If you don't care for fish that is unmistakably, well, fishy, and have an abnormal fear of fine bones, it's a sure bet that you won't care for shad. Unlike popular mild white fish such as grouper and flounder, there's nothing meek and retiring about a shad: its flavor is as assertive as it is unique. It's also exceptionally bony, containing upward of a thousand fine bones, not only in the usual places that most fish have them, but perversely in places where most other fish usually *don't*. A popular old way of cooking shad was to poach the whole fish in vinegar to partly dissolve the fine bones and make them edible. But that tactic unfortunately interferes with the flavor, and filleting the fish is no easy job. It isn't just a matter of taking out the wide, comblike backbone. Each side of the fish has three rows of bones: a center row running through the thickest part perpendicular to the backbone, and two more fine, hairlike rows running down both sides of the back and belly. As if that were not complicated enough, these bones interlock and splay out in three directions at the tail end. It takes a lot of practice to do the job in a way that doesn't leave the fish looking like a couple of cats have fought over it, which is why it is well worth your money to pay a professional fishmonger to do it for you.

BROILED SHAD

This is by far and away the most popular way to cook filleted shad; it's also the best. The flesh stays moist and delicate, yet there is just enough light caramelizing of the top and butter to deepen and enrich the flavor. Keep the recipe handy out of season; it needn't be limited only to shad; it's an excellent treatment for any smaller fillets—especially flounder, sole, catfish, snapper, or pompano.

The quantities given here will serve 4 as a part of a larger menu that includes more than one course, but 2 when the menu is simple and appetites are large.

2 shad fillets weighing about 3/4 pound each

1 set shad roe (about 6 ounces), optional

6 to 8 tablespoons unsalted butter, softened

Juice of 1 lemon

Salt and whole black pepper in a peppermill

Sweet paprika

Dry vermouth or white wine

2 lemons cut into wedges

1. Position a rack about 8 inches below the heat source and preheat the broiler for at least 10 minutes. Rinse the shad (and roe, if using) and pat it dry.

2. Rub a flameproof gratin dish (such as copper or enameled iron) or a rimmed baking sheet well with butter and put in the shad fillets, skin side down, and roe, if using. Sprinkle with lemon juice, dot generously with butter, and season liberally with salt, a few grindings of pepper, and paprika. Carefully pour a little vermouth around the edges of the pan—not enough to come up over the fish, but just enough to keep the edges moist.

3. Broil 8 inches from the heat until cooked through, about 12 to 15 minutes. If using the roe, turn after 7 or 8 minutes. Serve directly from the dish, or, if you've used a baking sheet, transfer it carefully to a warm platter or individual serving plates. Scatter the lemon around it and serve at once.

SERVES 2 TO 4

BROILED SHAD ROE with BACON

From the venerable *Christ Church Cook Book*, 1978 edition, comes this classic. It is traditionally served for breakfast or supper with hot grits and was a specialty of the elegant old Desoto Hotel that once stood on Liberty Street. It also makes a wonderful first course for a formal dinner. The recipe serves 2 but multiplies easily.

1 set shad roe

Bacon drippings or butter for greasing

Salt and whole black pepper in a peppermill

Ground cayenne pepper

4 strips thick-cut bacon

4 cups hot Cooked Grits (page 98)

1. Position a rack 8 inches below the heat source and preheat the broiler 10 minutes. Rinse the roe, pat dry, and separate the two roe sacs. Rub a small, rimmed, metal pan (such as metal pie plate) with drippings or butter. Season the roe well with salt, pepper, and cayenne, wrap the bacon around them (2 pieces per sac), and secure with toothpicks.

2. Broil 5 to 7 minutes, or until the bacon is beginning to brown, turn, and broil until roe is firm and bacon is browned, about 5 minutes longer. Serve at once with hot grits.

SERVES 2

BAKED SHAD STUFFED with ROE

1 set (pair) shad roe

Juice of 2 large lemons

5 tablespoons unsalted butter, divided

2/3 cup chopped Vidalia green onions or scallions

2 large cloves garlic, lightly crushed, peeled, and minced

2 tablespoons chopped fresh parsley

1 tablespoon chopped fresh oregano or thyme

1 cup fine, soft breadcrumbs

Salt and whole black pepper in a peppermill

Ground cayenne pepper

2 large shad fillets (about 3/4 pound each)

1 large lemon, thinly sliced

1/2 cup dry vermouth or dry white wine

Paprika

1. Rinse the roe under cold water and put them in a covered, close-fitting pan. Add the lemon juice, cover, and bring to a simmer over medium

Baked shad, filled with a rich stuffing of its own roe, was a greatly anticipated delicacy of old shad season. Originally, the shad was not filleted but was simply split open, stuffed with roe dressing, and then tied up and baked in one piece. Broad-bladed fish knives and forks, which make it easier to detect and remove the fine bones, were not mere Victorian prissiness; they were necessary for tackling this extremely bony fish at the table. Today, most cooks let a professional fishmonger bone it, and the resulting pockets in the fillets are filled with the stuffing and baked open-faced. It may lack romance, but it is certainly easier to eat. For an elegant touch at formal dinners, many locals still like to use their old-fashioned fish cutlery.

heat. Reduce the heat to medium low and simmer until the roe are firm, about 20 minutes. Drain well and let them cool. Scrape the roe from the membranes.

2. Put 3 tablespoons of butter and the onion in a sauté pan over medium-high heat. Sauté, tossing frequently, until translucent, about 3 minutes. Add the garlic and herbs and sauté until fragrant, about a minute. Turn off the heat, add the crumbs, toss until well coated, and mix in the roe. Season well with salt, pepper, and cayenne.

3. Position a rack in the center of the oven and preheat it to 375 degrees F. Butter a baking dish that will hold the fillets snugly in one layer. Put them in the dish skin side down. Season lightly with salt and pepper and spread the stuffing evenly into the pockets created by the filleting. (There will be 3 on each fillet—1 down the center and 1 to either side). Cover with sliced lemon and pour the wine around them. Dust generously with paprika and dot with the remaining butter. Bake, uncovered and basting frequently, until the fish is cooked through, about 25 to 30 minutes. Serve hot with Baked Shad Beurre Blanc (page 130) made with the cooking liquid.

SERVES 4 TO 6

BAKED SHAD BEURRE BLANC

A frequent sauce for fish in old Savannah manuscript cookbooks is melted butter, often seasoned with lemon or Worcestershire sauce—essentially a classic French beurre blanc. It can be made with the pan juices of any baked or braised fish, or, for sautéed fish, by deglazing the pan with 1/2 cup of dry vermouth or white wine. Pour the wine into the pan and bring it to a boil, stirring and scraping to remove any cooking residue that may be stuck to the pan, and cook until it is reduced by half. Use the deglazing to make the butter sauce, seasoning it with Worcestershire sauce and lemon juice to taste.

The pan juices from Baked Shad Stuffed with Roe (page 128) or other fish pan juices

8 tablespoons cold unsalted butter, cut into 1/2-teaspoon-size bits

1/2 lemon

1. Put the pan juices in a wide saucepan and bring them to a simmer over medium heat. Reduce the heat to the lowest possible setting and whisk in 2 to 3 bits of butter until they are dissolved into the liquid.

2. Gradually whisk in the remaining butter, 2 to 3 bits at a time. If, at any time, the sauce begins to look oily, remove it from the heat and quickly whisk in 4 to 5 bits of butter to cool it down. When all the butter is incorporated, the sauce should be the consistency of a lightly thickened cream sauce. Taste and refresh it with a squeeze of lemon juice, whisk until smooth, and serve immediately.

MAKES ABOUT 3/4 CUP

SHARON'S PAN-SEARED STRIPED BASS
WITH ZUCCHINI

4 to 6 fresh zucchini

3-1/2 tablespoons olive oil, divided

3-1/2 tablespoons unsalted butter, divided

1 medium onion, trimmed, split lengthwise, peeled, and roughly chopped

Salt and freshly ground black pepper

3 cloves garlic, lightly crushed, peeled, and chopped

About 2 ounces Parmigiano-Reggiano cheese

1 cup unbleached all-purpose flour

Lawry's Seasoned Salt or sweet paprika (optional)

6 striped bass fillets, about 6 ounces each

2 large lemons, 1 cut in half, 1 thinly sliced

Chopped flat-leaf parsley

1. Position a rack in the center of the oven and preheat it to 400 degrees F. Scrub the zucchini under cold running water and pat dry. Slice them thinly into rounds. Heat 1-1/2 tablespoons each of oil and butter in a heavy-bottomed ovenproof skillet over medium heat. Add the zucchini and onion and season well with salt and pepper. Cook, stirring often, until tender but still slightly crisp, about 10 minutes.

2. Add the garlic and cook until it is very fragrant but not colored, about 1 to 2 minutes, stirring constantly. Turn the squash out onto a serving platter and generously grate Parmigiano over it.

3. Season the flour well with salt, pepper, seasoned salt or paprika, all to taste. Wipe out the pan and heat the remaining 2 tablespoons of oil and butter in it over medium heat. Lightly roll the fish in the seasoned flour, shake off the excess, and slip them into the pan. Sear until golden brown on all sides, about 4 minutes per side. The fish should not be completely cooked.

4. Transfer the pan to the oven and roast until the fish are cooked through, about 6 to 8 minutes longer. If liked, squeeze fresh lemon juice over them. Lay the fish on top of the bed of zucchini, sprinkle with parsley and garnish with the sliced lemon.

SERVES 4 TO 6

Savannah born and bred, Sharon Morris moved to Atlanta, where she discovered her husband Marc and a passion for cooking. Her eldest daughter, Lindsey was literally weaned on such things as artichokes alla Romana, and when she was little more than a toddler, loved helping with the shopping and cooking. After persuading Marc to move their family back to her hometown, she began sharing that passion with her friends and neighbors, catering sit-down dinners for fellow parishioners at St. John's Church and working as hostess for nearby Wesley Monumental Methodist.

One of Sharon's favorite fish is local striped bass. Here, she pairs it with another favorite, lightly cooked zucchini dressed with onions and a generous sprinkling of Parmigiano-Reggiano cheese. Sharon calls it a personal indulgence, claiming that she could eat squash for breakfast, but, actually, they are perfect complements for one another.

KIM POLOTE'S PARMESAN CATFISH

Kim Michael Polote is a golden-voiced Savannah native who is best known for her silky interpretations of all the great American songwriters, not least of them native son Johnny Mercer. A gold-medal winner of the American Traditions competition and headliner for numerous Johnny Mercer tributes, Kim's singing is justly famous. Fewer people know or appreciate that she is also a very good cook. Just as her voice simply and elegantly coaxes amazing things from a song, her cooking takes simple, inexpensive ingredients like farm-raised catfish to a whole new level.

Sometimes, Kim varies this recipe by substituting large local shrimp for the crabmeat. Allow about 12 large raw shrimp, peeled and deveined, adding them as you would the crabmeat in step 3, or pull out all the stops and use both crab and shrimp.

4 catfish fillets, about 8 ounces each
Seafood Boiling Spice (page 6)
Blackened fish seasoning (available at specialty grocers)
Garlic powder
Ground cayenne pepper
2 lemons, cut in half
12 ounces grated Parmesan cheese
1/2 cup finely chopped green onions
2 tablespoons unsalted butter, softened
3 tablespoons mayonnaise (Kim uses Duke's)
8 ounces (1 cup) lump crabmeat
Sweet paprika

1. Generously butter a rimmed baking sheet or wide casserole and lay the catfish on it, skin side down. Season liberally with Seafood Boiling Spice, a pinch of blackened fish seasoning, garlic powder, and cayenne. Generously squeeze lemon juice over all and refrigerate for at least 30 minutes.

2. Meanwhile, mix together the Parmesan, green onion, butter, mayonnaise, 1 tablespoon freshly squeezed lemon juice, and a liberal dash of cayenne. Pick over the crabmeat for any bits of shell. Position a rack 8 inches below the broiler and preheat it for 15 minutes.

3. Broil the catfish for 5 minutes, then scatter the crabmeat over the top of each fillet and spread it with the Parmesan-onion topping. Dust generously with paprika and broil until the top is golden brown and the fish is cooked through, 5 to 10 minutes longer.

SERVES 4

FLOUNDER IN LEMON-PECAN BUTTER

In the last century, pecans became a major money crop in Georgia, and local cooks use them with abandon. Here they are paired with another abundant Georgia staple, flounder—a mild, delicate white-fleshed flatfish that is plentiful along our coast—and capers, a Mediterranean staple that goes way back in Savannah's culinary history: as far back as the eighteenth century, dry-goods merchants have been importing and selling olives, salt-packed anchovies, and capers by the barrelful.

Though the capers used by early Savannahians were probably dry-packed in salt, today most cooks use more widely available brine-packed capers. If you can find dry-salt-packed capers, they are in every way superior, but they must first be rinsed thoroughly and soaked for a few minutes in water to cover. Drain them well before using.

2 pounds flounder fillets

Salt and whole white pepper in a peppermill

8 tablespoons unsalted butter, divided

1/2 cup unbleached all-purpose flour

4 tablespoons unsalted butter

1/2 cup pecans, slivered

3 tablespoons capers, drained

2 tablespoons chopped flat-leaf parsley

2 lemons, zest removed from one and cut into fine julienne, cut in half, and one thinly sliced, for garnish

1. Rinse the flounder under cold running water and pat dry. Season liberally on all sides with salt and white pepper. Warm a wide, shallow skillet or sauté pan that will hold the fillets in a single layer over medium heat. Add 4 tablespoons of the butter and let it get hot. Quickly roll the fish in flour, shake off the excess, and slip them into the pan. Sauté, turning once, until golden brown and just cooked through, about 2 to 3 minutes per side. Take care not to overcook them. Remove them to a warm platter or serving plates.

2. Put the remaining butter in the pan and return it to the heat, stirring and scraping to loosen any cooking residue. When it is fully melted, add the pecans and sauté, tossing frequently, until the butter and pecans are a uniform golden brown. Add the capers and let them heat through. Remove the pan from the heat and add the parsley, lemon zest, and the juice from half the lemon. Taste and adjust the salt and lemon juice as needed, and then pour the sauce evenly over the fish. Garnish with sliced lemon and serve at once.

SERVES 4

CRAB-STUFFED FLOUNDER

One of the great delicacies of the South Atlantic coast is small, whole flounder split open and filled with a rich, highly seasoned deviled crab stuffing. To enjoy it, however, you have to accept that it will be bony. There is no way to partly bone the fish without tearing it up and, besides, the flavor is sweeter when the fish is cooked whole. If you really don't want to deal with the bones, or if fillets are the only flounder you can get, I've included directions for doing rolled fillets filled with this same stuffing in the notes at the end of the recipe. Though not as wonderful as the whole fish, they're still awfully good.

4 small (about 1 pound each) whole flounder or 2 whole (2-pound) flounder

12 ounces (about 1-1/2 cups, tightly packed) picked crabmeat

8 tablespoons unsalted butter, divided

1/2 cup finely chopped shallots or yellow onion

1/2 cup finely chopped green or red bell pepper

2 large cloves garlic, lightly crushed and minced

1 cup soft, stale breadcrumbs

Salt and whole black pepper in a peppermill

Ground cayenne pepper

Worcestershire sauce

Sweet paprika

About 1/2 cup dry vermouth or white wine

1. Rinse the fish under cold water and pat dry. Cut a slit down the top (dark) side of the fish all the way to the center spine bone. Using a fillet knife or small paring knife, carefully separate the meat from the ribs, forming a pocket on both sides of the cut. Lightly grease a rimmed baking sheet or casserole and put in the fish, cut side up. Pick through the crab for any lingering bits of shell. Position a rack in the center of the oven and preheat it to 375 degrees F.

2. Warm 2 tablespoons butter, the shallot, and bell pepper in a medium sauté pan or skillet over medium heat. Sauté, tossing often, until the shallot is translucent, about 4 minutes. Add the garlic and sauté until fragrant, about half a minute longer. Turn off the heat. Add the crumbs and crabmeat and toss until mixed. Season liberally with salt, pepper, cayenne, and a few dashes of Worcestershire, to taste. Toss well.

3. Sprinkle the insides of the pockets in the flounder lightly with salt and pepper. Stuff the deviled crab loosely into each pocket, mounding it up in the center. Dust lightly with paprika, dot with the remaining butter, and pour the vermouth around the edges of the pan. Bake until the fish is cooked through and the stuffing hot and lightly colored on top, about 20 minutes. Serve with pan juices spooned over each serving.

SERVES 4

CRAB-STUFFED FLOUNDER FILLETS

Crab-Stuffed Flounder.

Use four 6-ounce fillets. Lay them skin down on a work surface. Sprinkle lightly with salt. Mold the deviled crab stuffing into four equal lumps and put on each fillet, then roll each fillet around the filling. Generously butter a casserole that will hold the fillets snugly in one layer and put them in it seam side down. Dot generously with butter and dust with paprika. Pour the vermouth around the edges. Bake 15 minutes, baste well, and bake until the fish is cooked through and the stuffing hot, about 10 minutes longer (they actually take a bit longer than the whole fish). Spoon the pan juices over each serving.

Poultry, Meat, & Game

THE FIRST ENGLISH SETTLERS IN SAVANNAH continued to prefer the beef and salted pork they had known at home. They imported cattle and swine and bought supplemental stock from the more established colony in nearby Charles Town. Getting the animals here was apparently less of a challenge than controlling them in the still-wild, marsh-riddled land that surrounded the young colony. Trustee-owned herds were pastured on isolated marsh islands, but cattle can swim if they have to, and at any rate could easily ford shallow creeks at low tide; they proved difficult to contain. Pigs, craftier critters than cows and by far more resourceful, were notorious for getting loose and running wild. The wild boars on Georgia's barrier islands are actually descended from those first imported domestic swine. It shouldn't surprise, then, that some of the earliest legal conflicts involved cattle and the supply of both fresh and salt-cured red meat. Poaching was commonplace, and there were inevitably charges of favoritism and graft among the first proprietors of the Trustees' store.

Despite the plentiful supply of fish, shellfish, and game, then, imported domestic beef, mutton, pork, and poultry continued to be the preferred provisions, and they still have a prominent place on Savannah's table to this day. And then as now, they liked their beef best roasted and served medium to medium rare. If you ask any Savannah caterer for their most often-requested main dish, the one they are the most tired of cooking, without skipping a beat they'll tell you rare-roasted beef tenderloin. Savannahians also love slow-baked and braised beef

Facing: Veal Scallops with Oysters and Bacon.
Above: Jones Street, one of the historic district's most beautiful streets and coveted addresses.

dishes, from the Sauerbraten introduced by the Salzburger Lutherans to braised short ribs and Sabbath dinner brisket.

Unlike other parts of the Deep South, Savannahians also have a lingering fondness for lamb, probably thanks in part to its Jewish and Greek communities. A nearly vanished delicacy is barbecued lamb slow cooked over smoldering hardwood coals. Once very popular at private barbecues, home versions of lamb roast were often slow-baked with vinegar-laced sauce in imitation of barbecue. Today it is rarely done, though it can still be tasted at Johnnie Harris Restaurant on Victory Drive, an old Savannah institution. Failing that, heady compensation can be had in the traditional Roast Lamb with Lemon and Potatoes of Savannah's Greek community, found on page 162.

One favored domestic animal, however, was native: the turkey. Early settlers hunted them in the wild, but these birds were soon domesticated, and by the nineteenth century, a farm-fattened turkey stuffed with oyster dressing was the usual centerpiece for Christmas dinners and other celebrations. In some families it was had more often than was liked. One of the Telfair family properties was a turkey farm, and the birds appeared so often on Mary Telfair's table that it led her famous nephew, Ward McAllister, to half-jokingly accuse his aunt of being eccentrically parsimonious.

In those days, turkeys were often "boiled"—actually, poached in simmering liquid to cover—and served with oyster sauce, a thick version of Chafing Dish Oysters (page 38), a dish that has virtually disappeared from Savannah's tables. Today, turkey is still a popular main dish and not just roasted at Thanksgiving or Christmas. The breast and meaty thigh meat are used in exactly the same way as veal scallops, and African American cooks like my friend Shirley Cannon make spare parts such as the bony but flavorful wings into a feast by slow braising them with onions, peppers, and garlic, using the same basic recipe as for Lowcountry Smothered Pork Chops on page 149. Allow 1 to 2 wing joints per person and omit browning them.

ROAST TURKEY CHINESE-STYLE

3 tablespoons hoisin sauce

3 tablespoons tomato ketchup

2 tablespoons honey

1 teaspoon sugar

1/4 teaspoon Chinese five-spice powder

2 tablespoons sherry

1 small young turkey, about 9 to 12 pounds

Salt and whole black pepper in a peppermill

3 large cloves garlic, lightly crushed, peeled, and minced

2 to 3 tablespoons butter or vegetable oil

1 tablespoon cornstarch dissolved in 1/4 cup water

1. Make a seasoning paste by stirring together the hoisin sauce, ketchup, honey, sugar, five-spice powder, and sherry. Remove the neck and giblets from the turkey and rinse it well inside and out. Pat dry and rub the inside of the turkey with salt, pepper, garlic, and then the seasoning paste. Wrap it well and marinate, refrigerated, overnight.

2. Put the giblets and neck in a large saucepan. Completely cover them with water and add 2 to 3 tablespoons of the seasoning paste. Bring it to a simmer over medium heat and simmer gently for at least 1 hour—longer won't hurt. Strain the broth. Pick the meat from the neck and shred it. Chop the giblets. Add them back to the broth, cover, and refrigerate it.

3. Take the turkey from the refrigerator 30 minutes before cooking it. Position a rack in the center of the oven and preheat it to 325 degrees F. Put the turkey on a rack in a roasting pan. Rub the outside well with butter or oil and salt and pepper. Pour a cup of water into the roasting pan. Roast, basting often after the first half hour, until a meat thermometer inserted into the thickest part of the thigh registers 165 degrees F, about 2 hours. Let the turkey rest for 30 minutes before carving it.

4. Put the roasting juices and reserved broth in a saucepan and bring them to a simmer over medium heat. Stir in the dissolved cornstarch and bring it back to a simmer, stirring constantly. Simmer until thickened, about 3 minutes more, and turn off the heat. The turkey is carved in the conventional way except for the breast: cut each side from the turkey in one large piece and slice it across the grain. Serve with the gravy passed separately.

SERVES 10 TO 12

Descendants of the Woo family, who ran a grocery on Fahm Street, have become thoroughly American and have adopted much of their neighbors' cooking and food-ways into their own. Their traditional Thanksgiving dinner is roast turkey, just like everyone else, except that it is fragrant with Chinese seasonings that have been rubbed in the cavity and simmered in the broth that will supplement the pan juices. The recipe is from Catherine Woo Jue whose cooking is an elegant blend of her Chinese heritage and Deep South upbringing.

CHICKEN COUNTRY CAPTAIN

Since the nineteenth century, this spicy, tomato-based curry has been popular all along the Atlantic seaboard. While early twentieth-century legend claims that Country Captain originated in Savannah, truthfully, every major Southern port from here to Baltimore has made the same claim. Contrary to mythical tales of its origins in America, it's most likely an English adaptation of Indian cookery that came to our shores by way of Britain's East Indian spice and tea trade. Most recipes suggest raisins as substitutes for the currants, but more than one old Savannah recipe protested vigorously against it.

In Savannah, it is always accompanied by Lowcountry Steamed Rice (page 78). The other condiments (called "boys" in the old days) can be expanded to suit your own tastes. Try crumbled crisp bacon, peeled and sectioned oranges or tangerines, freshly grated lemon and/or orange zest, and chunks of fresh pineapple. But take to heart the advice of one seasoned Savannah host: "Anything more than a five boy curry is considered pretentious north of Gaston Street."

1 young chicken, about 2-1/2 to 3 pounds, disjointed and cut up for frying

4 tablespoons butter

4 tablespoons olive or vegetable oil

1 large yellow onion, peeled and chopped

1 large green bell pepper, seeded and chopped

2 large cloves garlic, crushed, peeled, and minced

2 to 3 teaspoons curry powder (more or less), to taste

1 tart, firm apple (such as Granny Smith), washed, cored, and diced

2 pounds ripe tomatoes, scalded, peeled, seeded, and chopped (page 15) or 2 cups canned Italian tomatoes, seeded and chopped, with their juices

1 teaspoon or more, to taste, turbinado (raw) sugar

1 cup currants

Salt

1 tablespoon chopped parsley

4 cups Lowcountry Steamed Rice (page 78)

1/2 cup freshly grated or thawed frozen unsweetened coconut

1/2 cup toasted peanuts or blanched, toasted almonds

1/2 cup St. John's Golden Mango Chutney (page 8) or Major Grey's Chutney

1. Wash the chicken under cold running water and pat dry. Heat the butter and oil in a deep, lidded skillet or sauté pan over medium heat. When it is hot, raise the heat slightly and add the chicken. Brown it well, turning frequently, and remove it from the pan.

2. Spoon off all but 3 tablespoons of fat and add onion and bell pepper. Sauté, tossing frequently, until softened, but not colored, about 5 minutes. Add the garlic and curry and sauté until fragrant, about half a minute more.

3. Add the apple and toss until uniformly coated with curry. Add the tomatoes, sugar, and currants and bring it to a boil. Return the chicken to the pan, turning it until it is well-coated with sauce and season lightly with salt to taste. Reduce the heat to low, cover, and simmer gently, turning the chicken occasionally, until tender, about half an hour.

Chicken Country Captain.

4. Remove the chicken to a warm platter. If the sauce is too thin, raise the heat to medium high and boil until it's thick, stirring frequently to keep it from scorching. Turn off the heat, stir in the parsley, and pour the sauce over the chicken. Ring the platter with hot rice and serve at once, passing coconut, peanuts, and chutney separately.

SERVES 4

VARIATION: SHRIMP COUNTRY CAPTAIN

Today, this same recipe is used for shrimp. Substitute 2 pounds peeled raw shrimp for the chicken. Reduce the butter and oil to 1 tablespoon each and omit step 1, adding the butter, oil, onion, and bell pepper to the pan and sauté over medium heat. Follow the remainder of the recipe, adding the shrimp after the sauce has been reduced in step 3. Simmer until the shrimp are pink and cooked through, 4 to 5 minutes.

Emma's Chicken in Champagne.

This exquisitely simple recipe, from the collection of Emma Morel (Mrs. Leopold) Adler, encapsulates in one dish all the old Savannah grace and elegance that typifies Emma herself. There is nothing here but chicken, champagne, and cream, but oh, my, what those three things do when they come together in the pan! The only change I've made is to do the initial browning in a flameproof casserole or ovenproof skillet so that the browning and baking are done in the same pan, and then bake it without a cover.

EMMA'S CHICKEN IN CHAMPAGNE

1 (2 to 2-1/2 pound) chicken, disjointed and cut up as for frying

Salt and whole black pepper in a peppermill

Sweet paprika

1/3 cup plus 2 tablespoons unsalted butter, divided

About 2 cups medium-dry champagne

2 tablespoons all-purpose flour

2 cups heavy cream

4 cups Lowcountry Steamed Rice (page 78)

1. Position a rack in the center of the oven and preheat it to 350 degrees F. Rinse the chicken under cold running water and pat dry. Season it well with salt, pepper, and paprika. Melt 1/3 cup butter in a flameproof casserole or ovenproof skillet over medium-high heat. Put in the chicken and brown it well on all sides, about 5 to 8 minutes.

2. Pour in enough champagne to completely cover the chicken and bake until it is almost tender, about 30 to 40 minutes. Emma covers the casserole, but I leave it open.

3. Meanwhile, melt the remaining 2 tablespoons of butter over medium heat and stir in the flour. Cook until bubbly and smooth, then slowly stir in the cream. Bring it to a simmer, stirring constantly, and simmer 3 to 4 minutes. When the chicken is almost tender, pour the cream over it, turning the chicken to mix, and bake, uncovered, 15 minutes longer. Serve with rice.

SERVES 4

QUAIL WITH CHAMPAGNE

Possibly the only other wine better loved than Madeira by nineteenth-century Savannahians was champagne. It was at the heart of every celebration, almost taken for granted in the punch bowl, and a picnic was not considered complete without it. Nothing has changed in the last hundred or so years.

Here it makes a delicate sauce for a delicate and well-loved game bird. The recipe is from T. Gongaware.

12 dressed quail
About 1 cup whole milk
1 tablespoon Worcestershire sauce
Salt and whole black pepper in a
   peppermill

4 tablespoons unsalted butter
1/2 cup all-purpose flour, spread
   on a plate
1/2 cup champagne
1 cup heavy cream

1. Rinse the quail. Put them in a glass or stainless-steel bowl with enough milk to completely cover. Add the Worcestershire and toss to mix. Let marinate for 30 minutes to 1 hour. Drain, pat dry, and rub them inside and out with salt and pepper.

2. Warm a large skillet or sauté pan over medium heat. Put in the butter and, when it is melted and hot, lightly roll the quail in flour, shake off the excess, and slip them into the pan. Lightly brown them on all sides and then pan-fry, turning once after the initial browning, until they are cooked through, about 14 minutes altogether. Remove the birds to a warm platter.

3. Deglaze the pan with the champagne, stirring and scraping to loosen any cooking residue, and then pour in the cream. Bring it to a simmer and cook until it is lightly thickened, about 5 minutes. Pour the sauce over the quail and serve at once.

SERVES 6

PAN-FRIED QUAIL WITH GRITS AND ONION GRAVY

If the catch doesn't happen to be quail, any small game bird such as dove or pheasant can be used in this recipe.

Fried quail, served with a creamy bed of grits and savory pan gravy, are traditional wintertime breakfast or supper fare wherever there are avid hunters in the South, especially during the holidays from Thanksgiving through Christmas morning. Of course, it doesn't hurt that frying may well be the most simply elegant and delectable way of cooking small birds, especially when they've been skinned rather than plucked.

In some modest households, and in the country, the accompaniment for fried game birds was always grits, whether the meal was breakfast or supper, but if the birds were served in a traditional two o'clock dinner, their accompaniment was inevitably rice. More well-to-do families rarely—if ever—ate grits at any meal other than breakfast, except when they were fried, laced with garlic and cheese (page 92), or otherwise gussied up.

8 dressed quail
Salt and whole black pepper in a peppermill
1 teaspoon or more crumbled dried sage
1/2 teaspoon garlic powder
8 strips thick-cut breakfast bacon

Peanut or other vegetable oil, for frying
1-1/2 cups unbleached all-purpose flour
1/4 cup finely minced onion
1-1/2 cups Basic Meat or Chicken Broth (page 57) or water
1 teaspoon Worcestershire sauce
4 cups hot Cooked Grits (page 88)

1. Rinse the quail under cold running water and pat dry. Season well with salt, pepper, sage, and garlic powder. Set them aside on a rimmed baking sheet or platter.

2. In a large, deep skillet or Dutch oven, cook the bacon over medium heat, turning frequently, until browned and crisp. Blot it well on absorbent paper, let it cool, and crumble it.

3. Add enough oil to the drippings in the pan to make the fat at least 1 inch deep, but no more than halfway up the sides of the pan. Heat it until the fat is shimmering but is not quite smoking, about 365 degrees F.

4. Roll the quail in the flour until each is well coated, shake off the excess, and slip them into the hot fat. Fry until the bottom side is well browned, about 7 to 8 minutes, turn, and fry until both sides are golden brown and the birds are just cooked through, about 7 to 8 minutes longer. Lift them from the fat with tongs or a wire frying skimmer, let them drain well, and blot briefly on absorbent paper. Transfer them to the wire rack in the oven and keep them warm while making the gravy.

5. Remove all but 1/4 cup of drippings from the pan and add the onion. Sauté, stirring often, until golden, about 4 minutes. Add 2 tablespoons of flour and cook, stirring constantly, until it is smooth and bubbly, about 2 to 3 minutes longer. Slowly stir or whisk in the hot broth or water and cook, again stirring

constantly, until it is lightly thickened and beginning to boil. Reduce the heat to medium low, season to taste with salt, pepper, and sage, and Worcestershire. Let simmer 3 to 4 minutes, stirring occasionally. Serve the quail with the gravy and crumbled bacon passed separately, accompanied by hot grits.

SERVES 4

Pan-Fried Quail with Grits and Onion Gravy.

Chicken Madeira

IN OLD SAVANNAH KITCHENS, cooks put the city's favorite wine to many uses, but a favorite pairing was with chicken. Here are two variations, making use of a whole fresh chicken and leftover cooked chicken.

CHICKEN MADEIRA

There is a little book published in the late seventies that is treasured by Southern food historians and Savannahians alike. Simply called *Four Great Southern Cooks*, the tattered copies of this book are fiercely guarded by locals because it contains the only known record of the legendary cooking of Savannah caterer Daisy Redman. One of Mrs. Redman's specialties was an elaborate version of this traditional chicken fricassee made with mushrooms and Madeira.

8 tablespoons unsalted butter, divided

1 chicken, weighing no more than 2-1/2 to 3 pounds, disjointed and cut up as for frying

Salt and whole white pepper in a peppermill

1 cup minced shallots or yellow onion (about 5 medium shallots or 1 onion)

8 ounces fresh brown (crimini) mushrooms, wiped clean with a dry cloth and thickly sliced

1 cup thinly sliced leeks

2 tablespoons chopped fresh sage

1 cup medium dry (Sercial) Madeira

1 cup Basic Meat or Chicken Broth (page 57) or 1/2 cup canned broth mixed with 1/2 cup water (even if label says ready to use or use full strength)

1/2 cup heavy cream

1 tablespoon all-purpose flour

1/2 cup thinly sliced green onions

1. Warm 6 tablespoons butter over medium heat in a deep, heavy-bottomed, lidded skillet that will hold the chicken in one layer. When the butter is hot, season the chicken well with salt and pepper and add it to the pan. Sauté, turning frequently, until it is browned on all sides, about 8 minutes. Remove it from the pan to a warm platter.

2. Add the shallots and sauté, tossing frequently, until golden, about 5 minutes. Add the mushrooms and sauté until they are beginning to color, about 2 minutes. Add the leeks and sage and sauté until fragrant.

3. Deglaze the pan with the Madeira, stirring and scraping the bottom of the pan, and bring it to a boil. Add the broth, let it come back to a boil, and return the chicken to the pan and reduce the heat to a slow simmer. Cook gently until the chicken is tender, about 20 minutes longer.

4. Remove the chicken to a warm platter. Raise the heat under the pan to medium high and add the cream. Cook, stirring constantly, until the sauce is lightly reduced. Knead the remaining butter with the flour and add it in bits to the pan, stirring constantly. Simmer until thickened, about 4 minutes longer, and stir in the green onion. Turn off the heat, pour the sauce over the chicken, and serve at once.

SERVES 4

Chicken Madeira.

CREAMED CHICKEN MADEIRA
ON RICE WAFFLES

Creamed Chicken Madeira on Rice Waffles.

This version, while less complex than Mrs. Redman's elegant sauté, is no less satisfying and makes a quick and elegant way to recycle leftover poultry.

8 ounces small button brown (crimini) mushrooms

4 tablespoons unsalted butter

1/2 cup finely chopped shallots (about 2 large)

Salt and whole white pepper in a peppermill

Whole nutmeg in a grater

1/2 teaspoon each dried sage and thyme (or 2 teaspoons each if fresh)

2 teaspoons all-purpose flour

1 cup Madeira

1 cup Basic Meat or Chicken Broth (page 57) made with chicken or 1/2 cup canned chicken broth and 1/2 cup water (even if broth says ready to use or use full strength)

1 cup heavy cream

8 divided sections of Savannah Rice Waffles (page 101)

2 cups cooked chicken, cut in 1-inch dice

1. Wipe the mushrooms clean with a soft cloth or mushroom brush. Trim the stems even with the caps. Have a toaster ready or position a rack in the upper third of the oven and preheat it to 350 degrees F.

2. Put the butter and shallots in a skillet or sauté pan over medium heat. Sauté, tossing frequently, until golden, about 5 minutes. Add the mushrooms and sauté, tossing occasionally, until just cooked through, about 5 minutes. Season well with salt, white pepper, and nutmeg, and add the sage and thyme.

3. Sprinkle in the flour and stir until smooth. Slowly stir in the Madeira, bring to a simmer, stirring, and add in the broth. Bring to a simmer, and cook, stirring occasionally, until thickened. Add the cream and bring it back to a simmer. Meanwhile, rewarm the waffles in a toaster or oven.

4. Stir in the chicken and cook until the sauce is lightly thickened and the chicken heated through. Arrange the hot waffles on four heated serving plates, ladle the chicken over them, and serve.

SERVES 4

LOWCOUNTRY SMOTHERED
PORK CHOPS

4 center-cut pork chops, 1/2 inch thick

Salt and whole black pepper in a
   peppermill

Ground cayenne pepper

2 tablespoons unsalted butter, bacon
   drippings, or vegetable oil

1/4 cup all-purpose flour, spread on a
   plate

2 medium green bell peppers, stem,
   core, and membranes removed, cut
   into strips

1 large or 2 medium yellow onions,
   trimmed, split lengthwise, peeled,
   and thinly sliced

2 large or 3 medium cloves garlic,
   lightly crushed, peeled, and minced

About 2 cups Basic Meat or Chicken
   Broth (page 57) or water

Worcestershire sauce

1. Trim the excess fat from the chops and season well with salt, pepper, and
   cayenne.

2. Melt the butter or drippings in a deep, lidded skillet or flameproof casserole
   over medium heat. When it's hot, lightly roll the chops in flour, shake off
   the excess, and slip them into the pan. Brown well, about 3 minutes per
   side, and remove them to a plate.

3. Add the bell peppers and onions and sauté until softened, but not colored,
   about 4 minutes. Add the garlic and sauté until fragrant, about half a minute
   longer. Push the vegetables to one side, return the chops to the pan, and
   then spoon the vegetables over them. Add enough broth to half cover the
   chops, a few dashes of Worcestershire sauce, to taste, and let it come to a
   boil. Reduce the heat to medium low, cover, and simmer gently until the
   chops are fork tender, replenishing the liquid as needed with broth, about
   45 minutes.

4. Remove the chops to a warm platter. If the pan juices are too thin, raise the
   heat and boil until lightly reduced and thickened. Pour it over the chops
   and serve at once.

SERVES 4

This simple, delicious braising technique is a standard one among Gullah and Geechee cooks. It's used for almost any meat and poultry—but especially chops, beef round steak, chicken, duck, beef short ribs, and pork spareribs. A more recent and delicious favorite is the two meaty joints of turkey wings. Substitute 1-1/2 pounds of 1/2-inch-thick round steak cut into 3-inch pieces, one 3-pound chicken or 5-pound duckling, disjointed and cut up for frying, 3-1/2 pounds of short or spareribs, separated into 1 or 2 rib sections, or 4 pounds of turkey wings, disjointed (save the tips for the broth pot). Adjust the simmering time until the meat is falling-off-the-bone tender.

Some local cooks finish this in the oven: use an ovenproof, lidded skillet or braising pan, preheat the oven to 300 degrees F. while the chops are browning, then transfer the pan to the oven for the slow simmer. Some African American cooks even omit the browning but and simply season the meat well, cover it with the raw peppers, onions, and garlic, and seal the pan tightly with foil, and bake it in a slow oven until the chops are falling-apart tender.

PORK MEDALLIONS
WITH SAGE AND MADEIRA

Old cookbooks frequently called cuts from the round and tenderloin of pork "steaks." Recipes for them were much like those for similar cuts of beef, mutton, or veal, and often included directions for "rolling" the meat—the logic of which eluded me until I watched chef Walter Dasher pound out pork scaloppine from thick-cut tenderloin medallions. The light finally dawned: they were doing exactly what he did with those medallions of pork—flattening them into tenderized, quick-cooking scallops.

The seasonings here are the traditional ones for pork in Georgia, but the Madeira gives away that a Savannah cook has gotten into the pot.

1 pound pork tenderloin

Salt and whole black pepper in a peppermill

About 2 teaspoons crumbled dried sage

2 tablespoons bacon drippings or unsalted butter

1/4 cup all-purpose flour, spread on a plate

1/2 cup Madeira

1/2 cup Basic Meat or Chicken Broth (page 57)

1. Rinse the pork under cold running water and pat dry. Trim away any fat and silver skin and cut it crosswise into 8 equal medallions about 1-inch thick. Lay them on a sheet of wax paper, cover with a second sheet of paper, and pound them until they are 1/4-inch thick. Season both sides well with salt and pepper. Rub the sage to a powder, sprinkle it evenly over both sides of the pork, and rub it into the surface.

2. Put the drippings or butter in a large skillet or sauté pan and heat it over medium heat until it is hot. Raise the heat to medium high, quickly roll the pork in the flour, and slip it into the pan until it is filled without crowding the pork (you may need to cook them in two batches). Cook until it is golden brown, about 2 minutes, turn, and brown the second side, about 2 minutes longer. Remove the meat from the pan.

Pork Medallions with Sage and Madeira.

3. Sprinkle in a teaspoon of flour and stir until it is mixed with the fat. Let it cook for a minute, then slowly stir in the Madeira. Cook, stirring and scraping the pan, until it is thick, then slowly stir in the broth. Bring to a simmer and cook until lightly thickened. Return the meat to the pan and cook, turning them several times, until they are heated through and the sauce is thick, about 1 minute. Turn off the heat, taste and correct the seasonings, and serve at once.

SERVES 4

Joan Levy's Brisket à la Bercy.

JOAN LEVY'S BRISKET À LA BERCY

Joan Levy is a born and bred Savannahian. Her grandmother, a direct descendant of Benjamin Sheftall, delivered Joan at home—and you do not get much more old Savannah than that. Joan's cooking, while infused with those traditions, is deeply colored by the years that she and her husband Gary lived in New Orleans and by extensive traveling all over the world. She did not grow up with the braised brisket that is traditional in so many Jewish families. However, now she often makes it for Sabbath dinners, especially at High Holy Days when the meal has to be made ahead, because it not only can be made a day ahead and reheated, it's actually better that way. It slices more evenly when cold and reheating in the gravy keeps it moist and tender.

3 pounds beef brisket

2 teaspoons salt

2 teaspoons seasoning salt

3 tablespoons brown sugar

1 cup chili sauce

1-1/2 cups cider vinegar

1 cup chopped celery leaves

2 medium yellow onions, trimmed, split lengthwise, peeled, and thinly sliced

1 tablespoon cornstarch, dissolved in 1/4 cup water

1. Rinse the beef under cold water, pat dry, and put it in a shallow glass, porcelain, or stainless-steel container. Stir together the salts, brown sugar, chili sauce, and vinegar and spread it on all sides of the meat. Cover and marinate overnight, refrigerated.

2. Position a rack in the center of the oven and preheat it to 325 degrees F. Lift the beef from the marinade and put it in a covered roaster. Pour the marinade over it and scatter the celery and onions over it. Roast slowly, uncovered, for about 2 hours, basting occasionally. Add a little water to the pan juices if it begins to get too dry.

3. After 2 hours, cover and roast slowly for about 3 hours more, or until the meat is fork tender. Let it rest at least 30 minutes before slicing across the grain about 1/4 inch thick. It is even better to let it cool completely and chill it, well covered, overnight, and slice it while still quite cold.

4. When you are ready to serve the brisket, strain the pan drippings, reserving the onions, and reheat gently over medium heat. When it is simmering, whisk in the dissolved cornstarch a little at a time until it is lightly thickened. Simmer about 2 minutes. Put the brisket and onions back in the roasting pan and pour the gravy over it. Cover tightly, and gently reheat in a slow (300 degrees F) oven, about an hour. Serve the brisket drizzled with some of the gravy and garnished with the onions, and pass the remaining gravy separately.

SERVES 4 TO 6

OLD SALZBURGER SAUERBRATEN

The Salzburger Lutherans first came to Savannah in 1734 after expulsion from the largely Catholic region of Austria surrounding Salzburg. They soon moved inland to found the community of Ebenezer and settled across Effingham County. More Austrian Lutherans followed, founding Ascension Lutheran Church in 1741, and they've been an enduring presence in Savannah ever since. A smattering of German-Austrian cookery survives here and has become an indelible part of the city's culinary heritage. This is an especial local favorite.

4 pounds boneless beef round, rump, or shoulder

2 cloves garlic, lightly crushed, peeled, and cut in half

Salt and whole black pepper in a peppermill

1 cup cider or red wine vinegar

1 cup water

2 medium white onions, trimmed, split lengthwise, peeled, and thinly sliced

2 to 3 bay leaves

1/4 cup tightly packed brown sugar

1 teaspoon whole peppercorns

2 tablespoons bacon drippings or unsalted butter

8 gingersnaps, crushed to fine crumbs

1. Rinse the beef and wipe it dry. Rub it well on all sides with the cut side of the garlic cloves and rub generously with salt and liberal grindings of pepper. Put the beef into a deep, nonreactive bowl.

2. Bring the vinegar, water, onions, garlic, bay leaves, brown sugar, and peppercorns to a bare simmer over medium heat. Do not allow it to boil. Pour the marinade over the beef (it should completely cover it). Let it cool, cover, and refrigerate for at least 7 and up to 12 days, turning the beef every day. Some cooks transfer the beef after it has cooled to a heavy-duty ziplock food storage bag. This works fine, but put it into a pan or bowl in case the bag springs a leak.

3. When you are ready to cook the sauerbraten, position a rack in the lower third of the oven and preheat it to 300 degrees F. Drain the beef, reserving the marinade, and wipe it dry. Heat the fat in a large Dutch oven over medium heat. When it is hot, but not smoking, put in the beef and brown it well on all sides, about 5 to 8 minutes. Meanwhile, remove the bay leaves and peppercorns from the marinade and discard them.

4. When the meat is nicely browned, pour the marinade over it (including the onions), bring it to a simmer, and turn off the heat. Cover tightly and bake until the beef is fork tender, about 3-1/2 hours.

5. Remove the beef to a platter and let it rest for at least 15 minutes. Bring the cooking liquids to a simmer over direct medium heat. Stir in the gingersnaps and simmer, stirring occasionally, until the sauce is thickened, about 5 minutes. Thinly slice the beef, drizzle it with gravy, and serve with the remaining gravy passed separately.

SERVES 6 TO 8

STEAK CASSEROLE

Regardless of whether the sauce is tomato or broth based, steak casserole is always served with dry steamed rice, but the tomato version makes a handsome sauce for just about any short, tubular pasta.

1-1/2 pounds round steak, cut 1/2 to 3/4 inch thick

2 slices thick-cut bacon, cut in 1/2-inch dice

Salt and whole black pepper in a peppermill

Ground cayenne pepper

Whole nutmeg in a grater

1 medium yellow onion, trimmed, split lengthwise, peeled, and diced small

1 medium green bell pepper, stem, core, and membrane removed, diced small

1 rib celery, washed, strung, and diced small

2 medium carrots, peeled and diced small

2 medium cloves garlic, lightly crushed, peeled, and minced

2 tablespoons red wine vinegar

2 tablespoons Worcestershire sauce

1/2 cup red wine or Madeira

2 pounds tomatoes, scalded, quartered, and put through a food mill (page 15), or 1 (28-ounce) can crushed tomatoes

4 cups hot Lowcountry Steamed Rice (page 78)

1. Position a rack in the center of the oven and preheat it to 300 degrees F. Trim the meat, cut it into even serving pieces, and wipe dry. Heat a flameproof casserole over medium heat. When hot, add the bacon and sauté until crisp. Remove it and add the steak. Fry until the bottom is well browned, about 2 minutes, turn, season with salt, pepper, cayenne, and nutmeg and let the other side brown. Remove it to a plate and season the second side.

2. Add the onion, bell pepper, celery, and carrots to the casserole and sauté, stirring often, until the onion is pale gold, about 5 minutes. Add the garlic and sauté until fragrant, about a minute more. Add the vinegar, Worcestershire, and wine. Bring to a boil, stirring and scraping the bottom of the casserole to loosen any cooking residue. Add the tomatoes, let it come back to a simmer, and reduce the heat to medium low and simmer 5 minutes.

3. Return the bacon, beef, and any juices that have accumulated in the plate to the casserole, turning several times to coat the meat with sauce. Cover tightly and bake in the center of the oven until the steaks are fork tender, about 2-1/2 to 3 hours. Thinner steaks will of course cook more quickly than thicker ones. Serve with rice.

SERVES 4 TO 6

This handsome old recipe, often called "smothered steak," survives in a few of Savannah's traditional home kitchens. Its tangy tomato sauce, with that ubiquitous blend of onion, peppers, garlic, and hot pepper, shares much with the Creole steak casseroles of the Caribbean and the Sauce Creole of New Orleans. There's a similar version without tomato sauce. To make it, follow the recipe for Smothered Pork Chops (page 149), substituting 1/2-inch-thick round steak for the chops.

WALTER DASHER'S PORT-BRAISED SHORT RIBS

Native son Walter Dasher was once named among the best chefs in the country by *Gourmet* magazine. His gifted professional cooking at such celebrated kitchens as La Toque, 45 South, and the Chatham Club set a standard that has had a major impact on Savannah's restaurant culture. However, his best contribution to local cooking has been through the hundreds of cooking classes that he and his wife, Alice, have taught over the years. Whenever they offer a class at venues like the cooking school of Kitchenware Outfitters, it sells out in less than twenty minutes.

This is the kind of cooking that Walter teaches in those classes, but more to the point, it's how he cooks at home. His advice on the port is to use an inexpensive one: don't waste a good wine on the braising pot.

2 tablespoons vegetable oil

2 tablespoons unsalted butter

6 large beef short ribs (about 3-1/2 to 4 pounds), trimmed of excess fat

Salt and whole black pepper in a peppermill

1 tablespoon dried thyme

2 tablespoons fresh thyme lightly chopped

1 cup diced yellow onion (about 1 medium)

1 cup diced carrots (about 3 medium)

1 cup diced celery (about 3 large ribs)

1 cup diced leeks (white and pale green parts only—about 3 medium)

4 large cloves garlic, lightly crushed, peeled, and minced

1/4 cup tomato ketchup

2 cups port

1 (28-ounce) can diced plum tomatoes

2 cups water

Celery Root Mashed Potatoes (page 179)

1. Position a rack in the center of the oven and preheat to 325 degrees F. Heat the oil and butter in a large, heavy-bottomed flameproof casserole or deep, ovenproof lidded sauté pan over medium-high heat. Rub the ribs well with salt and pepper, and thyme. Brown them well on all sides, about 8 minutes (in batches, if necessary—do not crowd the pan). Remove them to a platter and spoon off all but 3 tablespoons of fat.

2. Add the onion, carrots, celery, and leeks to the pan. Sauté, tossing frequently, until nicely browned, about 8 to 10 minutes. Add the garlic and ketchup and cook until fragrant and dry, about 3 minutes more. Add the port, stirring and scraping the bottom of the pan, and bring it to a boil. Let it cook until reduced by half, then add the tomatoes and water and bring them to a boil. Return the ribs to the casserole, cover tightly, and transfer it to the oven. Braise gently until the ribs are tender, about 2 hours. After the first 15 minutes, check to make sure that the liquid is barely simmering. If it is bubbling too much, reduce the oven temperature as necessary for a bare simmer.

3. When the ribs are tender, transfer them to a platter and cover loosely with foil. Let the braising liquid stand off the heat for 3 minutes to settle. Skim off the excess fat from the surface and return the ribs to the sauce or pour it over them. Serve with Celery Root Mashed Potatoes.

SERVES 6

*Walter Dasher's Port-Braised
Short Ribs.*

CORNED BEEF SAVANNAH-STYLE

For the beef:

1 (3 to 4 pound) corned beef brisket or eye of round

2 tablespoons cider vinegar

2 tablespoons pickling spice or Spice Mixture for Corned Beef (see box note)

For the glaze (optional):

1/2 cup light brown sugar

1/4 cup Dijon-style mustard

1 teaspoon dry mustard

Vegetables (optional):

12 small white "boiling" onions

1 medium head cabbage

12 small red-skinned potatoes

3 to 4 carrots, peeled and cut in 1-inch lengths

1. Rinse the beef well under cold running water to remove the brine. Put it, fat side up, in a heavy-bottomed flameproof casserole or Dutch oven. Add enough cold water to cover it by an inch and add the vinegar.

2. Bring slowly to a boil over medium heat, skimming away scum as it rises. Add the spices, reduce heat to a bare simmer, and gently cook until the meat is easily pierced through, about 2-1/2 to 3 hours. Check occasionally to make sure the liquid still covers the beef and add boiling water (never cold or hot tap water) as needed.

3. Turn off the heat, let the beef cool in the cooking liquid for a few minutes, and remove it to a warm platter. Let rest 30 minutes before carving. If you are cooking the beef primarily for sandwiches, it will make neater slices if it is thoroughly chilled first.

4. *Optional Glazing:* Corned beef is also occasionally glazed, especially when it is served with cabbage and other vegetables as a boiled dinner. Position rack in center of oven and preheat to 375 degrees F. Allow corned beef to cool slightly and place in shallow roasting pan, casserole, or gratin dish. Mix together the brown sugar and both mustards until smooth. Coat the beef well with glaze and, while preparing and cooking vegetables, bake until it is nicely browned, about 30 minutes.

5. For a full "boiled dinner" (Savannahians just call it "corned beef and cabbage"), bring a large pot of water to a boil. Trim the onions and cut a deep 'x' into the root ends. Put them in the boiling water for 1 minute, drain, and peel them.

6. Bring the beef cooking liquid back to simmer over medium heat. Add the onions and let it come back to a simmer. Meanwhile, remove the tough outer leaves of the cabbage and cut it into 8 wedges. When the onions are

---

Though native Irishmen may not think of corned beef as an especially Irish dish, when St. Patrick's Day descends on Savannah, it is to that day what turkey is to Thanksgiving. It was not, however, St. Patrick's Day that made corned beef popular here. Long before March 17 got out of control, corned beef was a regional favorite, as it was for most Anglo-Americans in the days before refrigeration, when corning (brine-curing) was the only way to keep meat for prolonged periods. Originally, the meat was soaked to remove as much of the salt as possible so that the meat would resemble fresh beef, but most have come to relish that salty tang as the whole point of corned beef.

Elsewhere, the common name for this is "Boiled Dinner"—a misleading moniker. Like a good "boiled" country ham, the secret to success in cooking corned beef is never to let it actually boil. That means that the bubbles should never break the surface of the cooking liquid but merely make the surface shiver gently.

half done (about 10 minutes), add the cabbage. Peel the potatoes (or only remove peel in a ring around center), and when the liquid is simmering again, add them to the pot. Bring it back to simmer, add the carrots and cook until all the vegetables are tender, about 20 minutes. Drain well.

7. Thinly slice the beef and surround it with the vegetables. Serve at once with horseradish mustard sauce (recipe follows) passed separately.

SERVES 8 TO 12

Spice Mixture for Corned Beef: For up to 5 pounds of corned beef, mix together 2 finely crumbled bay leaves, 1 teaspoon crumbled dried thyme, 2 teaspoons yellow mustard seeds, 1 teaspoon allspice, 1 teaspoon peppercorns, 1 teaspoon whole coriander seeds, and 3 to 4 whole cloves.

HORSERADISH MUSTARD SAUCE

Savannah cook and party diva Jeannie Knight, who spearheaded the award-winning cookbook *First Come First Served . . . In Savannah*, a fundraising cookbook by the St. Andrews Parent Teacher Organization, spreads the corned beef sandwiches in her St. Patrick's Day picnic basket with a sauce made of equal parts Dijon mustard, sour cream, and mayonnaise. With horseradish added to the mix it makes a great condiment for a warm corned beef, too.

1/2 cup prepared horseradish, well drained

1/2 cup sour cream

1/2 cup Herb Mayonnaise (page 23)

1/2 tablespoon Dijon-type mustard

1/4 cup finely minced green onion

1. Mix together the horseradish, sour cream, mayonnaise, and mustard.

2. Fold in the onion and let stand 15 to 30 minutes before serving.

MAKES ABOUT 2 CUPS

VEAL SCALLOPS
WITH OYSTERS AND BACON

Veal has not always had the cachet that it has today. Early Georgians found its mild, delicate flavor dull; Georgia's antebellum cooking authority Annabella Hill even called it "insipid." It was, however, usually cheaper than beef and chicken and, therefore, more prominent on colonial and antebellum tables than it is today. Naturally, cooks found many ways to bring it to life, among them the masterful pairing with oysters. The combination was old hat to the English colonials, and plentiful, cheap local oysters made it a rather obvious choice. Today, the two primary ingredients are no longer quite so cheap and plentiful, and their combination is no longer commonplace, so when this dish appeared on a downtown restaurant menu as a "nouvelle" Southern concoction, the chef had no idea that there was nothing new about it.

Our local cluster oysters are delicately sweet but very briny; if you can get them, they really make this dish sing, but you'll need to hold off on the salt. The oysters and bacon should provide all you'll need, so don't add any at all, but taste the sauce at the very end and add salt as needed.

12 to 16 freshly shucked oysters (about 1 cup), with their reserved juices

1 pound veal scallops, cut across the grain about 2 inches across by 1/2 inch thick

Salt and whole black pepper in a peppermill

2 slices thick-cut bacon, cut into 1/2-inch dice

1/4 cup all-purpose flour spread on a dinner plate

2 tablespoons bourbon

1 cup heavy (minimum 36% milk fat) cream

1/4 cup thinly sliced green onions

1. Drain the oysters in a wire sieve fitted over a glass or stainless-steel bowl containing their reserved juices. Spread wax paper or plastic wrap on a flat, sturdy work surface. Put the veal on it, cover with a second sheet, and lightly pound it with a mallet or scaloppine pounder to about 1/4-inch thick. Season very lightly with salt (especially if your oysters are very briny) and several generous grindings of pepper.

2. Fry the bacon in a large, heavy-bottomed skillet that will hold all of the veal in one layer, over medium heat, until lightly browned and most of its fat is rendered. Remove and drain on absorbent paper. Raise the heat to medium high. Lightly roll the veal in flour, shake off the excess, and add it to the pan. Sauté until golden brown, about 1 minute, turn and sauté until the second side is lightly browned, about a minute longer. Do not overcook; it should still be pink in the middle. Remove it to a warm platter.

3. Add the oysters to the pan. Sauté until they plump up and their gills begin to curl, about 1 minute, and remove them to a bowl using a slotted spoon. Add the bourbon and let it almost evaporate. Add 1/2 cup of the reserved oyster liquor, bring it to a boil, stirring and scraping to loosen any cooking residue, and cook, stirring frequently, until lightly reduced. Add the cream, bring it to a boil, and cook briskly until lightly thickened, about a minute.

4. Reduce the heat to medium low, return bacon and oysters to the pan and turn them several times in the sauce until lightly coated and just warmed through. Turn off the heat and pour the sauce over the veal. Sprinkle with thinly sliced green onion and serve at once.

SERVES 4

Veal Scallops with Oysters and Bacon.

ROAST LAMB
WITH LEMON AND POTATOES

Every October, St. Paul's Greek Orthodox Church holds its annual Greek Festival, and all of Savannah is invited to discover again the wonderful flavors and aromas of lemon-scented roast lamb and chicken, savory spanako-pita and pastitsio, briny feta and olive-laced salads, and dozens of filo-based Greek pastries.

Unlike English and French cooks, Savannah's Greeks tra-ditionally don't eat rare lamb but roast it gently in a fragrant bath of lemon juice, garlic, and oregano until it is well-done. If you're accustomed to eating lamb rare, trust them on this and follow the recipe exactly. You'll be surprised by how moist and flavorful it is. And the potatoes: simmered to perfection in the rich pan drippings—why, they're just this side of heaven.

2 large lemons
1 leg of lamb, about 6 to 7 pounds
2 large cloves garlic, lightly crushed, peeled, and minced
Salt and whole black pepper in a peppermill

1/4 cup chopped fresh oregano or 2 tablespoons dried
1/4 cup olive oil
3 pounds medium red potatoes

1. Position a rack in the center of the oven and preheat to 450 degrees F. Grate the zest from 1 lemon. Halve and juice both lemons through a strainer. Pat the lamb dry with a clean cloth. Cut small slits over the entire surface. Mix the garlic and a teaspoon each of salt and pepper and insert bits of it into each slit in the lamb. Rub the entire surface with the lemon zest and juice, and with more salt and pepper and the oregano.

2. Rub the bottom of a roasting pan well with oil and put the lamb in it fat side up. Drizzle the lamb with oil and roast at 450 degrees F until nicely browned, about 20 minutes. Add any remaining lemon juice and enough water to cover the bottom of the pan by 1/2 inch, lower the temperature to 350 degrees F and roast about 45 minutes more.

3. Meanwhile, peel the potatoes (if you like, you may leave the skins on) and quarter them. Place around lamb and roast, basting all with pan juices, about 45 minutes longer, or until the lamb is well done (about 170 degrees F on a meat thermometer inserted into the meatiest part of the leg without touching bone). Remove the lamb to a platter and let it rest 15 to 20 minutes before carving. Remove potatoes to serving dish and tent with foil to keep warm.

SERVES 6 TO 8

BOBOTIE

When made with fresh meat, the top tends to dome, making the egg custard slip to the sides when it is added. To get around this, one old Savannah recipe called for the custard to be gradually basted over the top during the last half hour—more trouble than it's worth. South African–born Judy Baker pokes the top at regular intervals with a fork before adding the custard so that it stays in place and seeps into the meat mix below it. It also helps to pack the sides a little higher than the center, lessening that tendency to dome. If, despite all this, the custard slips to the sides, just be sure to scoop a little of it onto each serving. It'll still taste wonderful.

1 large yellow onion, trimmed, split lengthwise, peeled, and chopped

2 tablespoons unsalted butter

1 thick slice firm, home-style white bread

1 cup milk

2 pounds ground beef or lamb, or both, mixed 2 parts beef to 1 part lamb

1 rounded tablespoon apricot jam

1/2 cup golden raisins (preferred) or dark raisins or currants

1/4 cup toasted slivered almonds

2 tablespoons curry powder

Salt and whole black pepper in a peppermill

6 to 8 small fresh or dried bay leaves, or fresh lemon leaves

2 large eggs

1. Sauté the onion in the butter in a heavy-bottomed sauté pan or skillet over medium heat until translucent, and let it cool slightly. Meanwhile, soak the bread in the milk for a few minutes, lift it out, and squeeze it dry over the bowl. Reserve the soaking milk.

2. Position a rack in the center of the oven and preheat it to 350 degrees F. Thoroughly mix the onion, bread, meat, jam, raisins, almonds, curry powder, salt, and pepper in a large bowl. Butter a 3-quart casserole, turn the mixture into it, and pat it flat. Roll the bay or lemon leaves and insert them into the meat. Bake in the center of the oven 30 minutes.

3. Meanwhile, beat together the eggs and reserved milk until smooth. Pour this over the meat and bake until the custard is set and golden, about 30 minutes more. Serve with grated coconut, chutney, and rice.

SERVES 6

There are strong and long-standing ties between South Africa and Savannah, and our city is enriched by a large community of South Africans who have imported much of their native cookery, including this traditional Cape Malay dish, which has been a part of Lowcountry cooking for at least seventy-five years. As is true of most dishes that are off their original turf, Bobotie has evolved over time. In Charleston, where its name was corrupted to "Hobotee," it was often made with leftover meat and baked in individual ramekins with a bay leaf or sliver of lemon stuck into each serving—an old-fashioned way of doing it that is no longer observed in South Africa. In Savannah, it was and still is baked in a single round casserole and includes apricot jam, a frequent ingredient in contemporary South African versions.

Vegetables, Salads, & Side Dishes

FROM THE DAY IT WAS FIRST LAID OUT in 1733, Ellis Square on Barnard Street has played an important role in the domestic and public life of the city. It was there that the first major citywide disaster began, when the bakery caught fire on a windy day in 1795 and leveled much of the young city's colonial fabric. There were the original sites of First Baptist Church and Independent Presbyterian Church. Just around the corner, the Sons of Liberty met at Tondee's Tavern to plan Georgia's role in the Revolution. And it was in Ellis Square that a doomed fight to save the old market building sparked a now legendary preservation movement that has conserved one of the largest historic districts in America.

But Ellis Square's real significance in the life of the city had nothing to do with Revolutionary politics, liberated protestant worship, cataclysmic disasters, or conservation. For more than two hundred years, until the mid-1950s, it was Savannah's public market, and as such was the center of its domestic economy and culinary life. Though the colonial plan had allowed for tithing lots large enough to sustain small kitchen gardens, with additional individual farming plots outside the old city walls, there was still a market for imported food, olive oil, wine as well as local dairy products, domestic and wild-caught meat, poultry and fish, and, significantly, fresh produce.

For nearly a century, the Polk family supplied that produce from their old location in the market district. Today that building, at the heart of a revitalized complex of shops, cafés, and art galleries, houses a restaurant, and the produce

Facing: Green Beans with Tomato Sauce.
Above: Fresh okra, a Lowcountry staple.

165

stand, operated by Jerry Polk and his wife, Diane, is across town on Liberty Street. But the family's dedication to providing quality produce is as strong as it was a century ago. The Polks are part of a committed effort to preserve more about the historic downtown than its lovely buildings.

SUSAN'S BUTTERBEANS

When people see Savannah's celebrity caterer Susan Mason at one of the parties she caters, dressed to the nines and working the crowd with her signature charm, they forget that her success owes a great deal to the fact that she is a good cook. Every year she and a group of friends take a busman's holiday to a rented house in France where, liberated from expectations of her professional life, she can spend all the time she wants in the kitchen, pleasing no one but her friends and herself.

Unlike the elegant cooking of her professional kitchen, Susan's home cooking, colored by that time in France and by deep roots in Southern Alabama, is forthright and unassumingly simple. One evening while talking shop over a glass of wine, Susan kept slipping out to her surprisingly tiny home kitchen to check on a supper she would later share with an old friend. When I exclaimed over the homey yet bewitching aromas that wafted out to the living room, she just shrugged, "Oh—that's *just* my butterbeans!"

Her secret was chicken broth rather than the usual bit of salt pork.

The terra cotta Griffon fountain at the Cotton Exchange (1886) on Bay Street.

1 pound (shelled weight) fresh or frozen small green butterbeans

2 teaspoons salt

3 to 4 tablespoons unsalted butter, optional

2 cups Basic Meat or Chicken Broth (page 57), or 1 cup canned broth mixed with 1 cup water (even if the label says to use it full strength)

1. Put the beans in a wire sieve and rinse them under cold running water. Drain well and put them into a heavy-bottomed 2-quart pot. Add the broth and bring them slowly to a boil over medium heat, skimming off the foaming scum as it forms.

2. Reduce the heat to medium low, add the salt, and simmer until tender and the cooking liquid is somewhat evaporated, about 25 to 30 minutes. Turn off the heat, mix in the butter, if using, pour them into a warm serving bowl, and serve at once.

SERVES 4

GREEN BEANS with TOMATO SAUCE

To the myth that Southerners historically had no subtlety with the vegetable pot, I submit this recipe from a late-nineteenth-century Savannah manuscript. The lovely wine and tomato sauce is full of flavor and yet it does not overpower the fresh taste of young, tender snap beans. Notice that there's not a scrap of salt pork in sight. Though the acidity of the tomatoes will affect the lively green color of the beans, they are even more flavorful if you let them simmer in the sauce for a few minutes. Leave the beans slightly underdone in the initial cooking and add them about halfway through the sauce's simmer. Simmer until the sauce is thickened and the beans are tender, about 8 minutes more.

1-1/2 pounds young, thin green beans

Salt

2 tablespoons olive oil

1 small yellow onion, trimmed, split lengthwise, peeled, and minced

1 tablespoon minced celery

1 tablespoon minced green bell pepper

1 large clove garlic, lightly crushed, peeled, and minced fine

1 tablespoon chopped flat-leaf parsley

1 teaspoon chopped fresh savory or marjoram

1-1/2 cups (about 2 medium or 3 plum tomatoes) scalded, peeled, seeded, and diced ripe tomatoes (page 15)

1/2 cup dry white wine

Whole black pepper in a peppermill

Cayenne pepper

1. Wash the beans in cold water, drain, and snap off the stem ends. Leave them whole. Bring 2 quarts of water to a boil in a 4-quart saucepan over medium high heat. Add a small handful of salt and the beans. Stir, bring it back to a boil, and cook until the beans are just tender, about 8 to 10 minutes. Drain well and put them in a warm serving bowl or platter.

2. While the beans are cooking, heat the oil, onion, celery, and bell pepper in a wide sauce or sauté pan over medium heat. Sauté, tossing frequently, until the onion is translucent and beginning to color, about 5 minutes. Add the garlic, parsley, and savory and sauté until fragrant, about a minute longer.

3. Add the tomatoes and wine and season well with salt, pepper, and cayenne. Bring to a boil, reduce the heat to medium low, and simmer 10 minutes, stirring occasionally. Pour it over the beans and serve at once.

SERVES 4 TO 6

A Vanished Treat

Until the early twentieth century, local children used to forage in the marshes for chinquapins, the nut-like seeds of the wild American water lotus. Not only a much-relished children's treat, they were also gathered and sold by the African American street vendors who plied the lanes of the old downtown.

NITA'S CABBAGE

1 small, fresh green cabbage

Garlic powder, or 1 to 2 large cloves garlic, crushed, peeled, and minced

Salt and whole black pepper in a peppermill

Ground cayenne

1. Strip off any tough, discolored, or withered leaves from the cabbage but don't remove any of the healthy-looking dark green leaves. Quarter it and cut out the core, then sliver each one lengthwise into the thinnest possible strips.

2. Put enough water in a 4-quart pot to cover the cabbage, cover the pot, and bring to a boil over medium-high heat. Add a healthy dash of garlic powder or fresh garlic to taste, a large pinch of salt, a few grindings of pepper and a small pinch of cayenne, and the cabbage.

3. Cover just long enough to bring the liquid back to a boil. Reduce the heat to medium, uncover and cook until the cabbage is just tender. It should still be bright green and not army-fatigue brown. Taste and adjust the seasonings, then drain and serve hot.

SERVES 4 TO 6

One of the most underappreciated (and underestimated) cooks in Savannah during the last decades of the twentieth century is Nita Dixon. Her career as a cook has known many ups and downs, but she always manages to roll with the punches, dust herself off, and turn right back to the stove. She put her children through school cooking for the dock workers in a mobile kitchen made from a converted bread truck.

Nita never puts salt pork or bacon in the vegetable pot and takes care never to overcook them. Like many African American cooks in Savannah, she uses powdered garlic prodigiously. Its flavor is brighter and more direct than fresh garlic, but finely minced fresh garlic can be substituted for it if you don't routinely have powdered garlic on hand.

STIR-FRIED COLLARDS

The Woo family has been in Savannah since the mid-1920s and for many years ran a grocery on Fahm Street. While life was not always easy, they always had plenty to eat, since, as Lily Woo Wong recalled, "Whatever we didn't sell, we ate." Often what they ate was foreign to them. Mrs. Wong thinks her father must have asked his customers how they cooked the things he sold them, but more often than not, their mother kept cooking new foods—like this Southern staple—the way she cooked other, more familiar vegetables. Collards are available anywhere in the South during fall and winter. Outside the South, look for them at markets that cater to African American and West Indian communities. If you can't find them, broccoli or cabbage can be cooked the same way.

1 pound young, tender collard leaves (inner section of head only) or cabbage

2 ounces (about 2 thick slices) thick-sliced streak of lean salt pork or bacon, rinsed well and patted dry

Soy sauce

1 cup Basic Meat or Chicken Broth (page 57) or 1 teaspoon bouillon dissolved in 1 cup water

2 teaspoons cornstarch, dissolved in 1/4 cup water

1. Wash the collards in several changes of cold water. Cut out the tough stems of the collards and cut the leaves into bite-size pieces.

2. Fry the salt pork in a wok or large sauté pan over medium heat until the fat is rendered. Remove the salt pork and raise the heat to medium high. Add the collard and stir-fry, tossing almost constantly, until bright green and hot through, about 3 minutes. Season well with soy sauce and pour in the broth.

3. Cover tightly and steam until crisp tender, about 3 to 5 minutes longer. Uncover and stir in the cornstarch a little at a time—you may not need all of it. Cook, tossing constantly, until the sauce is thickened, about half a minute longer. Taste and adjust the seasoning and serve immediately.

SERVES 4

TO STIR-FRY BROCCOLI:

Rinse it well under cold running water. Trim the stem and cut the florets from it, breaking them into bite-size pieces. Peel the stems and cut into bite-size chunks. Stir-fry the stems first, for about 2 minutes, before adding the florets.

BAKED EGGPLANT

While the details of how this vegetable came into North America are lost in time, two pieces of suggestive evidence point toward the African slave trade. First, contrary to the myth that it was not known in America until the end of the nineteenth century, eggplant had long been grown and enjoyed in the South for at least a century before that. More suggestive still is the fact that, in antebellum Carolina and Georgia, it was nicknamed Guinea squash, after the West African country.

1-1/2 pounds small to medium eggplants

Salt

4 thick-cut slices bacon

1 small yellow onion, trimmed, split lengthwise, peeled, and chopped fine

1 small green bell pepper, stem, core, and seeds removed, chopped fine

1 large clove garlic, lightly crushed, peeled, and minced

1 tablespoon chopped fresh parsley

1 cup roughly crushed saltine cracker crumbs, divided

Whole black pepper in a peppermill

Cayenne pepper

1/2 cup freshly grated Parmigiano-Reggiano cheese or very sharp cheddar

1. Peel and cut the eggplant into 1-inch dice. Put them in a colander, sprinkle well with salt, and toss to evenly coat. Let it stand in the sink for 30 minutes. Meanwhile, cook the bacon in a heavy-bottomed skillet over medium heat, turning several times, until it is crisp. Drain well on absorbent paper and roughly crumble it. Spoon off but reserve the drippings and measure 1 tablespoon back into the pan. Add the onion and bell pepper and sauté over medium heat until the onion is translucent and golden, about 5 minutes. Add the garlic and sauté until fragrant, about half a minute longer. Turn off the heat.

2. Position a rack in the upper third of the oven and preheat it to 375 degrees F. Prepare a pan with a steamer insert and put about 1 inch of water in the bottom of the pan. Bring it to a boil over medium-high heat. Wipe the eggplant dry and put it in the steamer basket over, not touching, the simmering water. Cover, reduce the heat to medium, and steam until tender. Let it cool enough to handle and mash it to a pulp.

3. Add the eggplant and parsley to the onion, bell pepper, and garlic. Mix in the crumbled bacon and half the cracker crumbs and season to taste with salt, pepper, and cayenne.

4. Lightly rub the inside of a 1-1/2-quart casserole with some of the reserved drippings. Put in the eggplant and smooth the top. Drizzle a teaspoon or so of drippings over the remaining cracker crumbs and toss until it is evenly absorbed (the crumbs should be loose and light, not greasy and clumping together). Sprinkle first the cheese and then the crumbs evenly over the eggplant and bake in the upper third of the oven until it is hot through and the top is golden brown, about 30 minutes.

SERVES 4

BAKED VIDALIA ONIONS

Martha Giddens Nesbit, the former *Savannah Morning News* food editor, fondly recalls this elegantly simple dish as her introduction to real Savannah style. It was the first course of a luncheon for two served on a polished mahogany table laid with delicate heirloom linens and her hostess' best china and silver. It remains a local staple during Vidalia onion season, served, just as it was then, at formal luncheons and dinners as a first course and as a side or vegetarian main dish at casual family meals. In the dead heat of a Savannah summer, when temperatures soar and the last thing anyone wants to do is add to the misery with a hot oven, local cooks often do the baking in a microwave. While it makes a respectable imitation, nothing concentrates their sweetness like a good slow baking.

4 large Vidalia sweet onions
About 5 tablespoons unsalted butter

1/2 cup freshly grated Parmigiano-Reggiano cheese

1. Position a rack in the upper third of the oven and preheat it to 375 degrees F. Trim off the roots and cut out the stem, making a shallow, cone-shaped well. Peel off the brown, papery outer skins (some Savannah cooks wash the onions and leave the skin on) and lightly rub each onion with butter. Put them, stem side up, in a snug-fitting, shallow baking dish and top each with a tablespoon of butter.

2. Bake in the upper third of the oven, basting frequently with the pan juices, until nearly tender, about 45 minutes.

3. Take them from the oven, mound the cheese up in the cut well of each, baste with pan juices, and bake until the cheese is melted and golden brown, about 15 to 20 minutes more. Let them sit for a few minutes and serve on individual shallow bowls or soup plates, pouring their pan juices over them.

SERVES 4

VIDALIA ONIONS STUFFED WITH SAUSAGE AND PECANS

Onions stuffed with sausage meat are a very old Southern classic that is ready-made for Vidalia sweet onions. The inherent sweetness is a perfect foil for the rich, spicy filling. They are so sumptuous and elegant that chef Elizabeth Terry served her version as a first course in her landmark restaurant, Elizabeth's on 37th, a practice that has been adopted by many Savannah hosts, but they are more commonly served on home tables as a main course at luncheons and family suppers.

4 large Vidalia sweet onions
Salt
1/2 pound bulk breakfast sausage
1/2 cup soft breadcrumbs
1/2 cup chopped toasted pecans
1 tablespoon chopped fresh, or 1 teaspoon dried, marjoram

1 tablespoon chopped fresh parsley
1 tablespoon chopped fresh, or 1 teaspoon dried, sage
Whole black pepper in a peppermill
Whole nutmeg in a grater
1/2 cup freshly grated Gruyère or sharp cheddar

1. Position a rack in the center of the oven and preheat it to 375 degrees F. Put the onions in a large pot and add enough water to cover them. Remove the onions, cover, and bring it to a boil over high heat. Add a small handful of salt and put in the onions whole (not peeled). Let it come back to a boil, reduce the heat to low, and simmer until the onions are almost but not quite done, about 20 minutes. Drain, reserving about a cup of their cooking liquid, and let them cool enough to handle.

2. Trim off the roots, leaving all the layers attached, and cut off about 1/4 inch of the stem end. Peel off the brown outer skin. With a melon-baller or sharp spoon, carefully scoop out the centers without breaking the root ends, leaving shells about 3 layers thick. Lightly butter a 9-inch square baking dish and put in the onions root side down. Chop the scooped out hearts of the onions.

3. Warm a skillet over medium heat and crumble in the sausage. Sauté until well browned, about 5 minutes. Add the chopped onion hearts. Sauté until the onion is beginning to color, about 4 minutes more. Turn off the heat.

4. Add the soft crumbs, pecans, marjoram, parsley, and sage. Toss well, taste, and season with salt, pepper, and nutmeg. Spoon the filling into the onion shells, mounding it on top. Sprinkle the tops evenly with grated cheese.

5. Carefully pour around them enough reserved cooking liquid to come about 1/4-inch up the sides. Bake in the center of the oven until the cheese is golden brown and the filling is hot through, about 40 minutes. Let stand for a few minutes to allow the intense heat to subside and serve hot or warm, basting each serving with pan juices. Serve them in shallow bowls with those pan juices—you won't want to waste them.

SERVES 4

Vidalia Onions Stuffed with
Sausage and Pecans.

SKILLET OKRA GUMBO
OR LOWCOUNTRY OKRA AND TOMATOES

Though bacon lends the most traditional flavor, now that good olive oil is regularly available, many local cooks use it instead.

2 pounds ripe tomatoes, or 4 cups canned tomatoes, seeded and chopped, with juices

3/4 pound tender young okra, preferably no longer than 2 inches

4 slices thick-cut bacon

1 medium white onion, trimmed, split lengthwise, peeled, and chopped

2 large or 3 medium cloves garlic, lightly crushed, peeled, and minced

Salt and whole black pepper in a peppermill

Ground cayenne pepper

3 cups Lowcountry Steamed Rice (page 78)

1. Scald, peel, seed, and dice the tomatoes as directed on page 15. Rinse the okra under cold, running water, gently rubbing each pod to remove the fuzz. Trim the caps. If the okra is very small (2 inches long or less), leave it whole; otherwise, slice it 1/4-inch thick.

2. Cook the bacon until crisp in a deep, heavy skillet over medium heat. Remove and drain it on absorbent paper. Spoon off all but 2 tablespoons of fat, put in the onion, and sauté, tossing often, until golden, about 5 minutes. Add the garlic and sauté until fragrant, about half a minute. Add the okra and sauté, stirring constantly, until barely tender.

3. Add the tomatoes and raise the heat to medium high. Bring it to a full boil and lower the heat to a gentle simmer. Season liberally with salt, pepper, and cayenne and simmer until the okra is very tender and the juices are thick, about 30 to 45 minutes. Taste and adjust the seasonings and simmer a moment longer to allow the flavors to meld.

4. Crumble the bacon and stir it into the gumbo or pass it separately so that each person can add it to taste. Serve hot with rice.

Facing: Skillet Okra Gumbo or Lowcountry Okra and Tomatoes.

SERVES 4 TO 6

GREEK-STYLE BLACK-EYED PEAS
WITH SPINACH

Stratton Leopold is known to the rest of the world for producing hit motion pictures like the *Mission: Impossible* series, but at home in Savannah, he's best known as heir to a family business whose tutti-frutti ice cream made Johnny Mercer want to write songs. When he closed the original Leopold's in the late sixties, fans of the homemade ice cream and secret recipe burgers did not let up until he was persuaded to come back with his wife, Mary, and revive the business on Broughton Street.

Stratton and Mary are both first generation Greek Americans and grew up eating mostly Greek food at home. But sometimes that food overlapped with the traditions of their adopted home, as here in Mary's traditionally Greek recipe for an old Southern staple—black-eyed peas. She frequently serves this as a dip, just like the black-eyed pea salads and salsas that have become popular in the last few years, but originally it was served as a vegetable side dish.

1 pound dried black-eyed peas
Salt
About 24 ounces fresh spinach, washed in several changes of water and drained, or 1 (10 ounce) package frozen whole leaf spinach, thawed and drained
About 4 tablespoons extra virgin olive oil, plus more for drizzling

1 large white onion, trimmed, split lengthwise, peeled, and chopped
1 bulb fennel, trimmed, cored, and chopped
3 bunches green onions, washed, trimmed, and thinly sliced
Whole black pepper in a peppermill

1. Soak the peas overnight in water to cover by at least 2 inches. Drain, add fresh water to cover by at least 2 inches, and bring them to a boil. Cook, replenishing the liquid with boiling water as needed, until they are tender, about an hour. When they are nearly tender, lightly salt them. Drain and rinse well. Coarsely chop the spinach.

2. Put 4 tablespoons of oil and white onion in a large skillet over medium heat. Sauté, tossing, until translucent, about 5 minutes. Add the fennel and sauté until it begins to soften. Add the green onions and spinach and toss until it is wilted, about 2 minutes. Add the peas. Season well with salt and pepper and let it heat through. Turn off the heat and serve hot or at room temperature.

SERVES 6 TO 8

Greek-Style Black-Eyed Peas with Spinach.

Anne Mingledorff's Squash Casserole.

Anne Mingledorff gets her extraordinary palate and culinary curiosity naturally. Her mother, Marjory (see Home-Fried Oysters, page 116), was a well-respected local caterer whose cooking was as legendary as her indomitable personality. Like her mother, Anne's own cooking is one part experience and two parts instinct. Here she applies those instincts to a traditional Deep-South staple, squash casserole, creating something that's at once as fresh and new as it is familiar and comforting. It's easier to put together than the more traditional versions and really lets the clean flavors of the vegetable shine through. Anne uses sweet, tender local yellow crookneck squash, but you can make this with young, small zucchini if yellow crookneck squash is not readily available. They will not taste quite the same, but they'll still be very good.

ANNE MINGLEDORFF'S SQUASH CASSEROLE

2 pounds young yellow crookneck squash or small yellow zucchini

3 tablespoons unsalted butter

1 medium yellow onion, trimmed, split lengthwise, peeled, and chopped

Salt and whole black pepper in a peppermill

3 tablespoons Italian seasoned dry breadcrumbs

6 tablespoons plain dry breadcrumbs

About 2 ounces grated Parmigiano-Reggiano cheese

About 4 to 6 ounces deli thinly sliced Swiss or Gruyère cheese

1. Position a rack in the center of the oven and preheat it to 350 degrees F. Scrub the squash under cold running water and pat dry. Trim and slice them crosswise into 1/4-inch thick rounds.

2. Melt the butter in a heavy-bottomed skillet or sauté pan over medium heat. Add the onion and sauté until translucent, about 3 minutes. Add the squash and sauté until softened and beginning to color, about 5 to 7 minutes more. Don't let the onions brown. Season well with salt and pepper and turn off the heat.

3. Lightly butter a 10-inch pie plate, or oval or rectangular 8 x 10-inch casserole. Mix the Italian and plain crumbs and sprinkle 2 tablespoons over the bottom. Add a sprinkling of Parmigiano and completely cover the bottom with a layer of Swiss cheese. Sprinkle the cheese with about 2 tablespoons of the crumb mixture and spread the squash and onion evenly over it. Scatter with 2 more tablespoons of crumbs and about 2 to 3 tablespoons of Parmigiano. Completely cover with a second layer of Swiss cheese, and then the rest of the crumbs and another sprinkling of Parmigiano. Bake in the center of the oven until golden brown, about 30 minutes.

SERVES 6

WALTER DASHER'S CELERY ROOT MASHED POTATOES

6 medium russet potatoes (about 3 pounds)
1 large celery root (about 1-1/4 pounds)
Salt

6 tablespoons unsalted butter, softened, divided
1 cup heavy cream, divided
Whole black pepper in a peppermill

This is what Walter serves with his Port-Braised Short Ribs (page 156), but they are also delicious with roasted or braised poultry and pork. When I tested the recipe, they were so good that they made up my entire supper. Celery root was not a common vegetable in Savannah until recent years, and it is largely thanks to chefs like Walter that locals know how to cook and enjoy it.

1. Scrub the potatoes and celery root well with a vegetable brush under cold running water. Bring enough water to completely cover the potatoes to a boil over medium-high heat in a large, heavy-bottomed pot. Add a large pinch of salt and the potatoes. Bring them to a boil, reduce the heat to a simmer, and cook until tender, about 30 minutes. Meanwhile, peel and roughly chop the celery root. Put it in a saucepan with enough water to cover, bring to a boil, loosely cover, and reduce the heat to a simmer. Cook until tender, about 30 minutes. It should be the same consistency as the cooked potatoes.

2. Drain the potatoes and, using a hot pad to protect your hands, quickly peel them while they're hot. Put them through a ricer and add 4 tablespoons of the butter and half the cream. Season well with salt and pepper and mix until smooth.

3. Drain the celery root and put it in a blender with the remaining butter and cream. Purée until smooth, using care, as the puree will be very hot. Lightly season with salt and pepper. Add the celery root puree to the potatoes and mix well. Taste and adjust the seasonings and serve warm.

SERVES 6 TO 8

Spanish Tomatoes.

SPANISH TOMATOES

Why this lovely mélange of tomato, bell pepper, and onion was called "Spanish" is lost in time. It goes back in Savannah at least to the 1870s, when Leila Habersham taught an elaborate version of it in her cooking school. Everything was sautéed in batches, and the whole thing was baked until the flavors were richly concentrated. One of Mrs. Habersham's students, probably quoting her teacher, wrote that they were "delightful to eat just so, or served for sauce, or as an entrée." So they are. Today, the preparation is more streamlined and the flavors are not as concentrated, though they're much fresher. Its secret is to use only good, ripe tomatoes and fresh, seasonal bell peppers.

2 pounds fresh ripe tomatoes

2 tablespoons bacon drippings or unsalted butter

1 large or 2 medium green bell peppers, stem, core, seeds, and membranes removed, thinly sliced

1 large Bermuda or yellow onion, trimmed, split lengthwise, peeled, and thinly sliced

Salt

Sugar

Ground cayenne pepper

1. Blanch, peel, and core the tomatoes (see page 15). Over a sieve set in a bowl to catch the juices, cut them into thick wedges and scoop out the seeds. Add the tomatoes to the bowl with their collected juices.

2. Melt the drippings or butter in a large skillet over medium heat. When it is hot, add the bell pepper and onion and sauté, tossing, until the onion is translucent and softened and the bell pepper is bright green, about 4 minutes. Add the tomatoes and their collected juices and bring them to a boil. Sprinkle lightly with salt, a pinch of sugar (if needed), and a dash of cayenne. Cook until the juices are evaporated and thick and the tomatoes are tender, about 20 minutes. Taste and adjust the seasonings, let it simmer half a minute longer, and turn off the heat. Serve warm.

3. Alternatively, you may bake the tomatoes instead. Position a rack in the center of the oven and, if the skillet is not ovenproof, transfer its contents to a shallow, lightly buttered baking dish. Bake, uncovered, until the juices are evaporated and thick, about 1 hour.

SERVES 4 TO 6

My own association with this dish goes back to my first summer in Savannah, nearly thirty years ago. It was one of the hottest on record and we all had ways of combating the heat. One of the most memorable for me was a White Christmas supper that a dear friend, the late Marilyn Whelpley, shared with me on an especially blistering August evening. We revived our heat-blunted appetites with a savory supper of these tomatoes, served over rice with a bit of sautéed local smoked sausage on the side, and pretended that cooler weather was imminent as we watched the classic film about waiting for snow.

MUSHROOM-STUFFED TOMATOES

Mushrooms and tomatoes are one of the world's great combinations, a notion well understood by the Savannah matron who added, as a footnote to the stuffed tomato recipe in a community cookbook from 1904, "Parmesan cheese and mushrooms all add nicety to the dish." They certainly do. Because of our mild climate, late tomatoes flourish well into the fall mushroom season in Savannah.

4 medium, ripe tomatoes

Salt

1/2 pound brown (crimini or portobello) mushrooms

2 tablespoons butter

3 medium shallots or 1 medium yellow onion, peeled and chopped fine

1 large or 2 small cloves garlic, lightly crushed, peeled, and minced

1/2 cup finely chopped (about 1 ounce) country ham or prosciutto

1 tablespoon chopped parsley

1 tablespoon chopped fresh (or 1 teaspoon dried) sage

1 cup soft breadcrumbs

Whole black pepper in a peppermill

Cayenne pepper

1/2 cup freshly grated Parmigiano-Reggiano cheese

1. Wash the tomatoes under cold running water and pat dry. Cut off the stem end just below the stem scar. Scoop out the seeds and discard them and, using a sharp spoon or melon baller, scoop out the inner pulp, leaving the outer pulp below the skin to form a shell. Drain the pulp well and chop it roughly. Lightly salt the insides of the hollowed-out tomato shells and in- vert them in a colander set over the sink for 30 minutes.

2. Meanwhile, position a rack in the upper third of the oven and preheat it to 375 degrees F. Wipe the mushrooms clean with a dry cloth and roughly chop them. Put the butter and shallots or onion in a large sauté pan. Turn on the heat to medium high and sauté, tossing frequently, until golden, about 5 minutes. Add the garlic and sauté, tossing frequently, until fragrant, half a minute longer. Add the ham and toss until heated through, then add the mushrooms, parsley, and sage and sauté until the mushrooms are wilted, about 3 to 4 minutes. Add the reserved tomato pulp, bring the liquids to a boil and cook quickly, stirring occasionally, until they are mostly evapo- rated. Turn off the heat.

3. Stir in the crumbs and season liberally with a large pinch or so of salt, sev- eral grindings of pepper, and a small pinch of cayenne. Toss well, then taste and correct the seasonings. Lightly butter a 9-inch square or round casserole. Wipe the tomato shells dry inside and out. Put them in the casserole and loosely spoon the filling into them. Sprinkle generously with cheese and bake in the upper third of the oven until the shells are tender and the filling is hot through, about 20 to 30 minutes.

SERVES 4

HONEY'S FRUIT THAIS

2 medium slightly under-ripe peaches

About 1/2 lemon, for juicing

2 to 3 ripe plums

1 cup fresh pineapple, cut into 1-inch chunks

1 cup Bing cherries, pitted and halved

1 slightly under-ripe banana, peeled and cut into 1-inch rounds

1 cup fresh blueberries

4 to 6 tablespoons light brown sugar

4 tablespoons butter, cut into small bits

1 cup slivered blanched almonds

1/2 cup medium-dry (amontillado) sherry

1/2 cup crushed almond or coconut macaroons or amoretti

Honey was the family pet name for Mildred Lee Guckenheimer Abrahams Kuhr, Joan Levy's great-grandmother, a direct descendant of Benjamin Sheftall. Her fruit compote is similar to those found in many old Jewish cookbooks but is especially fragrant with its sherry and macaroons. Why she named it "Thais" is lost to history, but that only adds to its charm.

Though intended as a condiment/side dish for roast meat or poultry, it would also make a delicious hot fruit compote to serve with short-bread cookies or pound cake for dessert.

1. Position a rack in the center of the oven and preheat to 350 degrees F. Peel the peaches, halve them, and cut out the pits. Cut them into thick wedges and sprinkle with lemon juice. Halve and pit the plums and cut them into wedges. Mix them and the rest of the fruit with the peaches.

2. Butter a 2-quart casserole and layer the fruit in it, sprinkling each layer with brown sugar, bits of butter, and almonds.

3. Pour the sherry over all and cover the top with macaroon crumbs. Cover and bake about 15 minutes, then uncover and bake about 20 minutes, or until the top is browned. Serve hot or warm.

SERVES 8

Honey's Fruit Thais.

Salads, Savannah Style

FROM MAY UNTIL WELL INTO OCTOBER, foods that can be served cold are an important part of Savannah's table, not only those set for entertaining but for more intimate family meals as well.

A popular salad in the spring and summer is seasonal green vegetables lightly cooked, cooled, and served cold or at room temperature in a light, mildly sweet-sour vinaigrette dressing. Early in the season, it will be asparagus, but as the balmy weather of spring gives way to the intense heat of summer, cold cooked green beans, black-eyed peas, squash, and even okra may be dressed in exactly the same way. The dressing that has been used for these vegetables has been virtually the same for more than a hundred years.

SAVANNAH VINAIGRETTE

1/3 cup wine vinegar (red, white, or sherry—your choice)

Salt and whole black pepper in a peppermill

1 tablespoon granulated sugar

Garlic juice, freshly squeezed through a garlic press

About 2/3 cup extra virgin olive oil

1 tablespoon chopped fresh herbs (basil, oregano, parsley, thyme, or tarragon, optional)

1. Whisk together the vinegar, a large pinch of salt, a liberal grinding of pepper, the sugar, and a few drops of garlic juice.

2. Gradually whisk in the oil. How much you will need will depend on the strength of the vinegar, the quality of the oil, and your family's tastes. Begin with 2/3 cup. Whisk in the herbs, if liked. Let it stand a few minutes, taste, and adjust the seasonings.

MAKES ABOUT 1 CUP

NOTE

To cook asparagus, young, slender green beans, sugar snap peas, or baby zucchini or yellow squash to serve cold with vinaigrette, wash and trim them but leave them whole (peel the tough stems of asparagus and break off the stem end of green beans and sugar snaps, but leave them attached to squash). Drop them in well-salted, rapidly boiling water and cook until they are barely tender and still bright green. Drain, refresh under cold running water, and let cool completely. To preserve the color of green vegetables, wait until just before serving them to dress them with the vinaigrette.

Southerners love sweet-sour dressings, and our version of the classic French-style vinaigrette is often softened with a touch of sugar or honey. In Savannah, we like a whisper of garlic, too. This is used not only for green salads, but for cucumbers, tomatoes, and lightly cooked, cold vegetables such as asparagus, sugar snap peas, green beans, and summer squash.

CUCUMBER SALAD
WITH DILLED SOUR CREAM DRESSING

The perfect thing to accompany almost any fish, shellfish, poultry, game, or lamb, this cool, refreshing salad has suggestive elements of Eastern Mediterranean cookery about it and probably came into Savannah by way of its Greek community.

2 large seedless ("English") cucumbers, about 1-1/2 pounds

Salt

1/2 cup thinly sliced green onions

2 tablespoons chopped fresh dill or 2 teaspoons dried

2 tablespoons freshly squeezed lemon juice

1-1/2 tablespoons Dijon-style mustard

1 cup sour cream

Whole black pepper in a peppermill

1. Scrub the cucumbers and, if the skin is tough and/or waxed, lightly skin them with a vegetable peeler. Slice as thinly as possible with a sharp knife or mandolin and put them in a colander. Sprinkle liberally with salt and toss. Let it stand in the sink for 1 hour.

2. Meanwhile, fold the onions, dill, lemon juice, and mustard into the sour cream. Season with a liberal grinding of pepper.

3. Press down on the cucumbers to remove as much moisture as you can without crushing them. Spread them on a dry kitchen towel, cover with a second towel, roll it up, and wring out as much moisture as possible. Transfer them to a glass bowl and fold in the sour cream dressing, mixing gently until they are well coated. Taste and correct the salt and pepper, cover, and chill thoroughly before serving.

SERVES 4 TO 6

WATERMELON SALAD

While developing recipes for my second book, *Beans, Greens, and Sweet Georgia Peaches*, I made what I thought was a clever, original salad with ice-cold watermelon, briny feta cheese, and crisp fresh mint, only to be informed by the late Mary Ellen Greenwood that my "invention" was an old Greek standard that was commonplace in Savannah's Greek community when I was in diapers. Her own recipe differed only in detail. Some local cooks add pitted and sliced Greek olives (about 1/3 cup), and you may add them if it suits you, but I prefer it without them.

Later still, I shared the recipe with longtime friend Paula Deen (Southern men know better than to refer to a lady as an "old" friend). When she made it on one of her early television shows, friends began calling to exclaim, "Paula Deen mentioned you on her show!" So, in a way, this old Greek salad has become my little claim to fame.

1/4 cup red wine, champagne, or sherry vinegar

Salt and whole black pepper in a peppermill

1/2 cup extra virgin olive oil

2 generous tablespoons chopped fresh mint

1/2 small watermelon, about 5 pounds, seeded and cut into bite-size pieces

1 medium Vidalia or other sweet onion, trimmed, peeled, and thinly sliced

4 ounces feta cheese, crumbled

6 whole sprigs mint, for garnish

1. Put the vinegar in a bowl and add a large pinch of salt, a few liberal grindings of pepper, and whisk until the salt is dissolved. Slowly whisk in the oil a few drops at a time. Stir in the chopped mint, taste and correct the seasonings, and set aside.

2. Combine the melon, onion, and feta in a bowl, pour the dressing over them, and toss gently until they are coated and evenly mixed. Garnish with the sprigs of mint or divide the salad among individual salad plates and garnish each serving with mint. Serve at once.

SERVES 6

Watermelon Salad.

CURRIED RICE SALAD

Cold rice salads are an old Savannah standard for warm weather buffets and luncheons. Unlike pasta, which can get gummy and flabby, rice holds its distinctly separate shape when cold and is firm yet tender. It not only can be made ahead, but is the better for it.

My first experience with this curried version was at a luncheon served in the subdued elegance of the Gothic-Revival Green Meldrim House, which today is the parish house for St. John's Church on Madison Square. It accompanied chicken salad and cold asparagus in vinaigrette. Like the architecture of that fine old house, it was complex yet perfectly balanced—the ideal complement to a cold buffet.

2 tablespoons sherry or white wine vinegar

2 teaspoons sugar

Salt

2 generous teaspoons curry powder

Whole white pepper in a peppermill

1 clove garlic, crushed and peeled but left whole

1/4 cup extra virgin olive oil

3 cups Lowcountry Steamed Rice (page 78), at room temperature

1/2 cup diced celery heart (pale inner ribs)

3/4 cup thinly sliced green onion

1/2 cup currants or roughly chopped raisins

1/2 cup toasted slivered almonds or pecans

1 tablespoon chopped fresh mint

1. Whisk together the vinegar, sugar, a large pinch of salt, curry powder, a light grinding of white pepper, and the garlic. Slowly whisk in the oil. Let it stand 15 to 30 minutes, taste, and adjust the seasonings. Remove and discard the garlic.

2. Gently toss together the rice, celery, onion, and currants. Fold in the dressing until it is evenly mixed. Chill thoroughly (at least 1 hour; overnight is better). Just before serving, taste and adjust the seasonings, add the nuts and mint, and gently toss to mix. Serve cold.

SERVES 4 TO 6

VARIATION: CURRIED SHRIMP AND RICE SALAD
To make a handsome main course salad, toss this with 1 pound small cooked shrimp (Poached Shrimp, page 18). Add a pinch more curry, salt, and a dash of cayenne.

ST. JOHN'S CRAB SALAD

This lovely salad comes from an old cookbook from the churchwomen of St. John's Episcopal Church on Madison Square. Part of its charm is the container in which it is served—the bright orange-red back shells of the crab—but you can make a respect- able crab salad from commercially packed crab and serve it on large scallop shells or lettuce leaves. The same recipe was used for any kind of flaked, cooked fish, especially salmon. Onions are not mentioned in the original recipes, but today no Savannah cook would make crab salad without it, and they are included here.

This same recipe is used to this day to make shrimp salad for the sell-out sandwiches served at the parish's annual bazaar luncheon. It can also be used for leftover cooked or canned fish. Substitute 3 cups of cooked, peeled, and deveined shrimp or flaked, cooked flounder, grouper, or salmon for the crab. For salmon, add a scant cup of peeled and small-diced cucumber. Serve on lettuce leaves garnished with chopped parsley, or as a sandwich filling on sturdy white or whole wheat bread.

1 dozen large blue crabs, or 1-1/2 pounds (3 cups) commercially packed crabmeat

1 cup minced celery hearts, including some of the leafy tops

1 cup minced green onion, including the green tops

Salt and ground cayenne pepper

About 1 cup Homemade Mayonnaise (page 22), made with olive oil and egg yolks, and omitting mustard

6 Romaine or Boston lettuce leaves

2 tablespoons chopped fresh parsley or snipped chives

1 lemon, cut into 6 wedges

1. Cook and pick the crab (see *To Cook and Pick Crabs,* page 16), reserving 6 whole back shells. Clean the shells and dry them.

2. Combine the crabmeat, celery, and onions in a glass or stainless-steel bowl. Season well with salt and a pinch or so of cayenne. Add the mayonnaise a little at a time until the crab is lightly, but thoroughly, coated. You may not need all of it.

3. Pack the salad into the reserved shells, mounding it at the center. Arrange the lettuce on a platter and arrange the filled shells on it in a pinwheel pattern, or put them on individual salad plates. Sprinkle with parsley or chives, garnish with lemon wedges, and serve at once.

SERVES 6

VARIATION: ANITA'S CRAB RAVIGOTE

The Lippitt family often served this variation on crab salad at picnics. Omit the onion and celery and add 1 teaspoon grated onion, 2 tablespoons of capers, and a dozen finely chopped pimiento-stuffed green olives. Stuff it into the back shells and sprinkle the top of each with 1 hard-cooked egg forced through a sieve.

SHRIMP SALAD

In a place where the weather is warm and fresh-caught shrimp are plentiful seven months out of the year, shrimp salad is, of course, a standard in any cook's repertory. The Savannah recipes are legion, but one of the most common is made pretty much like St. John's Crab Salad (facing). This is my own way of making it. It's terrific on sandwiches or, when the shrimp are left whole, as a first course for a formal meal or, stuffed into hollowed-out vine-ripe tomatoes, as a luncheon main course. When I'm not stuffing them into a tomato casing, I often stir in a generous cup of diced ripe tomato just before serving.

2 pounds (headless weight) Poached Shrimp (page 18), preferably small
1/2 cup diced heart of celery

About 1/2 cup Herb Mayonnaise (page 23)
Salt and ground cayenne pepper

1. Peel the shrimp and, if they're large, cut them into 2 or 3 pieces, but leave small ones whole. Toss them in a bowl with the celery.

2. Fold in enough mayonnaise to lightly coat them (you may not need all of it). Taste and season with salt and a dash or so of cayenne. Toss well, taste and adjust the salt and cayenne, and chill well before serving.

SERVES 4 TO 6

Cakes, Cookies, Pastries, & Desserts

THE FAMOUS AND OFTEN-QUOTED list of "Nostrums that are used at Fashionable Entertainments" (page 194), scrawled by Mary Telfair or her sister, Margaret, in one of their mother's manuscript recipe books, dashes off a heady selection of dainty sweets and other refreshments offered at early Savannah receptions and balls. Many would not be out of place at a Savannah party to this day: almonds and other nutmeats, butter cakes, ice cream, fresh and preserved fruits, wines of all descriptions, and punch. Others, fanciful spice cordials, fluffy creams, and sparkling gelatins flavored with wine and citrus fruit, having been displaced or debased by soft drinks and packaged foods like instant gelatin, have long since fallen out of use, at least for fashionable entertaining. But the list reminds us that, then and now, sweets have always been a fixture at Savannah receptions, balls, and teas. They're even served at modern cocktail parties, particularly those billed as "drinks with heavy hors d'oeuvres"—which means the hostess is really serving a buffet supper that you'll probably have to eat standing up.

The manuscript books in old Savannah family collections tended to be heavy on sweets, but that does not mean that they were used more often than savory recipes or that sweets were more important then than they are now. In those days, the baking, preserving, and dessert making were the provenance of the mistress of the household. That did not necessarily mean that she did it herself; there are many letters and journal entries boasting of a particular servant's skill at making excellent pastry or at whipping up a creditable Charlotte Russe. All it means is

Facing: Madeira Pots de Crème.
Above: Heirloom manuscript recipe book of Perla Sheftall Solomons, c. 1840–1850.

that a good hostess paid particular attention to the dessert board, just as they do now. Most community cookbooks in Savannah are heavy on recipes for sweets, not because we're inordinately fond of them, but because the end of the meal is important and we're always looking for something new, easy, and fashionable. No matter how seriously and earnestly the guests profess to be dieting, if they request any recipe of their hostess at all, it's sure to be the dessert.

SAVANNAH SPONGE CAKE

1 large lemon
5 large eggs
1 cup sugar

4 ounces cake flour (about 1 light cup sifted or whisked before measuring)

1. Position a rack in the center of the oven and preheat to 300 degrees F. Grate the rind from the lemon into a small glass bowl. Juice the lemon through a strainer into the bowl and let it steep while you prepare the batter. Butter and flour a 9-inch cake pan. Separate the eggs, putting the whites in a clean glass, stainless-steel, or copper bowl and the yolks in a large mixing bowl.

2. Beat the yolks until they are fluffy and light and then gradually beat in the sugar a little at a time, and then beat in the lemon zest and juice.

3. Whisk the egg whites until they are stiff but still glossy, preferably by hand. Fold them into the yolk and sugar batter. Sift or whisk the flour until it is very light and lump free, then fold it in a little at a time by sifting it over the top.

4. Pour the batter into the prepared pan and bake in the center of the oven until golden and set (a straw or toothpick inserted into the center comes out clean), about 45 minutes.

SERVES 4 TO 6

SERVING SUGGESTIONS

Dusted with finely powdered sugar, this makes a light and delicious tea or coffee cake. As a dessert, it is a perfect foil for fresh berries or sliced peaches, and is elegantly delicious with Savannah Sweet Madeira Sauce (facing). It is the classic cake to use for trifle, Charlotte, and Pineapple Charlotte (page 206), and makes a stellar strawberry shortcake.

Sponge cake was a common and popular teatime sweet both in England and America. Thomas Jefferson, the founding father as famous for his discerning palate as for his stirring patriotic prose, was fond of the French version known as Savoy biscuits, and copied out a recipe for them to send to the cooks at Monticello. The confection was not, however, by any means exclusive to Mr. Jefferson's table. In Savannah, it was at one time synonymous with our city and to this day figures prominently in two much loved composed desserts, trifle and charlotte. It is deceptively easy to make as long as you use a light hand for the mixing and a slow oven for the baking.

Savannah Sponge Cake with Savannah Sweet Madeira Sauce.

SAVANNAH SWEET MADEIRA SAUCE

1/2 cup medium dry Madeira

3 to 4 tablespoons sugar

10 tablespoons or 1-1/4 sticks cold unsalted butter, cut into small bits

1/4 to 1/2 teaspoon freshly grated nutmeg, and/or a light grating of lemon or orange zest, optional

1. Put the wine in a small saucepan and add the sugar, stirring until dissolved. Bring it to a simmer over medium heat. Reduce the heat as low as possible and remove the pan from the heat.

2. Whisk in 3 or 4 bits of butter until almost melted. Whisk in 3 or 4 more bits and return the pan to the heat. Continue adding butter a few bits at a time, whisking constantly, until all are incorporated and the sauce is the consistency of thick cream. If it overheats and begins to separate, take it off the heat and whisk in 4 or 5 bits of butter all at once to cool it.

3. If you like, you may whisk in nutmeg and/or citrus zest. Serve at room temperature.

MAKES ABOUT 1 CUP

Wine sauce was a common finish for simple cakes and baked, boiled, or steamed puddings. Though most manuscripts specified port or sherry, Madeira was probably used a good deal and makes an especially lovely, delicate sauce. Its one drawback is that it cannot be made ahead and should not be allowed to get cold, so last minute timing is critical. If you can't avoid having it get cold and it does set, or if you have leftovers, it can be whisked to a thick cream and dolloped like hard sauce over warm steamed or baked pudding.

Nostrums that are used at
fashionable Entertainments,
circa 1820

*Butter Cake Iced Plain, D[itt]o.
Caraway, Do. Dill Seed Cakes,
(Fruits) Apples, Oranges (In
Winter Season) In Summer,
Peaches, Nectarines, Figs,
Melons, Grapes, &c.—
Chestnuts, Filberts, &c.
(Cordials) Aniseed, perfect
Amour, Cinnamon, and Peach
Cordial, Wines, White & Red,
Sweet, Do. Punch, Do. &
Mead Wines. (Dried Fruits)
Raisins, Almonds, Prunes
Creams—Orange, Lemon,
Ice &c., Jellies orange, quince,
Do. & Swine's foot, Do.
Matrimony*

[Georgia Historical Society,
Manuscript Collection box 793.
There were at least two manuscript recipe books, the most
extensive of which, from the
third decade of the nineteenth
century, contained detailed
recipes for many of the things
on this list.]

SOUR CREAM POUND CAKE

Though this cake has become a standard all over the South, Savannah bakers have made it peculiarly our own. It knows no racial or social boundaries and is often the first cake that a young cook will learn to make. Though the recipes usually vary only in minor detail, each cook is usually fiercely loyal to their mother's version and will readily argue its superiority to anyone who will listen. This particular recipe comes from my pound cake mentor, Bonnie Carter, whose beautiful collection of antique china and crystal grace many of the photographs in this book.

3 cups unbleached all-purpose flour	6 large eggs
1/8 teaspoon salt	1 cup sour cream
1 cup or 2 sticks unsalted butter	1 teaspoon almond extract, Homemade Bourbon Vanilla (page 14), or vanilla extract
3 cups sugar	

1. Position a rack in the center of the oven and preheat oven to 325 degrees F. Butter and flour a tube cake pan. Whisk or sift together the flour and salt. With a mixer, at medium speed, cream the butter and sugar until very light and fluffy—about 2 minutes.

2. Mix in the eggs one at a time, and then the sour cream. Mix in the flour in several additions until smooth. Stir in the flavoring. Pour the batter into the prepared pan, run the blade of a table knife through it to get out any large air pockets, and give it a few solid taps on the counter to bring big air bubbles to the surface.

3. Bake in the center of the oven about 1-1/4 hours, or until a straw, toothpick, or cake tester inserted in the center comes out clean. Remove the cake to a wire cooling rack and cool it in the pan for 10 to 15 minutes, then invert it onto a plate and let cool completely before cutting. Many local cooks invert the cake onto a plain plate, and then lay the cake plate on the top and invert again onto the cake plate so that the crusty top is face up.

MAKES 1 10-INCH TUBE CAKE, SERVING 12 TO 16

Sour Cream Pound Cake.

One of the vivid memories that good friend Nancy Mercer Keith Gerard had of her Savannah childhood was of helping her grandmother, Lillian Mercer, make fruitcake every November in the kitchen of her old house on Gwinnett Street, where Nancy, her mother, and her uncle, songwriter Johnny Mercer, grew up. "I loved it," she said, "because it had all the good stuff that I liked—the pineapple and cherries—and none of that stuff that I didn't. We mixed it in one of those big tan earthenware bowls with a blue ring around the rim and baked it in white enameled bowls with a red ring. I helped cut the paper bags up to line the pans and floured the fruit. After they cooled, we would wrap them in wax paper and then brown paper, tied it up with a string and let them age until Christmas. And then we'd send two to Uncle Bubba."

You have got to love someone who could call Johnny Mercer "Uncle Bubba."

LILLIAN MERCER'S WHITE FRUIT CAKE

3/4 pound crystallized pineapple
3/4 pound crystallized cherries
1 pound shelled pecans
1 pound (about 3-1/4 cups) sifted all-purpose flour, divided
1 cup or 2 sticks butter, softened

2 cups sugar
6 eggs, separated
1-1/2 nutmegs, grated
1 tablespoon baking powder
3/4 cup medium dry (amontillado) sherry wine or bourbon whiskey

1. Position a rack in the center of the oven and preheat to 325 degrees F. Cut the pineapple and cherries into small pieces. Combine them in a bowl with the pecans and toss with about 1/4 cup of the flour.

2. Cream the butter and gradually add the sugar, beating until it is light and fluffy. Alternately, beat in the yolks of eggs and flour. Fold in the fruit, nuts, and nutmeg and baking powder. Gently stir in the wine or whiskey.

3. Beat the egg whites until they form soft peaks and fold them into the batter.

4. Grease two 12-cup tube pans with lard or butter and line the bottoms and long sides with a single piece of parchment or brown paper bag or wrapping paper cut to fit. Lightly grease the paper and spoon in the batter. Bake slowly for 2 hours, or until a straw, toothpick, or cake tester inserted into the center comes out clean. Let the cakes cool in the pans and wrap well in wax paper. Let them age for at least 4 weeks before cutting.

MAKES 2 TUBE CAKES

BENNE WAFERS

In Savannah and throughout the Lowcountry of Carolina and Georgia, you will find a number of variations for these traditional cookies. Some are more like brittle candy than cookie; some are more like teacakes; other are so airy and delicate that they practically evaporate on your tongue. These tend toward the latter variety—delicately scented and yet intensely flavorful.

You can usually find sesame seeds in the spice aisle of supermarkets, but they are expensive and often not very fresh. You'll find that they are fresher and much more economical at Asian and natural food markets, where they are often sold in bulk. The kind of seeds you want for this cookie are white, or hulled, sesame.

Benne Wafers.

3/4 cup white (hulled) sesame seeds

3/4 cup unbleached all-purpose flour

1/4 teaspoon salt

1/4 teaspoon baking powder

3/4 cup or 1-1/2 sticks unsalted
butter, softened

1-1/2 cups light brown sugar

1 large egg, lightly beaten

Grated zest of 1 lemon

2 tablespoons freshly squeezed
lemon juice

Whenever I make Benne Wafers, I always think about Emmeline King Cooper, who grew up on Hall Street and later lived on Monterey Square in downtown Savannah. An artist, writer, and leading force in Savannah's cultural life, she was a lovely hostess and wonderful cook. I can still taste her gumbo. Though she seldom baked, Benne Wafers were a specialty she shared generously with friends and neighbors.

1. Position a rack in the center of the oven and preheat it to 350 degrees F. Spread the sesame seeds on a 9-inch metal pie plate or cake pan and put them in the oven. Toast, stirring frequently, until they are a rich golden brown. Let cool. Reduce the oven temperature to 300 degrees F. Line 2 large cookie sheets with cooking parchment. Whisk or sift together the flour, salt, and baking powder.

2. In a separate mixing bowl, cream the butter and sugar until light and fluffy. Beat in the egg, and then mix in the flour, sesame seeds, lemon zest, and lemon juice. Drop by scant half-teaspoonfuls onto the parchment, leaving at least an inch between them (the cookies will spread a good deal).

3. Bake in batches until nicely browned, about 10 to 12 minutes. Place the pans on wire cooling racks and let the cookies cool completely before peeling them off the parchment or pads. Store in airtight tins.

MAKES ABOUT 14 DOZEN

SISTER SADIE'S HEAVENLY BITS

3/4 cup or 1-1/2 sticks unsalted butter, softened

4 tablespoons confectioners' sugar, plus more for rolling the cookies

2 cups unbleached all-purpose flour

1 tablespoon water

1 cup finely chopped pecans

Sister Sadie was the neighborhood pet name for Sadie Gottlieb, youngest daughter of Isadore and Jenny Gottlieb, who founded the famed family bakery in 1884. Sadie's whole life revolved around the family business, and by all accounts, she was a gifted baker and remarkable spirit. Her recipes survive, carefully transcribed in a kind of baker's shorthand, in an worn old leather-bound ledger that has become a family heirloom. These delicious little butter cookies were a favorite of her nephew, Isser.

1. Position a rack in the center of the oven and preheat to 350 degrees F. Cream the butter and mix in 4 tablespoons of the sugar, and then the flour, water, and pecans. Roll the dough into walnut-size balls and put them on ungreased baking sheets, spaced about an inch apart.

2. Bake the cookies in batches (1 pan at a time), rotating the pan in the oven if necessary to ensure even browning, for about 20 to 25 minutes. They're done when the bottom is a very pale brown and they can be easily picked up from the pan. While the first batch is baking, sift about a cup of confectioners' sugar into a shallow bowl.

3. While the cookies are still quite hot, roll them in the sifted sugar and let them cool on wire racks.

MAKES 4 DOZEN

IRISH LACE COOKIES

The only thing remotely Irish about these cookies is that they're made with oats and Irish whiskey, and they're a standard at many a St. Patrick's Day picnic in Savannah. They're exquisitely delicate and delicious, and they hold their own at the most formal afternoon tea or reception. I like to bump them up a notch by making them into sandwich cookies with bittersweet chocolate spread in the middle. If you'd like to try it, allow 4 ounces of bittersweet chocolate and barely melt it in a double boiler over simmering hot water. To help them set, spread them on a parchment-lined cookie sheet and refrigerate them until the chocolate is hard again.

Irish Lace Cookies.

1/2 cup or 1 stick unsalted butter, softened

1/2 cup sugar

1/2 cup light brown sugar

1 large egg

1 teaspoon Homemade Bourbon Vanilla (page 14) or vanilla extract

2 teaspoons Irish whiskey (your choice, but I'm a Jameson's man, myself)

1/4 teaspoon salt

2 tablespoons all-purpose flour

1 cup quick-cooking oats

1. Position a rack in the center of the oven and preheat it to 350 degrees F. Line 4 large baking sheets with parchment or silicone baking pads.

2. With a mixer, cream the butter and both sugars until light and fluffy. Beat in the egg, vanilla, whiskey, and salt. Mix in the flour and oats and drop by level half-teaspoonfuls onto the prepared pans, leaving 2 inches between (these will spread a lot as they bake).

3. Bake in batches until golden brown, about 6 to 7 minutes. Cool them in the pans on wire cooling racks.

MAKES 4-1/2 TO 5 DOZEN

Marika Leopold was the matriarch of a Greek American family who is best known for the diner and ice cream parlor that they operated on the corner of Gwinnett and Habersham streets. Her koulouria, a mildly sweet, sesame-topped butter cookie, were a legend in their Savannah neighborhood. The recipe comes from her son, Stratton, who used to help her make them, and who today has revived the old family business in a new location on Broughton Street.

Marika's Koulouria.

MARIKA'S KOULOURIA
(SESAME SEED COOKIES)

For the cookies:
3 cups unbleached all-purpose flour
2 cups cake flour
3 heaped teaspoons baking powder
Baking soda
1-2/3 sticks unsalted butter, softened
1 cup sugar

3 large eggs
3 teaspoons vanilla extract

For the sesame topping:
1 large egg
About 1/4 cup hulled (white) sesame seeds

1. Whisk together both flours, the baking powder, and a pinch of baking soda.

2. Cream the butter until fluffy, then gradually beat in the sugar until very fluffy and light, and beat in 3 eggs, one at a time. Work in the dry ingredients, and then the vanilla.

3. Turn the dough out onto a lightly floured work surface and knead it until it is smooth. Cover well with plastic wrap and refrigerate for 20 to 30 minutes. Position a rack in the center of the oven and preheat it to 350 degrees F. Line a baking sheet with cooking parchment or wax paper.

4. Pinch off a walnut-size lump of the dough and roll it out into a cylinder a little less than 1/2 inch in diameter and 5 inches long. Bring the two ends together and twist the dough. Put the cookie on the prepared baking sheet and repeat with the remaining dough.

5. For the topping, lightly beat the egg until smooth. Using a pastry brush, lightly brush the egg wash over the cookies and sprinkle them with sesame seeds. Bake until golden, about 15 to 18 minutes. Cool and store in airtight tins.

MAKES ABOUT 5 DOZEN

TELFAIR CURRANT SHORTBREAD

Several manuscript cookery books, attributed variously to Miss Telfair, her sister, and her mother, survive. These delicate currant-laced shortbread cookies are adapted from one of them.

1 cup sugar, plus more for dusting the tops of the cookies

1 pound (about 3-1/2 cups) all-purpose flour

1/2 teaspoon salt

1 teaspoon ground cinnamon

1 teaspoon freshly grated nutmeg

1 cup or 2 sticks unsalted butter, softened

1 cup currants

1 large egg, separated

1/2 cup whole milk

1. Whisk together the sugar, flour, salt, and spices in a large mixing bowl. Rub the butter into it with your fingers until the mixture resembles coarse meal. Add the currants and toss until evenly mixed. In a separate bowl, lightly beat the egg yolk and add the milk, beating until it is evenly mixed.

2. Make a well in the center of the dry ingredients and pour in the egg and milk. Mix together into a smooth, moderately stiff dough. Cover it with plastic wrap and let it rest in the refrigerator for half an hour.

3. Position a rack in the center of the oven and preheat the oven to 325 degrees F. Flour a work surface and the dough and roll it out about 1/4 inch thick. Cut into cookies with a 2-inch round or small decorative cutter and transfer them to ungreased baking sheets.

4. Lightly beat the egg white with a tablespoon of water until smooth. Brush the egg wash over the cookies, dust them with sugar, and bake until lightly colored, about 16 to 20 minutes. Cool them on the sheet and then store them in an airtight jar or tin.

MAKES ABOUT 5 DOZEN

Mary Telfair is one of Savannah's best known historical figures, a well-educated woman of letters who is famous for founding the first art museum in the Southeast, the Telfair Academy of Arts and Sciences. Until after the War Between the States, most society women in Savannah did not cook, which is why Leila Habersham was able to build a valuable career as a cooking teacher when those same society women fell on hard times and no longer had a cook to rely on. This did not, of course, mean that Miss Telfair did not care about the food on her table, nor did it stop her from trying to cook when the occasion warranted. Every Christmas, for example, she and her sister gave all their servants the day off and prepared dinner for their entire household. No one knows how well the servants dined, since little has been said of the Misses Telfairs' culinary prowess and the servants tactfully kept silent, but the potent Christmas punch that probably preceded the meal was no doubt a good sauce to cover most deficiencies.

Almost a hundred years to the day after Leila Habersham gave her first cooking lesson to the elite matrons of her day, Savannah artist Bailee Kronowitz began giving similarly intimate classes to her friends and neighbors. Until then, cooking had been more of a hobby for Bailee, but to everyone's surprise, including her own, she was a natural teacher and the popularity of those classes launched a new career that has spanned more than twenty years and inspired more than three generations of cooks. Though Bailee has retired from teaching, her recipes remain favorites in many local kitchens and have graced the pages of several books.

One cool October morning, she reflected with me on three decades of teaching and shared two notebooks overflowing with her singular recipes. These delicate nut clusters, a favorite of her son Lowell, were one of her original creations. Because they are flourless, Bailee likes to have them at Passover but is quick to point out that there's no reason to limit them to the holiday.

BAILEE'S GEORGIA PECAN CLUSTERS

2 large egg whites
1 cup dark brown sugar

2 cups pecans, coarsely broken by hand

1. Position a rack in the center of the oven and preheat to 450 degrees F. Beat the egg whites in a metal bowl until they are stiff. Mix in the brown sugar and fold in the nuts, holding back a few.

2. Line 2 large cookie sheets with parchment or lightly butter them. Drop the meringue by teaspoonfuls onto the prepared pans, spacing them at least an inch apart. As you get to the bottom of the bowl, you'll find that you'll need to add the reserved pecans in order to have the nuts evenly distributed among the last cookies.

3. Turn off the oven and put the cookies into it. Leave for 30 minutes without opening the oven door. Check them and leave a few minutes longer, if needed, until they're lightly colored and set.

4. Cool in the pan on wire racks and store them in airtight tins.

MAKES 2 DOZEN

OLD-FASHIONED PECAN BROWNIES

These gooey-rich brownies are from Emma Adler, adapted over time from a recipe given to her by an old friend, Jeannie Clapp. They're a snap to put together and need only a watchful eye while they are in the oven, because they should not be allowed to overbake. The only problem you'll have is restraining yourself from eating the entire batch while they're still warm from the oven.

1/2 cup pecans
1/2 cup or 1 stick unsalted butter
4 ounces (4 squares) unsweetened baking chocolate
1 cup firmly packed light brown sugar
2 cups granulated sugar

Salt
2 large eggs, well beaten
4 ounces (1 light cup) unbleached all-purpose flour
1 teaspoon vanilla extract

Old-Fashioned Pecan Brownies.

1. Position a rack in the center of the oven and preheat to 375 degrees F. Butter and flour a 9 x 13-inch pan. Spread the pecans on a pie plate and lightly toast them in the oven until they begin to color, about 8 minutes. Cool and roughly chop them. Reduce the oven temperature to 350 degrees.

2. Melt the butter and chocolate together over low heat. Stir together both sugars, a pinch of salt, and the eggs, and stir in the butter and chocolate. Stir in the pecans, and then the flour, sifting it a little at a time over the top of the batter. Stir in the vanilla and pour it into the prepared pan, spreading it thin with a spatula. Bake until a toothpick inserted into the center comes out with cohesive clumps clinging to it, about 15 to 20 minutes. They bake more quickly than most brownies, so don't overcook them. Let cool completely before cutting.

MAKES ABOUT 2 DOZEN

JULIE'S LEMON SQUARES

Lemon Squares are popular all over America, and Savannah is no exception. They're an indispensable element for many of our picnics and buffet parties, especially when the dessert needs to be bite-size and finger-friendly yet rich and elegant. Every local caterer makes them, and nearly every Savannah hostess has a prized recipe, but none of them can make them quite like my friend Julie Hooper, who allowed me to publish her recipe in *New Southern Baking*. After the book came out, however, she took me to task for "messing around with it," particularly for changing the butter.

Usually, unsalted butter is preferable for baked sweets, and I'd routinely called for it in the ingredients list. But in this instance, Julie used salted butter—on purpose—and it really does make an important difference. Here's her recipe again, this time purged of the cookbook author's fiddling. However, when I make them, I always add the grated zest of a lemon. Sorry, Julie.

For the shortbread crust:
1/2 cup powdered sugar
2 cups all-purpose flour
Salt
1 cup or 2 sticks salted butter, softened

For the custard filling:
4 eggs, well beaten
2 cups sugar
1/3 cup plus 1 tablespoon freshly squeezed lemon juice (about 2 large or 3 medium lemons)
1/4 cup flour
1/2 teaspoon baking powder

1. Position a rack in the center of the oven and preheat to 350 degrees F. Make the shortbread crust: sift together the powdered sugar and flour and a pinch of salt. Work the flour into the butter with your fingers, or begin by cutting it in with a pastry blender and then finish it with your hands until the butter is evenly incorporated and the dough is crumbly but uniform and holds together when you press a lump in your hand. (The initial cutting-in can be done in the food processor. Process until the mixture resembles coarse meal and then finish it by hand.) Clean your hands and press it evenly over the bottom of a 9 x 13-inch sheet cake pan. Prick the dough at even intervals with a fork. Bake in the center of the oven until the edges are golden brown and the top is beginning to color, about 20 minutes. Remove from the oven and cool slightly.

2. To make the custard filling, stir together the eggs, sugar, optional lemon zest, and juice. Sift the flour and baking powder over it and stir until smooth and lump-free. Pour it evenly over the crust, return it to the oven, and bake until the custard is set, about 25 minutes.

3. Cool completely and then sift powdered sugar evenly over the top. The squares usually pull away from the sides of the pan as they cook, but if they don't, run a thin, sharp knife around the edge of the pan and cut evenly into 1-1/2- to 2-inch squares.

MAKES ABOUT 3 DOZEN

PEACH TART

10 ounces (about 2 cups) all-purpose flour

4 tablespoons sugar, divided

1/2 teaspoon salt

1/2 cup or 1 stick unsalted butter, cut into small bits

2 tablespoons chilled lard or vegetable shortening

About 1/2 cup ice water, divided

Cinnamon Sugar (sidebar)

6 to 8 ripe freestone peaches

Whole nutmeg in a grater

3 tablespoons peach or apricot jam

1. Whisk or sift together the flour, 2 tablespoons sugar, and salt. Add the butter and lard and cut it into the flour with a pastry blender until it resembles coarse meal or grits. Add about 1/3 cup of ice water and work it in. Keep adding water by spoonfuls until the dough is just holding together. Gather it into a ball, cover with plastic wrap, and chill 20 minutes.

Note: You may make the pastry in a food processor fitted with a steel blade. Chill the blade 5 minutes and put in the flour, sugar, and salt and pulse several times to sift. Add the fat and process until the mixture resembles coarse meal. Pulse in the water a little at a time, starting with 1/3 cup, until it is holding together. Wrap and chill as in the hand method.

2. Position a rack in the center of the oven and preheat to 375 degrees F. Line a 12-inch round tart pan with the dough. Prick well with a fork, line with buttered foil (buttered side down), fill with pie weights or dried beans, and bake 20 minutes. Carefully remove the foil and weights and bake 8 to 10 minutes more, or until just beginning to color. Sprinkle the bottom with cinnamon sugar and let it cool while preparing the peaches.

3. Peel the peaches, cut them in half, remove the pit, and slice them into thick wedges. Arrange them on top of the crust in a single layer of slightly overlapping, concentric circles. Sprinkle well with cinnamon sugar and generously grate nutmeg over the top.

4. Bake until the peaches are tender and the crust is golden, about 40 minutes. Meanwhile, simmer the jam with 2 tablespoons sugar over medium-low heat until the sugar is dissolved, about 3 to 5 minutes.

5. Let the tart cool slightly and brush the entire surface with the jam glaze. Serve warm or at room temperature.

SERVES 6

Since peaches are Georgia's universal symbol, it's ironic that the first efforts to grow them in Savannah's Trustees Garden were reportedly less than successful. Spanish missionary monks on St. Simon's, St. Mary's, and St. Catherine's islands had better success, and it is the trees they planted that naturalized and spread across the state, giving Georgia its original connection with the fruit. Today the best Georgia peaches grow to the west of Savannah, in and around Fort Valley, and are shipped into our markets. But no Savannahian could imagine going through a summer without at least one serving of homemade peach ice cream, warm, buttery cobbler, or thin, crisp tart.

This simple yet elegant tart is one of the easiest ways of preparing peaches and may well be my favorite dessert. It's delicious on its own or sent over the top with a scoop of homemade vanilla, caramel, or Ginger Ice Cream (page 212).

To make Cinnamon Sugar, mix 1 cup sugar with 2 tablespoons ground cinnamon in a jar. Seal and shake until blended, then taste and adjust the cinnamon to suit.

Charlotte Russe has been popular throughout the South for more than a hundred and fifty years. In Savannah, where its name is often foreshortened simply to "Charlotte," it was until recent times the ultimate dessert for company or special occasions. Though today it is not as commonplace as it once was, natives like Chef Walter Dasher wistfully recall their grandmother's company Charlotte, molded in a bowl lined with store-bought ladyfingers, or with home-made Savannah Sponge Cake (page 192). Still others omitted the cake altogether and spooned it into stemmed compote or champagne glasses.

Charlotte Russe has long been popular across the South and can still be found in many published cook-books. Here are two unusual Charlottes that are unique to Savannah.

EGGNOG CHARLOTTE
(CONGEALED EGGNOG)

From the family recipe collection of Emma Morel Adler, this was a favorite dessert in her family for Christmas dinner. It is best made at least a day ahead so that the flavors fully develop. When you do serve it, be generous with the nutmeg grater.

1 tablespoon powdered gelatin	2 ounces rye or bourbon whiskey
1/2 cup cold water	A few drops dark rum
2 large eggs, separated	2 cups heavy cream
1/2 cup sugar	Whole nutmeg in a grater

1. Soften the gelatin in the cold water and set it in a basin of warm water until melted. Whisk the egg whites in a glass or metal bowl until they hold stiff but not dry peaks.

2. In a separate bowl, beat the yolks with a wooden spoon until they are light, and then gradually beat in the sugar until it is very light and fluffy. Stir in the whiskey and the rum. In a separate bowl, beat the cream until it is thickened and about double its volume but still pourable. Fold first the cream, then the egg whites, and, finally, the gelatin into the yolk mixture.

3. Pour the eggnog into 8 punch or pots de crème cups or 6-ounce ramekins. Chill until set, at least 4 to 6 hours; it is at its best made at least a day ahead. Dust each serving generously with freshly grated nutmeg.

SERVES 8

PINEAPPLE CHARLOTTE

24 3-inch-long by 1/2-inch-thick strips of Savannah Sponge Cake (page 192), or 8 ladyfingers split length-wise into 3 pieces	1/4 to 1/2 cup plus 3 tablespoons sugar, divided
3 cups fresh pineapple, peeled, cored, and cut into small chunks	2 cups heavy cream
	Thinly sliced, unpeeled pineapple wedges and sprigs of mint, for garnish

Before canning made them universally available and, therefore, somewhat ordinary, pineapples were a special treat in Charleston and Savannah, and a symbol both of prosperity and gracious hospitality. Stylized carved pineapples were common over doorway pediments and gateposts, and in the detailing of the doorjambs, knockers, and gate ironwork of the tall, elegant townhouses of the old historic district. When the real fruit appeared on the dessert board, it marked a really special occasion.

This delicate, easy fruit cream is an exquisite example of the simply elegant treatment given this luscious fruit. It isn't really a "charlotte," but an old-fashioned fruit fool, in which whipped cream is set by the acid in the crushed fruit that is folded into it.

1. Stand the sponge cake strips or ladyfingers 3 pieces per serving along the sides of 8 parfait glasses, footed compotes, or dessert bowls. Crush 1 cup of the pineapple to a pulp with a potato masher or in a food processor fitted with a steel blade. Combine it with the chunk pineapple and about 1/4 to 1/2 cup of sugar, to taste. Let stand for at least 15 minutes.

2. In a cold glass or stainless steel bowl, whisk the cream until frothy and thick. Sprinkle with 3 tablespoons sugar and whip until it holds firm peaks. Fold in the crushed and chunk pineapple. Taste and adjust the sugar. Spoon it into the prepared glasses or bowls, mounding it a little on top, and chill until very cold and set, at least 2 hours.

3. Just before serving, garnish each serving with a pineapple wedge and sprig of mint.

SERVES 8

Syllabub.

This rich, whipped wine-flavored cream is very old-fashioned, long predating America's colonization. The most charming of the old recipes directed the house-wife to put sweetened wine into a silver pail and milk the cow directly into it so that the warm, rich milk formed a thick froth as it streamed into the wine. Later, the froth was made with a churn specially designed for the job and became thicker and stiffer until, by the mid-nineteenth century, it resembled the firm whipped dessert given here.

Eventually, ice cream and other frozen treats made syllabub somewhat passé, but it was still popular in Savannah as late as the 1930s and has recently made something of a comeback. It survives in two distinct and completely differ-ent forms: this firm but deli-cate whipped dessert and a frothy ice-cold milk punch made with wine or whiskey.

SYLLABUB

1/2 cup medium-dry white wine, sherry, or Sercial Madeira

1 pint heavy cream

Sugar

3 large egg whites (use pasteurized eggs if you are concerned about eating them raw)

Grated zest of 1 lemon

1. Stir the wine into the cream and whip until it is frothy. Add sugar to taste and whip until it is blended. Add the egg whites and the lemon zest and whip until it holds firm peaks.

2. Spoon the syllabub into parfait or sherbet glasses and chill thoroughly before serving, at least 2 hours.

SERVES 6

This is of the milk punch persuasion, from The St. Andrews Academy Parent Teacher Organization's award-winning cookbook, *First Come, First Served . . . In Savannah.* For 12 to 16 servings, blend 2 pints of cream with 1 cup each of half-and-half and whiskey. Stir in 1 cup sugar until dissolved. Beat with an electric mixer or whisk until a thick froth has formed. Serve immediately, beating it again as necessary to renew the froth.

BLENDER POTS DE CRÈME

This is a very rich custard—almost like a chocolate truffle in a cup, so serve it after a meal that is not too heavy.

6 ounces (1 cup) semi-sweet chocolate chips or chopped bits

Salt

2 tablespoons sugar

1 large egg, at room temperature

1 scant cup heavy cream

1 tablespoon bourbon, white crème de menthe, orange liqueur, or 1 teaspoon vanilla extract and 2 teaspoons bourbon

1 cup whipping cream, whipped to soft peaks without sugar

Mint sprigs and/or candied violet or rose petals

1. Put the chocolate, a small pinch of salt, and sugar in a blender and blend at a moderately high speed until it's ground fine. Add the egg and blend for 20 seconds, or until smooth.

2. Scald the cream until it is almost boiling. Take the center section out of the blender lid. Turn on the blender and slowly add the cream through the opening. Turn off the machine, scrape down the sides, and pulse until smooth. Add the flavoring and pulse to blend.

3. Divide the custard evenly among 6 pots-de-creme or demitasse cups. Cover and chill until firm, about 2 hours. They may be served plain or garnished with unsweetened whipped cream, mint, and/or candied violets or rose petals.

SERVES 6

These sumptuous, drop-dead-easy pots de crème were a specialty of the late Dean Owens, who was one of Savannah's great wits and hosts, and who often let me share his wit, wisdom, and table. One Thanksgiving, now many years ago, illness and family obligations whittled our respective Thanksgiving guest lists down to just two people—us. We patched together a dinner for two, put a small turkey on to roast, and then put our feet up and a bottle of bourbon down on the table between us. It was one of my best Thanksgivings ever.

Beautiful antique pots de crème sets are a common ornament on the fine mahogany sideboards in Savannah's historic downtown homes. Though they're used mostly for the popular chocolate custard that is almost synonymous with their name, they are also perfect for this old-fashioned local favorite. Sherry is the wine most often used in the old manuscripts, but Savannah's favored Madeira makes a distinctive difference.

Candied flowers make a beautiful and appropriately old-fashioned garnish for pots de crème. They're available from specialty grocers, confectioners, and some bakeries. If you can't get them and can't make your own, just use a sprig of fresh mint all on its own.

MADEIRA POTS DE CRÈME

1 cup whole milk
3/4 cup heavy cream
1 (2 inch) stick of cinnamon
4 large egg yolks
1/2 cup sugar
Freshly grated zest of 1 orange

1/4 cup sweet Madeira or cream sherry
1 cup Whipped Cream (below), omitting the bourbon
6 candied rose petals, violets, or candied orange peel, and/or small sprigs fresh mint

1. Position a rack in the center of the oven and preheat to 300 degrees F. Bring a teakettle filled with water to a simmer. Meanwhile, heat the milk, cream, and cinnamon stick in a heavy-bottomed saucepan over medium heat, stirring frequently to prevent scorching. Simmer for 3 to 4 minutes, remove it from the heat, and let it cool slightly.

2. Whisk the egg yolks in a mixing bowl until light, then gradually beat in the sugar, and then the orange zest. Continue beating until it is very light and lemon-colored and falls in ribbons from the whisk. Remove the cinnamon from the hot milk and cream (it can be rinsed, dried, and reused) and gradually whisk the milk into the yolks. Stir in the Madeira.

3. Set 6 pots de crème, small custard cups, or ramekins in a deep, rimmed pan or casserole. Divide the custard among them and carefully pour enough simmering water into the pan to come halfway up their sides. Loosely cover with foil and bake until set, about 30 minutes. They should still be jiggly at the center.

4. Remove them to a wire rack, cool completely, then cover and chill for at least 2 hours. Serve cold, garnished with whipped cream, candied flowers if you have them, and mint.

SERVES 6

WHIPPED CREAM

Bourbon is almost taken for granted in Savannah's version of this universal topping, but you may substitute crème de menthe, amaretto, or almost any liqueur, half a teaspoon of vanilla, or, when only the clean taste of rich cream is wanted, omit them altogether.

Madeira Pots de Crème.

1 cup chilled whipping cream	2 teaspoons bourbon
2 to 3 tablespoons granulated sugar	

1. Put the cream in a cool stainless-steel, glass, or ceramic bowl and whip it by hand with a whisk or with a mixer at medium-high speed until frothy and beginning to thicken.

2. Sprinkle on sugar, to taste, and continue whipping until it forms firm peaks. Fold in the bourbon, cover, and refrigerate for 15 to 30 minutes.

MAKES 2 CUPS

Ginger Ice Cream.

GINGER ICE CREAM

Ginger was one of the major spice imports of the eighteenth century. Colonial newspapers often carried advertisements that included "ginger, for preserving." Later on, when everyone figured out that the lily from which the rhizome is taken was easily cultivated and grew almost wild in the garden, it became a pantry staple. This rich yet refreshing ice cream, a version of which was popularized by Asian cooking teacher Ellen Lew, is a popular dessert for Savannah curries, fish dinners, and, if you'll pardon the expression, for gilding the lily of such standard homey desserts as apple and peach pies, cobblers, and pound cakes.

2 cups whole milk

1 whole vanilla bean, cut in half and split lengthwise

1 cup sugar

6 large egg yolks

2 cups heavy cream (minimum 36 % milk fat)

Salt

1 generous tablespoon freshly grated gingerroot

2/3 cup chopped crystallized ginger or preserved ginger in syrup, drained

1. Prepare the bottom of a double boiler with at least 1 inch of water and bring it to a simmer over medium heat. In the top of the double boiler, over direct medium heat, scald the milk and vanilla bean until it is almost boiling. Stir in the sugar until it is completely dissolved. Beat the egg yolks in a separate bowl and gradually beat in a cup of the hot liquid. Place the top of the double boiler over the simmering water and gradually stir the egg yolk mixture into the hot liquid. Cook, stirring constantly, until it thickly coats the back of the spoon. Remove it from the heat.

2. Stir in the heavy cream, a small pinch of salt, and both kinds of ginger. Stir until completely cooled, remove the vanilla bean (it can be rinsed, dried, and reused), and chill for at least 2 hours. You can make the base a day ahead and chill it overnight.

3. Freeze the cream in an ice cream churn, following the manufacturer's instructions, until it is the consistency of commercial soft ice cream (set, but still not quite hard).

4. Pack the ice cream into a deep container and put it in the freezer to ripen and harden. The flavor of this ice cream really develops when it has ripened for at least 6 to 8 hours.

MAKES 1-1/2 QUARTS, SERVING ABOUT 6

VARIATION: PEACH ICE CREAM

No Savannah book is complete without ice cream made from Georgia's sweet iconic fruit. To the above custard, omit the fresh and preserved ginger, and add 1 cup of puréed and 1 cup roughly chopped fresh, ripe peaches. Peel, split, and pit 4 to 6 peaches and roughly chop them in a food processor fitted with a steel blade, then remove 1 cup and process the remainder to a puree. Sweeten all to taste with sugar (they won't need much) and let it dissolve completely before adding them to the custard. I also like to add a fresh grating of nutmeg. Chill thoroughly before freezing.

A Cook's Savannah Reading List

FORTUNATELY, THERE HAVE BEEN MANY EFFORTS over the years to capture Savannah's singular cookery in print, whether in published cookbooks by individuals and community groups, family manuscript household notebooks and recipe collections, or in the written impressions of visitors like Eugene Walter and such homesick expatriates as Ward McAllister and Ogden Nash. There were also a number of general cookbooks from without that were very influential in Savannah homes. A complete list of them would be difficult, if not impossible, to compile, and would easily double the size of this book. What follows is a list of the books and manuscripts that were used in compiling this collection. Four of them are from outside Savannah: *Mrs. Hill's New Cook Book* (1867), *Mrs. Dull's Southern Cooking* (1928/41), *Four Great Southern Cooks* (1980), and *Eugene Walter's American Cooking: Southern Style* (1971). The first two contained recipes from Savannah connections and were, in their day, the "kitchen bible" for generations of Savannahians. The last two contain important records of Savannah cooking within their pages.

Adler, Emma Morel. *A Few of Our Favorite Things*. Savannah: Privately Published, 1988. Reprint, 2002.

Baker, John H., III. *Savannah Heritage: A Collection of My Grandmother's Receipts*. Savannah: Privately Published, 2003.

Candler, Leonora. Manuscript recipes, Private Collection. Shared by her great niece Teeny Fulenwider.

Christ Church Cook Book. Savannah: Women of Christ Episcopal Church, 1956 (1978 edition consulted).

Colquitt, Harriett Ross. *The Savannah Cook Book*. Charleston: Walker Evans & Cogswell, 1933.

Common-sense Cook Book. Savannah: First Baptist Church, 1913.

Cooper, Ben Green. *Savannah's Cookin'*. Mableton, Ga.: Been Green Cooper Press, 1967.

Cox, Eugenia Barrs, editor. *Low Country Cooking: A Collection of Recipes from Liberty County and the Georgia Low Country*. Hinesville, Ga.: Liberty County Historical Society, 1988.

DeBolt, Margaret Wayt, and Emma Rylander Law. *Savannah Sampler Cookbook*. West Chester, Pa.: Whitford Press, 1978.

———, with Emma Rylander Law and Carter Olive. *Georgia Entertains*. Nashville, Tenn.: Rutledge Hill Press, 1988. (Originally published as *Georgia Sampler Cookbook*, 1983.)

Deen, Paula Heirs. *The Lady & Sons Savannah Country Cookbook*. New York: Random House, 1998. (Originally published privately by Paula Heirs Deen, *Favorite Recipes of The Lady & Her Friends*, 1997.)

———, with Martha Giddens Nesbit. *Paula Deen & Friends*. New York: Simon & Schuster, 2005.

Dull, Henrietta Stanley. *Southern Cooking*. Atlanta: Ruralist Press, 1928. In facsimile, Atlanta: Cherokee Press, 1989. Expanded edition, New York: Grosset & Dunlap, 1941. In reprint, with commentary by Damon Lee Fowler, Athens: University of Georgia Press, 2006.

The Ever Ready Cook Book. Savannah: Rector's Aid Society of St. John's Episcopal Church, n. d., c.1910.

Favorite Recipes from Savannah Homes, Many Before Unpublished: A Collection of Well Tested and Practical Recipes. Savannah: Ladies of Bishop Beckwith Society, 1904.

Freeman, Mary H. *Colonial Receipts & Remedies*. Savannah: Historic Savannah Foundation, n. d., c.1970.

First Come, First Served . . . In Savannah. Savannah: Parent Teachers Organization of St. Andrews School, 1999.

Four Great Southern Cooks. Atlanta: DuBose Publishing, 1980.

Fowlkes, Alida Harper. Manuscript collection, c.1930–1935. Private Collection. Mrs. Fowlkes owned The Georgian Tea Room in The Olde Pink House from 1930 to 1943. Though no recipes are included in the collection, the food purchases and menus are illuminating and reflect the homey fare of the tearoom's service.

From Savannah Kitchens. Savannah: Women of Christ Episcopal Church, 1959.

Gaede, Sarah. *The Pirates' House Cook Book*. Savannah: The Pirates House Restaurant, 1982.

The Geechee Cook Book. Savannah: Woman's Auxiliary of St. Michael's Episcopal Church, 1956.

Gems From Georgia Kitchens. Atlanta: The Garden Club of Georgia, Inc., 1963.

Georgia Heritage: Treasured Recipes. Atlanta: The National Society of Colonial Dames of America in the State of Georgia, 1979.

Gordon, Arthur. "Low-Country Christmas" from *Woman's Day Encyclopedia of Cookery*, Vol. 3. New York: Fawcett Publications, Inc. 1966.

Gordon, Eleanor Kinzie (Mrs. William W.). Household Notebook, c. 1858–1910, in 2 manuscript volumes. Collection of The Juliette Gordon Low Birthplace, Savannah. Mrs. Gordon was the mother of Juliette Gordon Low, founder of the Girl Scouts of America.

Gottlieb, Irving, and Isser Gottlieb, with Sarah Gaede. *Gottlieb's Bakery: 100 Years of Recipes*. Savannah: Gottlieb's Bakery, 1983. 1996 edition consulted.

Gottlieb, Sadie. Manuscript Cookbook, c.1910–1950. Private collection.

Heavenly Dishes. Savannah: All Saint's Episcopal Church Women, n. d.

Heritage Receipts from St. John's. Savannah: Episcopal Church Women of St. John's Church, n. d. (c. 1978).

Hill, Annabella P. *Mrs. Hill's New Cook Book*. New York: James O'Kane, 1867. In Facsimile with historical commentary by Damon Lee Fowler, editor: Mrs. Hill's Southern Practical Cookery and Receipt Book. Columbia, S.C.: University of South Carolina Press, 1995.

Iocovizzi, Celeste, and Alberta Mallione. *Savannah Cooks The Italian Way*. Savannah: Italian Classics, Ltd., 1982.

Kuhr, Mildred Lee Guckenheimer Abrahams. Manuscript Recipes, c.1910–1970. Private Collection. Mrs. Kuhr was Joan Levy's great grandmother, nicknamed Honey, and a descendent of Savannah Revolutionary War patriot, Benjamin Sheftall.

Kronowitz, Bailee. *Bailee's Best: A Collection of Recipes From Bailee's Best Cooking School*, Savannah, GA (in manuscript).

Levy, Joan. Manuscript recipe collection, c.1970–present.

Lew, Ellen. *Far East Favorites*. Hartwell, Ga.: Calico Kitchen Press, 1989.

Lippitt Family Collected Recipes, in manuscript, c. 1950. Collection of Anita Lippitt Clay.

Malone, Georgia Lamar. Household notebook, c.1880–1900. Private Collection.

McCallar, Herschel S., Jr., and D. Jeffrey Keith. *Recipes From The Olde Pink House*. Atlanta: DuBose Publishing, 1981.

Meldrim, Frances Casey (Mrs. Peter W.) and Sophie Meldrim Shonnard. Household Notebook In Manuscript. Private collection, Savannah, c.1890–1945.

Morel Family Manuscript Recipes, Private Collection, c.1890–1950.

Nesbit, Martha Giddens. *Savannah Collection*. Savannah: Privately Published, 1986.

———. *Savannah Entertains*. Charleston: Wyrick & Company, 1996.

100 Years of Cooking, Jones, Hill & Mercer. Savannah: Jones, Hill, & Mercer, 1985.

Pacesetters Circle, Wesley Monumental Methodist Church. *Tasteful Traditions*. Kearney, Neb.: Morris Press, 2001.

Robinson, Sallie Ann. *Gullah Home Cooking, the Daufuskie Way*. Chapel Hill, N.C.: University of North Carolina Press, 2003.

———. *Cooking the Gullah Way, Morning, Noon, & Night*. Chapel Hill, N.C.: University of North Carolina Press, 2007.

Rutledge, Sarah. *The Carolina Housewife*, or *House and Home*. Charleston, S.C.: W. R. Babcock, 1847. In facsimile, with introduction by Anna Welles Rutledge, Columbia, S.C.: University of South Carolina Press, 1979.

The Savannah Cook Book. Savannah: Ladies of Westminster Presbyterian Church, 1909 (not to be confused with the Colquitt book of 1933).

Savannah Style. Savannah: The Junior League of Savannah, Inc., 1980.

Savoring Savannah: Feasts from the Low Country. Berkeley, Ca.: Ten Speed Press/Design Press, 2001.

Smart, Elizabeth Malone. Household Notebook, c.1910–1950, in manuscript. Private collection.

Smith, Anna Habersham Wright, editor. *A Savannah Family, 1830-1901*. Milledgeville, Ga.: Boyd Publishing, 1999. A compilation of the papers in the Clermont Huger Lee Collection, including a manuscript memoir by Leila Elliott Habersham, 1863.

Solomons, Perla Sheftall. Household Notebook, c.1840–1850, in manuscript. Private collection.

Telfair, Sarah Gibbons, Mary Telfair, and Margaret Telfair Hodgson. Household Notebooks, c. 1810–1840, in 2 manuscript volumes. Georgia Historical Society, manuscript collection 793.

Terry, Elizabeth, and Alexis Terry. *Savannah Seasons*. New York: Doubleday, 1996.

Trustees Garden Club Recipes. Savannah: Trustees Garden Club, n. d., c. 1990.

Tybee Island Recipes. Tybee Island, Ga.: Tybee Museum, n. d., c. 1983.

Victor, Irving, et al. *From Black Tie to Blackeyed Peas: Savannah's Savory Secrets*. Nashville: Favorite Recipes Press, 2000.

Walter, Eugene. *American Cooking: Southern Style*. New York: Time-Life Books, 1971. Walter includes a long essay on his visit to Savannah while researching the book.

Weeks, Carl Solana. *Savannah In the Time of Peter Tondee*. Columbia, S.C.: Summerhouse Press, 1997.

White Bluff Presbyterian Church Cookbook (Savannah). Olathe, Kan.: Cookbook Publishers, Inc., 1988.

Wilkes, Sema Americus (Mrs. L. H.). *Famous Recipes From Mrs. Wilkes' Boarding House in Historic Savannah*. Savannah: Privately Published, 1978.

———, with Introduction by John T. Edge. *Mrs. Wilkes Boarding House Cookbook*. Berkeley, Ca.: Ten Speed Press/Design Press, 2001.

Woodbridge, C. L. Manuscript Notebook from Leila Habersham's Cooking School, March/April 1895, Georgia Historical Society, manuscript collection 878, item 16, folder 4.

Ye Old Time Salzburger Cook Book. Ebenezer, Ga.: Georgia Salzburger Society, n. d.

Index

641.5975 FOWLER
Fowler, Damon Lee.
The Savannah cookbook /
R0111657748   NRTHSD

NORTHSIDE

ATLANTA-FULTON COUNTY LIBRARY

10-2004